Movement, Knowledge, Emotion

Gay activism and HIV/AIDS in Australia

Movement, Knowledge, Emotion

Gay activism and HIV/AIDS in Australia

Jennifer Power

THE AUSTRALIAN NATIONAL UNIVERSITY

E PRESS

E PRESS

Published by ANU E Press
The Australian National University
Canberra ACT 0200, Australia
Email: anuepress@anu.edu.au
This title is also available online at: http://epress.anu.edu.au/

National Library of Australia Cataloguing-in-Publication entry

Author: Power, Jennifer.

Title: Movement, knowledge, emotion : gay activism and HIV/AIDS in Australia /
                   Jennifer Power.

ISBN: 9781921862380 (pbk.) 9781921862397 (ebook)

Notes: Includes bibliographical references and index.

Subjects: Gay liberation movement--Australia

                   AIDS (Disease)--Australia--Political aspects.

                   HIV infections--Government policy--Australia.

                   Homosexuality--Australia--Political aspects.

                   Gay activists--Australia.

                   AIDS activists--Australia.

                   Australia--Social conditions--1976-

Dewey Number: 306.7660994

Cover design and layout by ANU E Press

Printed by Griffin Press

This edition © 2011 ANU E Press

Contents

Acknowledgements

There are a number of people who assisted me through the process of writing this book and who deserve thanks. Firstly I would like to thank Dr Kevin White who supervised my research for this text along with Dr John Ballard and Professor Frank Lewins.

I am grateful to the staff at the Noel Butlin Library and the National Library of Australia, Petherik Reading Room, for their assistance in gaining access to archival material and interview transcripts for my research. Gary Janes and Graham Carbery from the Australian Lesbian and Gay Archives also offered wonderful and enthusiastic (volunteer) assistance with this.

Thankyou to my friends and family for ongoing support, particularly Prue Power and Rachel Power who assisted me with editing.

Publication of this manuscript was made possible through the support of a publishing prize offered by the ANU College of Arts and Social Sciences. I am very grateful for this opportunity and would like to thank all involved. Thankyou also to Jan Borrie for her editing expertise.

Finally, I would like to extend my greatest thanks to those who so generously offered their time to talk to me about their experiences with HIV/AIDS politics. In particular, Ian Rankin and Phil Carswell spent many hours telling me their stories and discussing ideas for this work. Thankyou also to Ken Davis, Bill Whittaker, Bill Bowtell, Robert Griew, Levinia Crooks, David Lowe, David Plummer, Dennis Altman, Don Baxter, Peter Baume, Steve Mark, Terry Thorley and Jennifer Ross. Phil Carswell and Ken Davis also reread drafts of this manuscript, for which I am very grateful.

Introduction

Acquired Immune Deficiency Syndrome (AIDS) entered the public arena as a 'mystery disease' for which there was no known cause and no cure. Concerns that this unknown killer would sweep rapidly across whole populations provided it with media and political attention few medical conditions receive. But more significantly, AIDS achieved rapid infamy through its association with a set of social and sexual practices considered by many to be deviant and highly immoral: homosexuality, illicit drug use and prostitution.

In May 1983, doctors from St Vincent's Hospital in Sydney announced that the first known case of AIDS in Australia had been diagnosed the previous October in a gay man who had been visiting Sydney from New York.[1] Hindsight would prove that there were almost certainly many more undiagnosed cases of both Human Immunodeficiency Virus (HIV) and AIDS in the community at this time, but the official identification of that first case was enough to prompt acknowledgment that this mystery disease from the United States had found its way to Australia.

From this first diagnosis in 1982 until the end of 2009, there had been 29 395 reported diagnoses of HIV[2] in Australia. Of these, 10 446 people had been diagnosed with AIDS and 6776 AIDS-related deaths had been recorded. It is estimated that 20 171 Australians were living with diagnosed HIV at the end of 2009.[3] The virus spread most rapidly through the Australian community in the early years of the 1980s, with the incidence of new HIV diagnoses peaking in 1984. But despite predictions that there would be a significant resurgence of the virus (the so-called 'second wave'), the rate of new HIV infections in Australia remained relatively steady until the early 2000s, when there were indications that rates of new HIV infections were increasing in Australia for the first time in more than a decade.[4]

---

1 Editorial, 'Twenty Years', *Positive Living*, November–December 2002, <http://www.afao.com.au>; Menadue, David 2003, *Positive*, Allen & Unwin, Sydney.
2 Human Immunodeficiency Virus (HIV) is the virus that leads to a breakdown of the immune system causing the collection of illnesses and infections that is known as Acquired Immune Deficiency Syndrome (AIDS). HIV is not the same as AIDS and the acronyms should not be used interchangeably. A person living with HIV is not necessarily a person who has AIDS. An HIV-positive diagnosis is different to a diagnosis of AIDS. When I use the term AIDS, rather than HIV/AIDS or HIV, I am referring either to the physiological condition of AIDS or to the period, before 1985, when HIV had not yet been discovered.
3 National Centre in HIV Epidemiology and Clinical Research 2010, *HIV, Viral Hepatitis and Sexually transmissible Infections in Australia Annual Surveillance Report 2010*, National Centre in HIV Epidemiology and Clinical Research, The University of New South Wales, Sydney.
4 Australian Federation of AIDS Organisations 2003, HIV on the Rise in Three States: Australia's National AIDS Strategy Must Be Revitalised, Press release, 29 May 2003, viewed 2 June 2003, <http://www.afao.org. au>; Wilkinson, David and Dore, Greg 2000, 'An Unbridgeable Gap? Comparing the HIV/AIDS Epidemics in Australia and Sub Saharan Africa', *Australian and New Zealand Journal of Public Health*, 24(3), pp. 276–80.

Gay men have been affected by HIV/AIDS more than any other population group in Australia. While the rate of HIV transmission among heterosexuals—particularly those in marginalised groups such as Indigenous Australians—has increased slightly in recent years, the majority of HIV infections (more than 80 per cent of all infections between 1982 and 2009) have occurred through male-to-male sexual transmission.[5] This pattern differs from that seen in other Western countries, including France, the United States and Germany, where HIV has moved much more widely into the heterosexual population. In the United States, for example, heterosexual sex accounted for 33 per cent of all newly diagnosed HIV cases in 2004, with 47 per cent attributed to men who have sex with men.[6] In comparison, in Australia, 85.4 per cent of new diagnoses of HIV in 2005 were attributed to male-to-male sex—a similar proportion to earlier years.[7] Alongside this, the rate of HIV among intravenous drug users and women in these countries is much higher than in Australia.

Public perceptions of HIV/AIDS in Australia have shifted and changed over the years to the point where HIV/AIDS is increasingly viewed in a global context as a disease of poverty and underdevelopment. When AIDS first emerged in the early 1980s, however, many people suspected that it was a disease exclusive to gay men. Before HIV was identified as the virus causing AIDS—even before the term AIDS was established—the syndrome was being called Gay Related Immune Deficiency (GRID), the 'homosexual cancer' or the more derogatory 'gay plague'. Early theories regarding the cause of AIDS pointed to factors such as excessive semen in the bloodstream from anal intercourse or the 'fast-paced' lifestyle of many gay men.[8] Although it was not long into the 1980s when the first cases of AIDS among heterosexual people began to appear in Australia, the belief that there was an inherent association between AIDS and the lifestyle and sexual choices of gay men seemed to be entrenched in Australian public consciousness.

There were indications, and fears, that the contagious nature of the illness would provide licence for a formal crackdown on the recently won social freedoms of gay men, such as the decriminalisation of homosexual sex in some States and

---

5   National Centre in HIV Epidemiology and Clinical Research 2006, *Australian HIV Surveillance Report*, 22(2), National Centre in HIV Epidemiology and Clinical Research, University of New South Wales, Sydney, pp. 1–16; World Health Organisation 2002, 'Australia 2002 Update', *Epidemiological Fact Sheets on HIV/AIDS and Sexually Transmitted Infections*, viewed 2 June 2003, <http://www.unAIDS.org>; National Centre in HIV Epidemiology and Clinical Research, 2010.

6   Wilkinson and Dore, 2000; Centers for Disease Control 1985, *Acquired Immunodeficiency Syndrome (AIDS) Weekly Surveillance Report—December 30*, US AIDS Activity Center for Infectious Diseases, Centers for Disease Control, Atlanta, Ga; Centers for Disease Control 2005, *HIV/AIDS Surveillance Report 2004*, US Department of Health and Human Services, Centers for Disease Control and Prevention, Atlanta, Ga, viewed 21 November 2005, <http://www.cdc.gov/hiv/topics/surveillance/resources/reports/2004report/>

7   National Centre in HIV Epidemiology and Clinical Research, 2006.

8   Seidman, Steven 2002, 'AIDS and the Discursive Construction of Homosexuality', in Kim Phillips and Barry Reay (eds), *Sexualities in History: A Reader*, Routledge, New York.

Territories of Australia. As well as threatening lives, AIDS made vulnerable the civil liberties and public acceptance of lesbians and gay men that had slowly been expanding throughout the 1970s.

It was in this context that AIDS activism first emerged. Gay men in Australia began to organise politically not only to protect people afflicted with AIDS and draw attention to their needs, but to defend the broader social rights of gay men and lesbians.

The 1980s and 1990s witnessed the rise of consumer-based health movements, both in Australia and across the Western world. But when AIDS first appeared in the early 1980s the sophistication and breadth of the organised response to it by the gay community were unheralded. To date in this country, no other community or consumer-based health movement has captured the same level of public and political influence as that of the AIDS movement.[9]

In part this was due to the extent to which the politics of HIV/AIDS became connected with the broader gay and lesbian movement.[10] Organisational structures that had been established through the 1970s in campaigns for gay and lesbian rights were drawn upon, and the cultural and political framework of the gay movement was reoriented towards the immediate problem of AIDS.

At issue for the AIDS movement was the way in which HIV/AIDS and the people most affected by it were constructed in the public's imagination. It was this that would inform policy and direct the treatment of HIV/AIDS by government and public health authorities. If HIV/AIDS continued to be seen as a disease of immorality, of 'blameworthy deviants', then punitive and restrictive measures to control its spread could potentially be considered justifiable. AIDS activists campaigned on a number of fronts: to reduce stigma and discrimination against gay men and people with HIV/AIDS; and to ensure that the concerns of the gay community were taken into account in public health responses.

---

9   While it is common to refer to HIV and AIDS in conjunction with each other, as in HIV/AIDS, to signify the medical and social association between the two, I have chosen to use the terms 'AIDS activism' or 'AIDS movement' rather than 'HIV/AIDS activism'. This is, in part, a stylistic decision. AIDS activism is shorter and more readable; however, it is also indicative of the fact that AIDS activism in Australia emerged before HIV had been diagnosed and named. As such it is historically accurate to refer to early activism as AIDS activism. Further, before the antibody test for HIV became available, the only way of knowing that someone was infected were the physical symptoms of AIDS. Hence much of the stigma around AIDS in the early 1980s was associated with the visible attributes that came to signify AIDS-related conditions such as Karposi's sarcoma.
10   This text focuses on the response of gay male activists to HIV/AIDS. While there were a number of lesbians who were involved in AIDS activism, and a study of their role would be a worthy project in its own right, I do not discuss in detail the role of lesbians in Australian AIDS activism.

The Influence of History

In 1932, a clinical study into the efficacy of syphilis treatment began in the American town of Tuskegee, Alabama. Although originally planned as a six-month trial, the study continued for nearly 40 years. It finally ended in 1972, when a journalist revealed that the researchers involved had intentionally denied 399 African-American men knowledge of the existence of effective treatment for their syphilis infection. Although penicillin had been discovered as a simple cure for syphilis as early as 1947, researchers chose not to inform their research subjects about this so they could observe the long-term effects of syphilis on African-American bodies. The *Tuskegee Study of Untreated Syphilis in the Negro Male* resulted in the unnecessary deaths of more than 100 men from syphilis or its complications. Many of these men also infected their wives or partners. The legacy of the Tuskegee study—the so-called 'Tuskegee effect'—has been described as a collective memory of experiences that shaped a powerful mistrust of medical authorities among African Americans.[11]

This mistrust was still apparent in the early 1980s when HIV/AIDS first emerged in America. In 1990, a *New York Times/WCBS TV* news poll found that 10 per cent of African Americans 'genuinely and definitely' believed that HIV/AIDS had been 'deliberately created in a laboratory in order to infect black people'. A further 20 per cent agreed that this could 'possibly be true'.[12] For many African Americans, AIDS was perceived within a context of several centuries of racial discrimination and abuse.

In Australia, AIDS has overwhelmingly been a disease that affects men who have sex with men. When the first diagnosed Australian cases were reported in 1983, public reaction was layered in homophobia. Fear of AIDS was dressed as a fear of gay men.

By the same token, the response of gay men to the illness occurred on the back of a long history of homophobic discrimination and a mistrust of authorities stemming from many years of legal, religious and medical efforts to control or punish homosexuality.

Comparisons between the history of racism in America and the experiences of gay men in Australia might seem tenuous. But both cases are illustrative of the way in which the responses of people and communities to an issue or threat in the present are influenced by the past. For groups that have experienced

---

11   Jones, James 1992, 'The Tuskagee Legacy: AIDS and the Black Community', *Hastings Centre Report*, November–December pp. 38–40; Bates, Benjamin and Harris, Tina 2004, 'The Tuskegee Study of Untreated Syphilis and Public Perceptions of Biomedical Research: A Focus Group Study', *Journal of the National Medical Association*, 96(8), pp. 1051–64.
12   Ibid., pp. 38–40.

discrimination throughout history there is every reason for fear of continued discrimination to frame many of their actions and decisions. This can sometimes be whittled down to more specific instances of abuse on behalf of specific authorities, as with the Tuskagee study. But it can also manifest as a more general mistrust.

This idea is the starting point for this account of gay activists' responses to AIDS in Australia. The gay community's response to AIDS was arguably the most significant consumer health movement Australia has ever witnessed. Many thousands of people became involved in the community response to AIDS and the AIDS movement achieved considerable political and public influence. But the gay community did not mobilise such a response to AIDS in the context of the immediate threat of AIDS alone. Rather, the threat posed by AIDS sat within the context of a history of homophobia and the way in which gay men and women had come to respond to homophobia over many decades in Australia.

'Sodom of the South': Homophobia in Australia's history

Homosexuality—often defined and conceptualised primarily by the act of sodomy—has been part of public consciousness in Australia since early settlement. The first Governor of the Australian colony established in 1788, Captain Arthur Phillip, is recorded as saying: 'There are two crimes that could merit death—murder and sodomy. For either crimes I would wish to confine the criminal till an opportunity offered of delivering him as a prisoner to the natives of New Zealand, and let them eat him.'[13]

In the early days of Australian settlement, the threat of severe punishment ensured any sexual act between two men remained extremely covert. As such there is minimal documented evidence of homosexuality from this period.[14] Despite this, by the early 1800s Australia had developed a reputation of being the 'Sodom of the South'—an image articulated in the testimonies of Roman Catholic clergyman Dr William Ullathorne, Vicar-General of the colonies at the time. In his report on the state of the Catholic mission in Australia, prepared for the *Cardinal Prefect of Propaganda Fide*, Ullathorne provided considerable detail of the existence of a 'class of crime...which St Paul, in detailing the vices of the heathens, has not contemplated'.[15] Similarly, the 1837–38 Molesworth

---

13   French, Robert 1993, *Camping by a Billabong*, Blackwattle Press, Sydney.
14   Lewis, Milton 1998, *Thorns on the Rose: The History of Sexually Transmitted Disease in Australia in International Perspective*, Australian Government Publishing Service, Canberra.
15   Cited in Fogarty 1992, Walter, '"Certain Habits": The Development of a Concept of the Male Homosexual in New South Wales Law, 1788–1900', in Robert Aldrich and Gary Wotherspoon (eds), *Gay Perspectives:*

Committee on (convict) Transportation heard evidence from Superintendent James Mudie that homosexuality at the Sydney Cove Settlement was far from uncommon.[16] Mudie stated that '[u]pwards of 150 male couples may be pointed out who habitually associate for this most detestable intercourse, whose moral perception is so completely absorbed that they are said to be "married", to be husband and wife.'[17]

Sodomy[18] was an offence punishable by death in the early Australian colonies, the first hanging for this 'crime' taking place when a man named Alexander Brown was committed to die in 1828. Despite all evidence suggesting that Brown's sexual partner was willing (the partner's death sentence was commuted), the hanging went ahead. The last execution in Australia for the charge of sodomy took place in Tasmania in 1863. Capital punishment for homosexual sex then ceased when the 1885 *(British) Criminal Amendment Act* was introduced. This Act still made sure all male homosexual acts (including mutual masturbation) were criminal offences, but deemed the maximum punishment to be life imprisonment rather than death.[19]

In its first period of settlement, Sydney would not have been large enough to allow the anonymity that made possible the extensive gay subcultures that existed in London and other major cities at the time, although there is evidence of a few gay 'beats' around Sydney in the early decades of the 1900s. By the 1920s there was an emerging gay underground in all major Australian cities.[20] Publicly, however, there was a veil of silence around homosexuality and Australian social attitudes tended to remain fairly conservative through the first half of the twentieth century. There are numerous reports from this time of police raids on gay and lesbian gatherings. For example, in 1942, five men were arrested in a raid on a house party in Annandale, Sydney (journalists must have been ecstatic with the possibilities for scandalous headlines when four of the accused fronted up to court the following day still dressed in drag).[21]

Throughout the 1940s, the Australian media began to promote the idea that an increase in the number of men appearing in court for homosexual-related offences was indicative of a growing culture of 'sex perverts' in Sydney. Various organisations began to respond to this, particularly conservative groups

---

Essays in Australian Gay Culture, Department of Economic History, University of Sydney, NSW, p. 63.

16   Simes, Gary 1992, 'The Language of Homosexuality in Australia', in Aldrich and Wotherspoon, 1992.

17   Cited in Stannard, Bruce and Murphy, Kevin 1989, 'More Than a Million Australians? Still Glad to be Gay?', *The Bulletin*, 10 October, pp. 50–7.

18   The intention of 'anti-sodomy' laws seems to have been to prevent homosexual sex rather than sodomy itself as acts of sodomy within heterosexual relationships are very rarely mentioned within the context of anti-sodomy legislation.

19   French, 1993.

20   Ibid.; Lewis, 1998.

21   French, 1993; Lewis, 1998.

such as the Country Women's Association, which passed a resolution at its 1949 conference to urge the Government to implement heavier penalties for (homosexual) sex crimes.[22]

Despite this, there were some indications that social and sexual conventions were becoming more relaxed during the post–World War II period, and gay subcultures began to grow. For instance, in 1949 an article appeared in Sydney newspaper *The Sun* documenting the workings of the Sydney gay scene. The article discussed the lives of gay men without the usual references to perversion and sex crime—a rarity in mainstream media and possibly a sign of changing attitudes.[23]

This was short-lived, however, as the Cold War atmosphere of the 1950s ushered in a new climate of intolerance towards any signs of non-conformism or radicalism. All things perceived to be morally or politically 'deviant' were a target of sanction.[24] Communism and homosexuality were considered close associates—'Reds' and 'Pinks' equally suspect and both a threat to the nation. This suspicion played out within government bureaucracy, particularly those agencies concerned with national security. The Australian Security Intelligence Organisation (ASIO) put requests to the Federal Cabinet on more than one occasion to disallow homosexuals from employment in the Federal Public Service.[25] Other countries had enacted similar bans. For instance, an article published in the *Melbourne Truth* in April 1950 discussed a crackdown on lesbians and homosexual men employed by the US Federal Government. In all, 91 people were forced to resign from the US Civil Service following investigations into their personal lives. This purge was explained on the basis that gay people were considered a security risk, more likely to be loyal to each other than to their country.[26] While homosexuals were never banned from Australian Government jobs, in the early 1960s, Prime Minister Robert Menzies issued a directive that no homosexual would be allowed access to classified information. Further, heads of departments were directed to observe staff to detect character defects such as homosexuality, drug addiction or serious financial irresponsibility.[27]

The 1950s also bore witness to increasing media concern about 'moral indecency'. In November 1951, church leaders and judges broadcast on ABC Radio a 'Call to

---

22   Lewis, 1998.
23   French, 1993.
24   Hilliard, David 1997, 'Church, Family and Sexuality in Australia in the 1950s', *Australian Historical Studies*, 28, pp. 133–46.
25   Willett, Graham 1997, 'The Darkest Decade: Homophobia in 1950s Australia', *Australian Historical Studies*, 28, pp. 120–32.
26   French, 1993.
27   Willett, 1997.

the People of Australia'. This announcement aired concerns about the so-called moral decay of Australia. It was accompanied by media reports of an 'alarming' increase in male homosexuality.[28]

Police attention began to focus much more closely on homosexual 'crimes', leading to a sharp increase in the number of people charged with committing 'unnatural offences'.[29] In many States, special 'vice squads' were formed specifically to target 'parks and lavatories frequented by perverts and prowlers'.[30] In 1958, the NSW Police Commissioner Colin Delaney was widely reported in the media as having identified homosexuals as 'Australia's greatest menace'.[31] Delaney was known to be an ardent campaigner against the 'homosexual threat' and his claims were reported not only in the tabloid press—the arena in which stories relating to 'moral indecency' were traditionally aired—but also in the broadsheet newspapers, including the *Sydney Morning Herald Quarterly Index*.[32]

It is difficult to assess conclusively where public attitudes towards homosexuality stood during this period. Despite legal and moral concerns about homosexuality in the Cold War era, it was still relatively hidden and not of academic or political interest. The first public opinion polls on the issue were not conducted until the late 1960s. It is, however, reasonable to assume that few people (knowingly) had contact with, or knowledge of, gay men or lesbians beyond what was reported in the mainstream press, putting the media in a powerful position to influence public perceptions. If the average heterosexual Australian relied on 1950s media reporting alone to gain an understanding of homosexuality, their perception would have been one of crime and perversion, and a lifestyle dedicated to cross-dressing and sex in public parks. Sensationalist reporting was common practice for topics related to homosexuality. For example, following a series of arrests at a gay party in Newcastle in June 1952, the media claimed that '[a] society of perverts, membership of which was quite large, existed in Newcastle'.[33]

Medicine, Psychiatry and the 1960s

The 1960s saw a new profile of homosexuality emerging as the medical and psychological professions began to take an increasing interest in sexuality. The Kinsey Reports of the late 1940s and early 1950s had been among the first

---

28   French, 1993.
29   Willett, 1997; Wotherspoon, Garry 1991, 'From Sub-Culture to Mainstream Culture: Some Impacts of Homosexual and Gay Sub-Cultures in Australia', *Journal of Australian Studies*, 15(28), pp. 56–62.
30   Willet, Graham 2000, *Living Out Loud: A History of Gay and Lesbian Activism in Australia*, Allen & Unwin, Sydney; Reynolds, Robert 2002, *From Camp to Queer: Remaking the Australian Homosexual*, Melbourne University Press, Vic.
31   French, 1993; Willett, 1997.
32   French, 1993.
33   Cited in ibid., p. 90.

of a number of new studies into human sexuality. In the 1960s, 'sexology' as a discipline became more prominent and the study of sex and sexuality was increasingly a topic of interest to medical and psychological researchers. Following this upswing in medical interest, psychological studies began to adopt a medicalised definition of homosexuality, positioning it not in terms of a criminal or deviant act but as a mental illness or, in some cases, a peculiar character trait. While some psychologists saw it as evidence of mental problems or moral insanity, others followed the theory first articulated by Havelock Ellis in 1915 that homosexuality was a 'congenital and a relatively harmless "anomaly" that should not be criminalised'.[34] Either way, one consequence of a medical or pathological perspective on homosexuality was that psychological researchers and practitioners began to explore the possibility of a 'cure'. Psychological and medical therapies, such as electroshock therapy, began to be trialled.[35] In October 1966, the *Sydney Morning Herald* ran a feature article on the 'new hope for deviants'. It discussed results of research being undertaken at Prince Henry Hospital into the treatment of a range of psychological disorders including homosexuality. The treatment involved electroshocks and other forms of aversion therapy.[36]

New ideas started to emerge advocating 'help' rather than 'punishment' for gay men and lesbians, and criticism of laws criminalising homosexuality began to circulate in public discourse. For example, in 1965 a Sydney judge, Justice Hiddens, drew on medical and psychological theories as he reluctantly sentenced two men who had been found guilty of indecent assault. Hiddens complained that the law had not kept pace with modern thought on homosexuality and that it should now be seen as a 'disease not a crime'.[37]

As this medicalised definition achieved more common acceptance, the idea that homosexuality could be viewed as something other than criminal, or deliberately perverted, behaviour gained credibility. The underlying message of the medical model of homosexuality was, however, that gay men and lesbians still required surveillance and intervention. Homosexuality was now seen as a condition or illness that needed, instead of legal surveillance, to be diagnosed, and possibly cured, by professional intervention. In effect, the medical profession overtook the criminal justice system as the authority with the legitimate right to manage and control homosexual lives. As Robert Reynolds has written: 'By the very

---

34 Weeks, Jeffrey 1981, *Sex, Politics and Society: The Regulation of Sexuality Since 1800*, Longman, London; Thompson, Denise 1985, *Flaws in the Social Fabric: Homosexuals and Society in Sydney*, Allen & Unwin, Sydney.
35 Willet, Graham 2005, 'Psyched In: Psychology, Psychiatry and Homosexuality in Australia', *Gay and Lesbian Issues and Psychology Review*, 2, pp. 53–7.
36 Reynolds, 2002.
37 Ibid.

nature of their neurotic condition, homosexuals were denied an autonomous sexual existence—experts represented homosexuality and their official prognosis neatly encapsulated the constraints of a medical discourse'.[38]

The Beginnings of Law Reform

Unlike the United States and Britain, where demands for decriminalisation of homosexuality came from a radicalising gay movement, in Australia, the early push for law reform came from welfare organisations and churches. As medical definitions of homosexuality gained more currency, religious and social organisations began to declare publicly that gay people were in need of treatment and support rather than criminal sanction. This was not necessarily indicative of more liberal attitudes emerging. Rather, the interest for many religious organisations was the potential for a cure. In the 1960s, Reverend Ted Noffs of the Wayside Chapel in Kings Cross, Sydney, urged the State Government to consider law reform so that homosexuals could seek 'treatment' without fear of arrest. Similar calls were made by a committee of inquiry established by the Presbyterian Church in 1967.[39]

Australia has not been subject to the fundamentalist zeal and political might of the far-right religious groups that dominate the social agenda in the United States. Religious leaders tend, however, to be considered legitimate commentators on matters of human sexuality and relationships, and they have a strong presence in public discourse on this issue. The media certainly regularly consults and quotes church leaders on such issues. Since the 1970s, several non-Catholic church groups in Australia, including the Religious Society of Friends (the Quakers) and the Uniting Church, have been in favour of law reform to decriminalise homosexuality. The SA Methodist Church also endorsed law reform at its 1972 conference, and the social questions committee of the Melbourne Anglican Diocese in 1971 stated that homosexual acts need not be considered criminal even though they did not accord with Christian values.[40] The Christian approach, while promoting tolerance, still maintained, however, the line that homosexuals needed 'help'. The NSW Presbyterian Assembly, for example, expressed their support for law reform in the 1970s while also appealing to the State Government for funds to research the causes and cure of homosexuality. Homosexuals were considered to be people who needed care, and a role was seen for the church in advocating these needs as perceived through religious values.[41]

---

38   Ibid.
39   Lewis, 1998.
40   Ibid.
41   Reynolds, 2002.

The notable exceptions to the 'compassionate' approach taken by Australian churches were the Sydney Archdiocese of the Anglican Church and the multi-denominational conservative grouping the Festival of Light (FOL). Along with the official voice of the Catholic Church, these both represented long-time vocal opposition to homosexuality in Australia. A Sydney Anglican Archdiocese report on homosexuality in 1973 stated that homosexual sex should remain criminalised as it threatened the institution of marriage and was 'intrinsically wrong'.

The conservative churches tend to receive regular media coverage and are generally consulted by journalists on their views regarding sexuality—if only as a source of controversy to spice up media stories. While it attracts a following in some areas, however, extreme religious conservatism has also often been depicted in the Australian press as irrational or 'loopy', particularly the antics of FOL spokesman, Reverend Fred Nile. As such, they have not always had the same impact as the far-right churches in other countries, particularly the United States. In Australia during the 1970s, those churches calling for decriminalisation of homosexuality probably had greater political influence.[42]

Lobbying for Law Reform

The first political lobby group dedicated specifically to gay law reform, The Homosexual Law Reform Society of the Australian Capital Territory, was formed in 1969 after two men were arrested for engaging in homosexual practices when they were found in a parked car on the outskirts of Canberra. This group comprised academics, lawyers and civil libertarians, some of whom were gay but certainly not all. The make-up of the group was reflective of a general left-wing support base for gay law reform that was emerging in Australia. Support for law reform also came from individual Members of Parliament. For example, in 1967, Bill Hayden, who would later become Leader of the Federal Opposition and Governor-General, suggested establishing a national committee on gay law reform and looked at ways the Federal Government could override the States on this issue.[43]

Don Dunstan, the Attorney-General and popular leader of the SA Labor Party, had been pushing for law reform in that State since the mid-1960s. When he became Premier in 1970, the campaign reached new ground and South Australia became the first Australian State to decriminalise homosexuality, in 1972. The Federal House of Representatives followed suit in October 1973, voting 60 to 44 in favour of a motion to decriminalise homosexual acts. It was not until 1975,

---

42   Lewis, 1998.
43   Ibid.

however, that draft law reform was sent to the Attorney-General so legislation could be amended in the Federal Territories. In the Australian Capital Territory, homosexuality became legal in 1976, although the law was not put in place in the Northern Territory until 1983.

In 1978, the Commonwealth Royal Commission on Human Relationships concluded that it was 'unnecessary' to put homosexuality on the criminal code and that it should be an offence only in the case of rape or where it offended public decency and order. Victoria complied with this, decriminalising homosexual acts in 1980. In Tasmania, despite a select committee set up in 1978 recommending decriminalisation of private homosexual acts, law reform was blocked by a conservative Upper House. This did not change until the late 1990s.[44]

In July 1982, the NSW Anti-Discrimination Commission released a report that made 35 recommendations, including: decriminalisation of homosexuality; better education within schools about homosexuality; and improving relations between gay people and the police force, beginning by ending the common police practice of surveillance and deliberate trapping of homosexuals. The report received publicity in all major newspapers but was ignored by the State Government.[45] New South Wales repealed laws criminalising homosexuality two years later, in 1984.

Law reform came much later in Queensland and Western Australia—1990 and 1989 respectively[46]—and when it did come it was not necessarily indicative of more progressive social attitudes among politicians. For example, when the new laws were introduced in Western Australia (the *1989 Law Reform, Decriminalisation of Sodomy, Act*), State parliamentarians insisted on inserting a preamble to the legislation that, while acknowledging that they felt it to be inappropriate for criminal law to intrude on personal sexual relationships, expressed their overt condemnation of homosexuality. Furthermore, while male-to-male sex was made legal, a range of new offences prohibiting the 'encouragement' or

---

44   Altman, Dennis 1989, 'The Emergence of Gay Identity in the USA and Australia', in Christine Jennet and Stewart Randal (eds), *Politics of the Future: The Role of Social Movements*, Macmillan, Melbourne; Lewis, 1998; Bull, Melissa, Pinto, Susan and Wilson, Paul 1991, 'Homosexual Law Reform in Australia', *Australian Institute of Criminology Trends and Issues in Crime and Criminal Justice*, 29, Australian Institute of Criminology, Canberra, <http://aic.gov.au>

45   See Mercer, Neil 1982, 'Board Reports on Homosexuality', *Sydney Morning Herald*, 6 July; 'NSW Study Finds One in 10 Are Gay', *Sunday Times* [Perth], 18 July 1982; 'Law Change on Homosexuality Recommended', *The Canberra Times*, 6 July 1982; 'Homosexuals Should Get Rights, Says NSW Board', *The Age*, 6 July 1982, p. 5; Cumming, Fia 1982, 'Homosexual Study Urged Law Reform', *The Australian*, 6 July, p. 3; Bull et al., 1991.

46   The relatively late change in law in Western Australia, Tasmania and Queensland also meant that in the mid-1980s Australia was one of only three other Western democracies (alongside Ireland, a number of states in the United States and Israel) to maintain consensual adult homosexual sex as a crime (Altman, 1989). Paradoxically, however, a few years later Australia also led the way in the area of anti-discrimination law. In New South Wales and South Australia, there were legal protections from discrimination on the grounds of homosexuality in place by the end of the 1980s (ibid.).

promotion of homosexual behaviour was introduced. This included a section on the illegality of 'promoting' or 'encouraging' homosexuality within educational institutions.[47]

Homosexual law reform was also limited to the notion of 'actions undertaken in private'. While this was no doubt considered to be the most acceptable— or at least a less controversial—way to approach the debate, it had the effect of containing the laws, maintaining only limited acceptance of homosexuality. Public displays of homosexuality could still be considered indecent or offensive in a legal sense. Nevertheless, the debate over law reform did open space for public discussion on homosexuality that was not immediately associated with criminality, illness, sinfulness or immorality. Ideas of human rights and minority representation began to carve out a new frame for the public treatment of gay men and lesbians.[48]

Public Opinion

Criminologists conducted the first Australian survey of public attitudes towards homosexuality in 1968, with the results published in the *Australian Law Journal*. The survey indicated that only 22 per cent of respondents favoured homosexual law reform and many felt that punishment for engaging in homosexual acts should be 'severe whipping' or 'a long period of imprisonment'.[49] When the same survey was repeated in 1971, however, more than half of respondents (56 per cent) indicated their support for law reform.[50] In 1965, an article was published in *The Bulletin* by criminologist Gordon Hawkins discussing myths and stereotypes about homosexuality and changing public attitudes towards law reform in the United Kingdom and America. Hawkins was, at the time, one of the few high-profile authors seriously bringing homosexuality to public attention and he was able to gain a sense of attitudes through people's reactions to his publications. In 1970, Hawkins expressed optimism for law reform, commenting on what he observed to be a marked increase in positive public attitudes towards homosexuality.[51]

In 1973, Australian National Opinion Polls asked people what their reaction would be if they found out two men were living together in a relationship in

---

47   Pereira, Darryl 1999, 'HIV/AIDS and its "Willing Executioners": The Impact of Discrimination', *Murdoch University Electronic Journal of Law*, 6(4), <http://www.murdoch.edu.au/elaw/issues/v6n4/pereira64nf. html>; Bull et al., 1991.
48   Reynolds, 2002.
49   Ibid.
50   De Waal, Peter, Black, Ian, Trebilco, Peter and Wills, Sue 1994, *A Review of the 1976 Tribunal on Homosexuals and Discrimination*, The Tribunal Working Group, Sydney.
51   Reynolds, 2002; Lewis, 1998.

their neighbourhood. Of the respondents, 8 per cent said they would inform authorities or police and 75 per cent said they would consider it none of their business. In 1974, a Morgan poll indicated that just more than half of all respondents (54 per cent) thought sexual acts in private between consenting males should be legal.[52] While polls taken during the 1970s and early 1980s tended to indicate public support for decriminalisation and non-intervention in gay relationships, there was still, however, a view that homosexuality was morally wrong. For example, the 1984 Australian Social Science Survey found that 64 per cent of respondents indicated that they believed homosexual behaviour was always wrong. In the 1999–2000 survey, 48 per cent of respondents felt it was always wrong.[53]

Simon Watney once wrote that 'a specific cultural agenda imposes its values via the very questions it asks'.[54] While opinion polls tend to be inconsistent and are unlikely to be the most reliable reflection of broad public opinion, the fact that such polls exist on the issue of homosexuality is in itself indicative of a belief that homosexuality is a 'public issue' in a way that heterosexuality is not. The history of regulation of homosexuality, whether medical or legal, has positioned it as a political and social 'problem' considered a valid topic for public debate. There is a sense that society and the state, rather than individual gay men and lesbians, have a right to decide if homosexuality is acceptable behaviour or not and sanction it accordingly. Similar debates rarely, if ever, occur on the topic of adult heterosexuality.

The history of homosexuality is one marked by professional intervention into the lives of gay men and lesbians. While homosexuality had been subject to much public debate, it was generally a debate played out in the media between medical and legal 'experts'. Gay men or lesbians had no voice in such discussion. Indeed, the construction of homosexuality as either 'illness' or 'crime' meant gay people were, on the whole, deliberately excluded from communicating their opinion. It was only with the emergence of organised gay and lesbian activism that this began to change.

The Gay Movement in Australia

Australia does not have long-established gay and lesbian political organisations, such as the Mattachine Society in the United States and other groups associated with the early 'homophile' movement of the 1950s. By the 1970s, however, there

---

52   De Waal et al., 1994.
53   Kelley, Jonothan 2001, 'Attitudes Towards Homosexuality in 29 Nations', *Australian Social Monitor Online Journal*, <http://www.international-survey.org/A_Soc_M/>, pp. 15–22.
54   Watney, Simon 1994, *Practices of Freedom*, Rivers Oram Press, London.

was a fledgling gay and lesbian movement in Australia and a number groups were forming around issues of gay law reform and challenging definitions of homosexuality as a psychological disorder. The largest of these groups was the Sydney-based Campaign Against Moral Persecution (CAMP).[55]

According to Graham Willett, '[i]f the Australian lesbian and gay movement can be said to have a birthday, 19 September 1970 is it'.[56] It was on this day that a feature article published in *The Australian* newspaper announced the formation of CAMP. Two friends, John Ware and Christabel Poll, conceived the idea for CAMP over a bottle of whisky. It was to be one of the first overtly political gay organisations in Australia. Prior to this, gay and lesbian groups had generally been social or support based and non-political. It seems, however, that in the 1970s the time was ripe for a shift to a more political orientation. A year after the feature on CAMP appeared in *The Australian*, the group had acquired more than 1500 members, and what began as a loosely structured collaboration developed into an established organisation with set procedures and a constitution.[57]

Encouraging gay people to 'come out' publicly was a core tactic of CAMP in the early 1970s and this resulted in some high-profile publicity in Australian newspapers and a growing membership of the organisation. Graham Willett describes well the significance of this, writing:

> Unquestionably it was the willingness of CAMP's leaders to come out publicly as homosexuals that elevated CAMP from a 'sort of book club' to the founding organisation of a social movement. Never before had anyone in Australia willingly identified, indeed proclaimed, themselves as homosexual to the media as Ware and Poll were doing. Their courage was the spark that lit the bushfire.[58]

CAMP first shifted its attention from publicity stunts to collective protest in October 1971, when they demonstrated outside the Liberal Party headquarters during preselection for the seat of Berowra in New South Wales. Berowra's sitting member, Tom Hughes, a man who had demonstrated cautious but relatively progressive support for gay law reform, was facing a conservative challenge from a contender known for his homophobic views, Jim Cameron. The protest had not been easy for CAMP to organise as fears of attracting anti-gay violence meant that the time and place were advertised only by word-of-mouth. The crowd that turned up was, however, fairly large and certainly vocal. They

---

55 Thompson, 1985.
56 Willet, 2000.
57 Thompson, 1985.
58 Willet, 2000.

carried banners proclaiming that 'Cameron hates homos, but he'll sure b-g-r the Liberal Party', and handed out leaflets explaining CAMP's position to delegates as they entered the meeting.[59]

While Tom Hughes easily won the preselection and the demonstration was deemed a success, CAMP did not continue to grow as a 'radical' organisation. Inhibited by the lack of any precedent in Australia for more radical gay action, major legislative or political change was not on CAMP's agenda—particularly in branches of CAMP outside Sydney. Instead, the organisation tended towards conciliatory statements aimed at convincing the broader public that gay men and women were just average people.[60]

However, it was around this time that other gay and lesbian activist groups began to focus more directly on achieving political change. In 1975, the Australian Union of Students (AUS) adopted a pro-gay policy and sponsored the first annual National Conference of Lesbians and Homosexuals.[61] The AUS engaged in a campaign to reduce homophobia on campuses and within teaching practices. They also mounted a major public defence of Queensland teacher Greg Weir who had been refused employment as a teacher on the basis of his homosexuality. From this, an action group called Melbourne's Gay Teachers' Group was formed, leading to an ongoing campaign to ensure job security for gay and lesbian teachers.[62] Actions such as this began to draw attention to the legal status of homosexuality and the lack of legal protections in society for gay men and lesbians. By the end of the 1970s, there was more consistent political organising occurring around the issue of the decriminalisation of homosexuality.

Gay and lesbian activism in Australia achieved perhaps its highest public profile with the event now marked as the first Sydney Gay and Lesbian Mardi Gras. On the night of 24 June 1978, a group of lesbian and gay revellers paraded down Oxford Street in Sydney. The celebration was held to commemorate the Stonewall riots that had begun in New York on 28 June 1969, while also drawing attention to the ongoing campaign for law reform in Australia. Dancing down Oxford Street, demonstrators hoped people would be drawn out of bars and pubs to join them. The gathering was peaceful and had been given all the necessary approval by authorities; however, as the marchers reached Hyde Park, police unexpectedly attempted to disperse the crowd. Protestors reacted angrily to this, and moved on to Kings Cross where a violent confrontation followed. This continued for some time and 53 women and men were arrested. Allegations of

---

59   Ibid.
60   Thompson, 1985.
61   Ballard, John 1992, 'Australia: Participation and Innovation in a Federal System', in David Kirp and Ronald Bayer (eds), *AIDS in the Industrialised Democracies: Passions, Politics and Policies*, Rutgers University Press, New Brunswick, NJ.
62   Willet, 2000.

police brutality soon followed.[63] Eventually, those demonstrators who had not been arrested held a frantic meeting outside Darlinghurst Police Station, at which bail was raised to release those now held by the police (although the amount was only $70–100 for each person, it required a fair amount of organisation to gather the cash very early on a Sunday morning in pre–ATM machine 1978). A meeting later that day was also arranged to devise a media communications strategy. Influential people within the gay community were contacted and mobilised. The demonstrators re-gathered outside the Courthouse on Monday morning where more arrests were made. Large solidarity protests were held all over Australia in response.[64]

The following year, in June 1979, another night time parade was assembled in commemoration of the violent events of the year before. Police did not prevent this parade and it went ahead, peacefully, as planned. The event became an annual gathering, growing over the years to become one of the largest street festivals in the world: the Sydney Gay and Lesbian Mardi Gras Parade. In 1983, six years after the first protest, more than 20 000 spectators attended the parade, which by this stage had been moved from June to March to catch the end of the Australian summer. By 1994, the 'Mardi Gras' audience had increased to four hundred thousand. In addition, Mardi Gras had become a month-long community festival incorporating arts and sporting events. While there is debate about whether or not the Sydney Gay and Lesbian Mardi Gras should be considered a 'social movement' or even a political initiative, there is no doubt that the annual event created unprecedented publicity for the Australian community of gay men and lesbians.[65] As author and academic Dennis Altman observed in 1993:

> Of course, now [Mardi Gras has] become a massive event that is recognised by almost everybody…as one of the things that happens in Australia in Summer: certainly, in Sydney…[For] example, [for] the last Mardi Gras the *Sydney Morning Herald* had a special Mardi Gras crossword that Saturday. Now, this is the newspaper which 20 years ago refused to use the word 'gay' in its pages. That change, I think, is symbolic of what's happened, which is, that the lesbian and gay community, which is now the term which is most often used, has actually become recognised as a legitimate community in Australian life—most obviously in Sydney, but to a considerable extent elsewhere. We see that reflected in politics. It was very clear in the last election when politicians were courting the votes of that community.[66]

---

63 Ariss, Robert 1997, *Against Death: The Practice of Living with AIDS*, Gordon and Breach, Amsterdam.
64 Phil Carswell, Personal Communication, 25 October 2006.
65 Marsh, I. and Galbraith, L. 1995, 'The Political Impact of the Sydney Gay and Lesbian Mardi Gras', *Australian Journal of Political Science*, 30(2), pp. 300–20; Ariss, 1997.
66 Dennis Altman, Interviewed by Heather Rusden, 7 July 1993, Oral History Project: The Australian Response to AIDS, TRC 2815/37, National Library of Australia, Canberra [hereinafter NLA].

Although 'Mardi Gras' had become a major focus of gay and lesbian activism over the past decades, in the early 1980s homosexuality remained on the criminal code in most Australian States and a number of organisations were being formed separate to Mardi Gras to tackle this issue. In Sydney, two gay activists, Lex Watson and Craig Johnston (both of whom would later go on to be involved in AIDS activism), established the Gay Rights Lobby (GRL), the first meeting of which was held in February 1981. The GRL began a campaign involving political lobbying, petitioning, media liaison and community education around the law reform issue. They also sought support from churches and other community groups. In late 1981, GRL mounted a campaign around the State election, lobbying candidates and voters in key seats. The organisation found support for their goals from a left-wing member of the NSW Parliament, George Petersen, when he announced his intention to try to repeal laws that criminalised homosexuality. The GRL worked closely with Petersen to draft his bill. They also continued to campaign among the gay community, generating enthusiasm for the prospect that law reform could become a reality. When the bill was to be tabled in April 1981, 500 people attended a demonstration outside the NSW Parliament. Although Petersen's bill was defeated and the laws remained unchanged, these actions still represented a surge in momentum for activism around gay law reform.[67]

The issue resurfaced in January 1983 when police raided a gay nightclub in Sydney's inner suburbs. During the raid, more than 100 men were detained and four people were charged with indecent assault. Police claimed that they had visited the club only following a complaint made by a patron. But once there, they had apprehended a number of men, taking their names and, in some cases, the contact details of their employers.[68] At the time, under the *Crimes Act*, a man charged with indecent assault against another man (sodomy) could be sentenced to 14 years' jail in New South Wales, and consent could not be used as a defence (this was despite the fact that a charge of 'rape without violence' attracted only a seven-year sentence). More than 1000 people demonstrated in angry protest of the nightclub raid. The GRL released a media statement that said: 'It is ironic that at the same time police are complaining about a lack of resources and overtime that 15 officers, four cars and two vans could be devoted to harassing homosexuals.'[69] Despite this protest, a second police raid on the same nightclub was conducted less than one month later. This time, 11 men were charged, some under the archaic common-law offence of 'scandalous conduct'. A second protest rally was organised, at which about 300 people

---

67   Willet, 2000.

68   'Homosexuals March', *Sydney Morning Herald*, 1 February 1983, p. 10; 'Gay Protest', *The Canberra Times*, 6 February 1983, p. 3.

69   Cited in Coultan, Mark 1983, 'Police Raid on Club Angers Homosexual Community', *Sydney Morning Herald*, 31 January, p. 3.

demonstrated outside Sydney Police Headquarters.[70] Actions continued, with 28 men presenting themselves to the Darlinghurst Police Station in Sydney in October 1983 with statutory declarations confessing to engaging in sodomy.[71] In 1984, NSW Premier Neville Wran finally announced that he would support a bill to decriminalise homosexual sex—although not to equalise the age of consent between homosexual acts and heterosexual sex.[72]

Community, Identity and Activism

Although law reform had involved many hundreds of gay men, the late 1970s had also produced increasing visibility of the non-political gay scene. People now spoke about the 'gay community', rather than gay activism or a gay movement. By the early 1980s there were a number of prominent non-political gay groups across the country, as well as a range of gay businesses including bars, pubs and nightclubs starting up in known 'gay areas' of the major cities. There is much debate among gay activists, and in academic writing, on the notion of community and whether a 'gay community' exists at all. Those who support the notion argue that gay men and lesbians share a community-like connection through shared social experiences, close friendship ties and strong social networks. The counterargument to this, however, asserts that similar experiences of sexuality do not create a basis for community and that the lives of lesbians and gay men are too diverse to warrant the term 'community' based on common social identity. There is also a concern that the growth of a gay 'community' represents the de-politicisation and increasing commercialism of gay identity. In this approach, gay community is seen to amount to the ghettoisation or containment of gay politics.[73] In the early 1980s, however, there was a sense of politics and activism present in the general gay community that reflected a collective consciousness of the marginalised status of gay men and lesbians and their history of activism. For example, the two major gay community publications at the time had overtly political titles: *Campaign*, published in Sydney since 1975, and *Outrage*, published in Melbourne from April 1983.[74] The history of (and ongoing) discrimination against gay men and lesbians also meant community events such

---

70   Mercer, Neil 1983, 'Anti-Labor Threat After Homosexual Club Raid', *Sydney Morning Herald*, 28 February, p. 3; 'Gay March on Police Station After Raids', *Border Morning Mail*, 28 February 1983, p. 8.
71   Willet, 2000.
72   According to Dennis Altman, it was only New South Wales that could claim law reform had been the result of movement action. Altman argues that in New South Wales continued pressure from activists caused enough embarrassment for the State Premier Neville Wran to push for conservatives within his party to allow law reform. In contrast, Victoria had no real mass gay movement. If law reform had been influenced by the work of activists, it was due to the more formal lobbying efforts of the Gay Legal Rights Coalition (Altman, 1989).
73   Ariss, 1997, p. 28.
74   The immediate precursor to *Outrage* was a publication called *Gay Community News*.

as the Sydney Gay and Lesbian Mardi Gras festival were grounded in a sense of politics in a way that mainstream festivals are not.[75] As Ariss writes: 'While not all gays participating in the Mardi Gras may consciously perceive it as a political event, participation is a very emotionally charged experience, much like a religious ritual.' Moreover, Ariss argues, the concept of gay community in itself has political utility.

Gay identity was now socialised via this link to a 'community' of like others. 'Gay' constituted a quasi-ethnic identity with geographical, social, behavioural and cultural features shared by its members. By socialising gay identity, political strategies were opened up to include more diverse forms of activities and greater participation in terms of the numbers of people involved.[76]

AIDS Activism

The fact that there was an existing gay and lesbian media and a history of organised activism among the gay and lesbian community meant that when AIDS first arrived in the early 1980s gay men were in a strong position to respond to it collectively.[77] The organisational structures necessary for political mobilisation were, to a large extent, already in place and people were drawn in to the politics of HIV/AIDS in some cases because they identified personally and socially with the visible gay community rather than because they considered themselves to be overtly political.

AIDS beckoned a whole new generation of political activity. Many hundreds of people—many of whom had not previously been part of the organised gay-rights movement—became involved with AIDS activism. Long-term Australian gay activist Lex Watson once wrote, 'AIDS has fundamentally changed the style, the content and, indeed, the whole notion of gay male politics. And it has done something—unfortunately, as it happens, but nonetheless in a very real way—that nothing else in the gay community did.'[78]

---

75   Carr, Adam 1988, '*Outrage* at 15 or the Rise and Fall of Practically Everyone', *Outrage*, April, [Republished by the author on his personal web site: <http://www.adam-carr.net/003.html>]; Lewis, Lynette and Ross, Michael 1995, *A Select Body: The Gay Dance Party Subculture and the HIV/AIDS Pandemic*, Cassell, London.
76   Ariss, 1997.
77   This point has been made by several authors writing on the Australian response to AIDS. See, for example, Altman, Dennis 1988, 'Legitimation Through Disaster: AIDS and the Gay Movement', in Elizabeth Fee and Daniel Fox (eds), *AIDS: The Burdens of History*, University of California Press, Berkeley; Ballard, John 1989, 'The Politics of AIDS', in Heather Gardner (ed.), *The Politics of Health: The Australian Experience*, Churchill Livingstone, Melbourne; Misztal, Barbara 1991, 'HIV/AIDS Policies in Australia: Bureaucracy and Collective Action', *International Journal of Sociology and Social Policy*, 11(4), pp. 62–82; Sendziuk, Paul 2003, *Learning to Trust: Australian Responses to AIDS*, UNSW Press, Sydney.
78   Watson, Lex 1988, 'Life After AIDS', *Australian Left Review*, October–November, pp. 12–15.

The organised response of the gay community has been one of the most striking features of the HIV/AIDS epidemic in Australia. Throughout the 1980s and the 1990s, the Australian gay community and their supporters established the first 'safe sex' HIV-prevention campaigns, created large volunteer-run care and support networks for people living with HIV/AIDS, produced volumes of information to educate people and inform policy debate, and established a presence at the forefront of public health policy making regarding HIV/AIDS.

Alongside this, the AIDS movement played an increasingly important role in shaping public attitudes towards homosexuality more generally. HIV/AIDS brought the gay community under intense public scrutiny. While issues around the nature, legality and social acceptance of homosexuality dominated public discussions around HIV/AIDS, the AIDS movement organised to ensure it had a presence in this discussion. Paradoxically, despite the devastation it caused the gay community, HIV/AIDS brought unprecedented opportunities for gay activists to present publicly a perspective on homosexuality and the gay community that was not bound by legal, moral or medical definitions. Instead, the community had a voice that was independent of these authorities.

This account of the emergence of the organised AIDS movement in Australia focuses on how the movement was able to gain enough political strength and public profile to influence the policy response to HIV/AIDS, and to shape public knowledge about the virus and those affected by it. The emphasis is not on the tangible or policy outcomes achieved by the AIDS movement. Rather, I am interested in how the actions of the movement contributed to changing public knowledge about, and attitudes towards, homosexuality, and how activists were able to inject a new perspective about the role of community into the Australian medical and public health systems.

AIDS Activism as a Social Movement

Throughout this text I refer to collective action in response to AIDS as a movement: the AIDS movement. There are no clearly definable elements that mark a social movement, and whether or not particular forms of collective action constitute a 'movement' is a source of much academic debate. But there are some key features that have been identified by a number of researchers as common to most social movements. First, many theorists agree that an analysis of movement tactics must be at the basis of any definition. Paul Burstein et al., for instance, construct a definition of social movements based on the willingness of actors to use 'non-institutionalised tactics at least part of the time'.[79] Social

---

79   Burstein, Paul, Einwohner, Rachel and Hollander, Jocelyn 1995, 'The Success of Political Movements: A Bargaining Perspective', in Craig Jenkins and Bert Klandermans (eds), *The Politics of Social Protest*, University

movements, they argue, must not be bound to any institutional structures or have formal alliances to a political party, institution or government. Movements are independent, organised, collective efforts aimed at achieving some form of social change.[80]

Researchers also generally consider the goals of collective mobilisation to be central to the definition of a social movement. Social movements in general are assumed to be aiming to achieve some measure of cultural, social or political change. Alberto Melucci and Leonardo Avritzer, for instance, explain a social movement as a form of collective action that produces solidarity among actors, presents an existing conflict to the public and challenges social or political systems.[81] Sidney Tarrow bases his definition on the structural location of movement actors, arguing that social movements involve contentious collective action. According to Tarrow: 'collective action becomes contentious when it is used by people who lack regular access to institutions, who act in the name of new or unaccepted claims.'[82] In other words, social movements are the main mechanism by which ordinary people can challenge more powerful or better resourced opponents. The basis of contentious action is movement actors' belief in the capacity of action to challenge authority.

I have no intention here of determining systematically whether or not the community response to AIDS in Australia constituted a social movement. I maintain the basic assumption that it did and that it is appropriate to discuss the AIDS movement within the framework provided by social-movement literature. It is certainly worth noting that the collective response to AIDS on the part of gay activists bears many of the indicators of a 'social movement' as defined by the authors mentioned above. The response to AIDS by community-based activists involved sustained, collective action over a number of years aimed at influencing public policy and improving social conditions for gay men and lesbians. People were drawn to the movement through their relationship with HIV/AIDS itself or because they broadly identified with the population group most affected in Australia—namely, gay men. AIDS activists utilised a range of tactics, from formal lobbying and participation in government advisory bodies to street demonstrations and pickets.

The response of community actors to AIDS was diverse. Some people volunteered for care and support roles, establishing charities and agencies that provided at-home care for people with AIDS-related illnesses. Others became more directly

---

of Minnesota Press, Minneapolis, p. 278.

80   Ibid.

81   Melucci, Alberto and Avritzer, Leonardo 2000, 'Complexity, Cultural Pluralism and Democracy: Collective Action in the Public Space', *Social Science Information*, 39(4), pp. 507–27.

82   Tarrow, Sidney 1998, *Power in Movement: Social Movement and Contentious Politics*, Cambridge University Press, p. 3.

politically engaged, lobbying for increases in government funding and action around HIV/AIDS. Education and HIV-prevention initiatives were also major focuses of community action, with many people involved in the production of HIV information materials and running 'safe sex' campaigns. When I refer to the 'AIDS movement' as an identified group, I seek to encompass the full range of initiatives taken up by activists. This is not an attempt to simplify or ignore the diversity of community responses to AIDS. Defining the community response to AIDS as a social movement, however, is an expression of my assertion that analysis of the history of the AIDS movement in Australia can be seen as an analysis of the history of a social movement.

Through analysing this history, I seek to explore the process by which the AIDS movement progressed from being a group of activists sitting far outside formal systems and institutions—and representing a highly stigmatised and marginalised group—to a relatively powerful and well-resourced political force that gained a legitimate and credible standing in the public eye, with government and the medical system. What factors enabled this shift to occur? Was it particular to the historical conditions into which AIDS emerged or the skills of individual activists?

I am also interested in the way in which AIDS activists were able to influence public knowledge and attitudes towards gay men and lesbians. How did this occur? What role do social movements play in constructing social knowledge? What is the cultural legacy of social movements such as the AIDS movement?

Exploration of these questions is not a matter of assessing in a positivistic sense the concrete achievements of the AIDS movement. Rather, I use a narrative-history approach to detail the rise of the AIDS movement in historical context and track the development of relationships between AIDS-movement actors and other social groups, such as medical doctors. I also look at the way in which the AIDS movement contributed to political and cultural discourse around homosexuality—an approach to the study of social movements that could be described as 'hermeneutic'.[83]

In part, this involves consideration of the content of mainstream media related to HIV/AIDS. My assumption is that what is expressed in the mainstream media will reveal shifts in public perceptions of HIV/AIDS and the people affected by it.[84] Given that a majority of the general heterosexual public had limited personal experience with either gay men or people with AIDS, the media was

---

83 Eyerman, Ron and Jamison, Andrew 1991, *Social Movements: A Cognitive Approach*, Polity Press, Cambridge.

84 Gamson, William and Modigliani, Andre 1989, 'Media Discourse and Public Opinion on Nuclear Power: A Constructionist Approach', *American Journal of Sociology*, 95(1), pp. 1–37; Lawler, Steph 2004, 'Rules of Engagement: Habitus, Power and Resistance', *The Sociological Review*, 52(s2), pp. 110–18.

their central means of acquiring knowledge. The way in which the media constructed images of HIV/AIDS was instrumental in determining how the general public perceived their level of risk with regards to HIV transmission.[85] This was confirmed in a study conducted through Macquarie University in which the media was identified as an important source of information through which Australians formed opinions and beliefs about HIV/AIDS and HIV-positive people. The authors of this study write:

> It was clear from the group discussions that people obtained information and constructed meaning from media sources. News reports were very frequently mentioned either implicitly or explicitly. Cases such as Holly Johnson,[86] Charleen,[87] the dentist in Miami who infected his patients, the prison officer who was injected with a blood filled syringe…were mentioned. When such cases were mentioned, the other group members had no difficulty in identifying them.[88]

An inquiry by the NSW Anti-Discrimination Board in 1992 also concluded that the media plays a central role in determining public attitudes towards HIV and AIDS. The inquiry report stated that the media could be responsible for either legitimising discrimination or promoting positive public attitudes.[89]

The AIDS movement employed campaign strategies that deliberately sought to influence media portrayals of both gay men and HIV-positive people. Activists also worked hard to position themselves as legitimate media spokespeople on HIV/AIDS-related matters. This was an important political strategy given

---

85   Wellings, Kaye 1988, 'Perceptions of Risk—Media Treatment of AIDS', in Peter Aggleton and Hilary Homans (eds), *Social Aspects of AIDS*, The Falmer Press, London.

86   Holly Johnson was a child who was infected with HIV by her mother, who had acquired the virus through a blood transfusion. The case received a great deal of media attention when Holly's father made a legal claim for compensation. Holly Johnson died in 1990. Riley, Mark 1990, 'Holly is Farewelled, But the Grief Stays', *Sydney Morning Herald*, 6 September, p. 9.

87   Charleen (sometimes spelt Sharleen) was a sex worker who achieved infamy when, in 1987, newspapers ran stories claiming she continued to have sex with clients despite knowing her positive HIV status. The then NSW Minister for Health, Peter Anderson, wanted to use the *Public Health (Proclaimed Diseases) Amendment Act* to detain her, but it was not until two years later, in 1989, following her appearance on the *60 Minutes* current affairs show, that the Department of Health arrested her, enforcing the *Public Health Act 1903*, which enables health authorities to detain an infectious patient for treatment. This led to outrage among AIDS activists and civil libertarians, and was a high-profile media story for some weeks. It was the first act of compulsory quarantine of an HIV-positive person ever seen in Australia. Perkins, Roberta 1991, 'Working Girls: Prostitutes, Their Life and Social Control', *Australian Studies in Law, Crime and Justice Series*, Australian Institute of Criminology, Canberra, viewed 12 November 2006, <http://www.aic.gov.au/publications/lcj/working/ch2-5.html>

88   Kippax, S., Tillet, G., Crawford, J. and Cregan, J. 1991, *Discrimination in the Context of AIDS*, Macquarie University Research Unit, National Centre for HIV Social Research, Sydney, p. 31.

89   NSW Anti-Discrimination Board (ADB) 1992, *Discrimination—The Other Epidemic*, NSW Anti-Discrimination Board, Sydney.

that the historical authority and respect afforded to medical authorities mean information from these sources tends to be privileged in the media over that of activists or non-medical sources.[90]

The media was important in debates about HIV/AIDS because to a large extent it is the media that makes or breaks the credibility of social actors or groups. If the media was willing to accept AIDS activists as legitimate contributors to debates about HIV/AIDS, this would in turn give them a higher standing in the public eye.[91]

Of interest in this historical account is whether or not, over time, AIDS activists managed to gain greater access to the media as 'legitimate experts' as well as the way in which HIV/AIDS issues were framed by the media and how this changed over time.

A Note About Emotions

Each section of this book is framed around a different emotion: fear, trust and mistrust, and grief. These themes emerged from the subject of the book itself. Emotion is a consistent, if not implicit and unacknowledged, presence throughout much of the literature on the social history of HIV/AIDS. It was certainly present in the interviews I conducted with AIDS activists. In the early days of HIV/AIDS, there was an obvious relationship between fear, anger and the mobilisation of the AIDS movement. Gay activists were motivated to begin campaigning because they were fearful, not only of AIDS itself but also of the potential social and political repercussions it brought. They were also angry about the lack of political attention being given to AIDS (if not in Australia then certainly in other dominant Western countries, most notably the United States). As the movement developed, the issue of trust and mistrust between AIDS activists and the medical profession was an important underlying factor in the negotiation of AIDS policy and practice. Underpinning all of this was an immense sense of grief. In the 1980s, many gay men attended a funeral every few weeks. Some people spoke of the early years of AIDS as a surreal experience—like the plot of a bad movie—in which they endured the deaths of so many friends and lovers from a largely unknown cause, not knowing if they would be next. In the final section of the book, I look more at the relationship between

---

90 Kippax et al., 1991, p. 41; Gamson and Modigliani, 1989; Klandermans, Bert 1992, 'The Social Construction of Protest and Multiorganizational Fields', in Aldon Morris and Carol Mueller (eds), *Frontiers in Social Movement Theory*, Yale University Press, New Haven, Conn.
91 Epstein, Steven 1996, *Impure Science: AIDS, Activism and the Politics of Knowledge*, University of California Press, London.

grief and stigma, exploring the way in which the AIDS movement challenged homophobic discrimination and stigma around AIDS through the creation of AIDS memorials as outlets for public grieving.

There is much academic work on the relationship between organised, collective action and emotion. Implicitly or explicitly, all social movements appeal to emotion in some way. Feelings of fear, anger, indignation or joy are emotions that can inspire and galvanise collective action. Rituals and demonstrations are also used to stir up emotional sensations and affirm connection with the group.[92] Early academic work on emotion and collective action focused on emotional reactions to events that led to crowds spontaneously reacting in anger or hatred 'in the heat of the moment'.[93] More recent scholarship has sought to examine the relationship between emotions that inspire collective action and the cognitive, rationalised decisions of movement actors. James Jasper, for instance, uses the term 'moral shock' to suggest that what might motivate a person to take political action are feelings of moral outrage or indignation towards events— such as anger following an environmental disaster or offence over government decisions. Jasper suggests that emotional reaction and rational political argument go hand in hand; morals are a culturally or cognitively framed assessment of the situation, but these generate an emotional reaction (anger, indignation).[94]

Of further interest to social-movement scholars is the question of how movement actors work to maintain the emotional reaction of groups and direct it towards a political target and substantive goals. Moral outrage sparks an emotional response, which social-movement organisers then steer towards a sustained political strategy.[95] As a movement progresses, the sensations of empowerment and elation that often accompany involvement in collective protest can serve to maintain motivation for movement action.[96]

I do not wish to make a generalised statement about the role of emotion in social processes. As Jack Barbalet has written: 'Rather than treat emotions in general it is absolutely necessary to treat particular emotions.'[97] I do maintain the view,

92 Taylor, Verta and Rupp, Leila 2002, 'Living Internationalism: The Emotion Culture of Transnational Women's Organisations 1888–1945', *Mobilization*, 7(2), pp. 141–58; Goodwin, Jeff, Jasper, James and Polletta, Francesca 2001, 'Why Emotions Matter', in Jeff Goodwin, James Jasper and Francesca Polletta (eds), *Passionate Politics: Emotions and Social Movements*, University of Chicago Press, Ill.

93 Goodwin et al., 2001.

94 Ibid.; Jasper, James 1998, 'The Emotions of Protest: Affective and Reactive Emotions In and Around Social Movements', *Sociological Forum*, 13(3), pp. 397–424.

95 Jasper, 1998.

96 Gould, Deborah 2000, Sex, Death and the Politics of Anger, Unpublished PhD Thesis, University of Chicago, Ill., p. xvii.

97 Barbalet, Jack 2001, Emotion in Social Life and Social Theory: Recovering the Leicester Tradition, Inaugural Lecture, 20 November 2001, University of Leicester, UK, p. 16.

however, that the relationship between emotions and the development of the political and ideological goals of a social movement (or what is often called the 'frame' of a social movement) is not coincidental.

Social-movement 'frames' can, in a nutshell, be described as the ideological position of a movement—the view of social reality adopted by movement activists, and their ideas about what social and political changes are required to achieve their ideal world.[98] I argue that the history of the Australian AIDS movement demonstrates the need to look at social-movement frames not just in terms of their intellectual content and form, but also from the personal and emotional perspectives of movement constituents. When HIV/AIDS first emerged, members of the gay community were incredibly fearful about what the future held for them. People were worried that the virus would, along with the devastation caused by AIDS itself, inspire a new wave of homophobia and prejudice in society. A social group that held a more dominant position in the social fabric, and that did not have a history of discrimination, would not have experienced the impact of HIV/AIDS in the same way. The gay community mobilised in response to the fears of their constituents and the grief and anger that followed AIDS deaths. The political outlook and strategies adopted by the AIDS movement were based on activists' knowledge and experience of past injustices as well as their emotional reaction to the current situation. In other words, the history of the AIDS movement demonstrates the way in which movement frames are informed at once by emotion, history and political strategy.

---

98   Snow, David and Benford, Robert 1992, 'Master Frames and Cycles of Protest', in Aldon Morris and Carol McClung (eds), *Frontiers in Social Movement Theory*, Yale University Press, New Haven, Conn.; Benford, Robert and Snow, David 2000, 'Framing Processes and Social Movements: An Overview and Assessment', *Annual Review of Sociology*, 26, pp. 611–39; Tesh, Sylvia 2000, *Uncertain Hazards: Environmental Activists and Scientific Proof*, Cornell University Press, Ithaca, NY.

Part One: Fear and Morality

1. The 'Homosexual Cancer': AIDS = gay

Reports about a lethal mystery disease began trickling into mainstream Australian media by mid-1982, some months before the first Australian case would be diagnosed. The reports told of an increasing number of unexplainable cases of Karposi's sarcoma and pneumocystis carinii pneumonia (PCP) among young gay men in America. Both these illnesses are relatively rare and indicative of problems with the body's immune system. What doctors could not explain was why so many previously healthy young men were presenting with damaged immune systems. They also could not explain why nearly all these young men seemed to be gay.[1]

Before HIV was identified as the virus leading to AIDS, a number of theories pointed to a causal link between homosexuality and AIDS. For example, the 'overload theory' suggested that the gay lifestyle, including a combination of drug use, poor health and a history of sexually transmitted infections, led to a collapsed immune system.[2] Similarly, a report in the *Launceston Examiner* in 1982 explained that researchers were 'studying the effects of drugs used by homosexuals to enhance orgasm, and have examined the possibility that frequent bouts of venereal disease among homosexuals might break down the body's ability to fight illness'.[3] In the absence of any information beyond an observed link between immune system problems and gay men, researchers began using the term 'GRID' (Gay Related Immune Deficiency) to describe the appearance of Karposi's sarcoma and other infections among this population group. The media followed suit, coining a number of terms including 'the homosexual cancer' and 'the gay plague'. Even when the clinical diagnosis of HIV was made, and people became aware that the virus could also be spread through heterosexual sex, the perception that there was an intrinsic link between homosexuality and AIDS tended to persevere in Western countries.[4]

The accepted beliefs about AIDS in the early 1980s, before HIV was discovered, were that it was contagious and deadly. This merged with existing homophobic attitudes to produce an image of gay men as diseased and dangerous—guilty not only of misdirected sexual predilections but of their newfound potential to infect and kill 'normal' Australians. All gay men came to be seen as potentially

---

1   Kraft, Scott 1982, 'New Illness Strikes Gays', *Launceston Examiner*, 13 July, p. 6; Chadwick, Paul 1982, 'States Warned of Mystery Killer Disease', *The Age*, 20 July, p. 16.
2   Seidman, Steven 2002, 'AIDS and the Discursive Construction of Homosexuality', in Kim Phillips and Barry Reay (eds), *Sexualities in History: A Reader*, Routledge, New York.
3   Kraft, 1982, p. 6.
4   Seidman, 2002; Watney, Simon 1994, *Practices of Freedom*, Rivers Oram Press, London.

contagious and deadly.[5] As Gary Dowsett has written: 'It is almost as if gay men were the virus and that they, rather than it, caused the pandemic.'[6] Steven Seidman agrees, arguing that the response to HIV/AIDS in Western society was structured by homophobia.

All diseases, particularly those that are communicable, lend themselves to some degree of moral interpretation: leprosy, for example, has long been associated with poverty and lack of hygiene and syphilis has been linked to prostitution, adultery and other behaviour considered 'immoral'. It is not difficult to understand how AIDS brought with it the potential to create a new social foothold for homophobia and why people feared it could become the basis of renewed calls for the punishment of homosexuality.[7] From the outset, AIDS was directly associated with a sexuality and lifestyle already subject to social stigma, disapproval and, in many places, illegality.

In October 1989, *The Bulletin* magazine published a cover story on homosexuality, discussing increasing reports of acts of discrimination against gay men and lesbians in the wake of AIDS. The article observed that the new awareness and tolerance of homosexuality that had been developing since the 1960s were giving way to increasing reports of anti-homosexual violence in the major Australian cities: 'Public ignorance associated with AIDS is believed to have had much to do with the slide back into the fear and loathing of the '50s when all queers, poofters and dykes were regarded as fair game.'[8]

There is some evidence to support this statement. For instance, in 1985, the two major Australian airlines—Ansett and TAA—imposed a ban on all HIV-positive passengers. Although short-lived, the ban came alongside increased complaints of workplace harassment and fears that gay men could be banned from jobs in the service industries. There were also increasing reports of gay bashings in major cities and indications that the public supported compulsory detainment of gay men.[9] A survey conducted by the National Centre for Epidemiology and Population Health in 1991 found respondents felt more sympathy for people who died as a result of excessive alcohol or tobacco consumption than for gay

5   Seidman, 2002.

6   Dowsett, Gary 1998, 'Pink Conspiracies: Australia's Gay Communities and National HIV/AIDS Policies, 1983–1996', in Anna Yeatman (ed.), *Activism and the Policy Process*, Allen & Unwin, Sydney, p. 173.

7   Pereira, Darryl 1999, 'HIV/AIDS and its "Willing Executioners": The Impact of Discrimination', *Murdoch University Electronic Journal of Law*, 6(4), <http://www.murdoch.edu.au/elaw/issues/v6n4/pereira64nf.html>

8   Stannard, Bruce and Murphy, Kevin 1989, 'More Than a Million Australians? Still Glad to be Gay?', *The Bulletin*, 10 October, p. 50.

9   Wilson, Paul, Walker, John and Mukherjee, Satyanshu 1986, *How the Public Sees Crime: An Australian Survey*, Trends and Issues in Australian Crime and Criminal Reporting Series No. 2, Australian Institute of Criminology, Canberra; Synnott, John 1985, 'Board Blames Hysteria for Gay Sackings', *Illawarra Mercury*, 1 August, p. 5; Steven Mark, Lawyer and President, NSW Anti-Discrimination Board, Interview with Diana Ritch, 12 August 1993, Oral History Project: The Australian Response to AIDS, TRC 2815/52, National Library of Australia, Canberra [hereinafter NLA].

men who died from AIDS.[10] By the early 1990s, approximately 20 per cent of complaints regarding homosexual discrimination put to the NSW Anti-Discrimination Board contained some element of HIV or AIDS discrimination.[11]

Internationally, there were reports that fear of AIDS was leading to overt acts of discrimination against gay men and lesbians. In 1983, New York City Council established an AIDS Discrimination Unit within the city's Commission on Human Rights. The unit recorded numerous complaints from healthy gay men and lesbians who had been fired from their jobs or thrown out of their homes on the basis of allegedly being 'AIDS carriers'.[12]

A study conducted in the early 1990s on HIV/AIDS-related discrimination in Australia found that people tended to justify their prejudice towards HIV-positive people because they assumed people with HIV/AIDS were likely to have engaged in 'deviant' behaviour (if not homosexual sex then illicit drug use). The study report states that, '[e]ven if deviance is not a central part of people's expressed attitudes to people with HIV, there is a level at which it underlies all discrimination, prejudice, and the excessive fear of HIV'.[13] The study found that HIV/AIDS-related discrimination could not be divorced from prejudice against risk groups such as gay men. People with HIV/AIDS were assumed to be members of risk groups and individual members of risk groups were automatically associated with HIV/AIDS regardless of their actual HIV status. That is, all gay men were seen as likely to be infectious. Furthermore, most people's reactions to HIV/AIDS were not determined by the fact that it was a presumed fatal disease, but by its association with gay men and drug users. The fear of being associated with these groups, and becoming the subject of such stigma oneself, was a large part of the fear of being infected with HIV.[14] The study's authors observed:

> The more prejudiced members of the community believe that people living with AIDS and HIV should be placed under the control of the law and of the state, in order to prevent the spread of 'the plague'. Others endorse the view that there should be compulsory testing of persons from 'risk groups' to ensure control and the prevention of further spread…Punishment and retribution is enacted both at an institutional

---

10   Editorial, 'AIDS Victims Receive Little Sympathy, Survey Shows', *Sydney Morning Herald*, 30 September 1991, p. 5.
11   NSW Anti-Discrimination Board 1992, *Discrimination—The Other Epidemic*, NSW Anti-Discrimination Board, Sydney.
12   Hollibaugh, Amber, Karp, Mitchell, Taylor, Katy and Crimp, Douglas (Interviewer) 1988, 'The Second Epidemic', in Douglas Crimp (ed.), *AIDS Cultural Analysis, Cultural Activism*, The MIT Press, Cambridge, Mass. For a detailed discussion on homophobic and AIDS-related discrimination in Britain, see Davenport-Hines, Richard 1990, *Sex, Death and Punishment*, Collins, London; also Watney, 1994.
13   Kippax, S., Tillet, G., Crawford, J. and Cregan, J. 1991, *Discrimination in the Context of AIDS*, Macquarie University Research Unit, National Centre for HIV Social Research, Sydney, p. 28.
14   Ibid.

level and an individual level in the refusal of treatment, gay bashing, incarceration, isolation, and avoidance of people suspected of being 'AIDS carriers'.[15]

Uncertainty about how far or how quickly HIV/AIDS would spread in Australia meant that in the 1980s fear of infection remained high even as the public became more educated about the physiology of HIV transmission. A second study, conducted in 1991 into public knowledge, attitudes and beliefs about AIDS, concluded that high levels of knowledge about HIV transmission did not reduce prejudice. The researchers concluded:

> [The] community's knowledge about the nature of AIDS transmission, treatment and risk reduction is approaching saturation level, with 95 per cent or more correctly agreeing with propositions that have been central to community AIDS education efforts...Although knowledge levels about most issues may be satisfactory, our findings also point to a disturbing level of community hysteria about AIDS.[16]

According to the study's authors, the survey responses indicated a deep and often misguided concern about catching HIV/AIDS. More than half of the people interviewed believed that a policy of compulsory testing was warranted and a further 5 per cent believed all homosexuals should be tested.[17]

It is difficult to judge with any certainty how deeply or widespread public fears about AIDS were held, or the extent to which this had an impact on actual cases of discrimination against gay men and lesbians. It is, however, certainly clear why gay men were fearful of discrimination and/or legal sanction as a result of AIDS. The public was concerned about contracting AIDS and fears were exacerbated and shaped by the association between AIDS and an identifiable group of people who were already marginalised and stigmatised. Former President of the NSW Anti-Discrimination Board Steven Mark describes AIDS as having afforded homophobic discrimination 'a new heightened respectability in the community', representing 'discrimination on a new level'.[18]

15   Ibid., p. 24.
16   Bray, Fiona and Chapman, Simon 1991, 'Community Knowledge, Attitudes and Media Recall About AIDS, Sydney 1988 and 1989', *Australian Journal of Public Health*, 15(2), pp. 107–13, at p. 112.
17   Ibid.
18   Steven Mark, TRC 2815/52, NLA.

The immediate response from the gay community and the fact that there was a gut response, but it was a united one, was critical. The fact that we had enough of an organised gay community to have a gay press, a gay bookshop, gay venues—we even had the argument about gay community versus gay movement. That was all going on. There was enough of that stuff and enough political self-awareness so that when this was on top of us we actually had a framework to respond with. It wasn't like we were just some little atoms of people, there actually was a centre—geographical and political—a heart where we knew the gay community was. And we knew each other very well. I don't know if we trusted each other very well, but I think we knew each other well enough to have a good working relationship. And that was enough to get started.

— Phil Carswell (2005a)

Discrimination was rife. So gay men were fighting on a number of fronts—for the right to have sex, for the right to work and live in the community as other people are able to do, for the right to anti-discrimination protection—a whole lot of things like that. So these were all motivators and there was a sense that a community was being built and here was something that threatened to decimate the community entirely. So they were part of motivating the gay community in Australia.

— Bill Whittaker (2004)

It wasn't really a particular person I knew who became positive, it was actually a general thing that, sometime late in '83 or early '84, the possible ramifications started to really come home to me—or what I thought the possible ramifications could be. And I was envisioning them as being quite drastic, because it seemed to me that it heralded the potential destruction of the community altogether. I always remember thinking quite clearly that what it could do would be to destroy most of the community institutions that we had. So that while we only had a sort of a relatively—or compared to now—a relatively small gay press, it seemed to me that that was very likely to go, that quite a number of gay businesses would collapse either because their proprietors would die or a lot of their customer base might die, so therefore the advertising base for the press would go as well.

— Don Baxter (1993)

Homophobia, Discrimination and Fear: The beginning of AIDS activism

It was this environment of uncertainty and fear—occurring within the context of the history of homosexual discrimination—that shaped AIDS activism in Australia. First, gay communities were confronting an illness that, as far as anyone was aware at the time, inflicted a possible death sentence on anyone infected. No-one knew how quickly or how far the epidemic would spread, and the only thing that seemed clear was a link between gay men and this new disease. As activist Ken Davis recalls:

> [Initially] I found it quite hard to believe that there was a viral agent causing cancer, because the initial attention was to the pneumonia and Karposi's sarcoma. That was hard to get your head around. But we knew that gay men were dying, we didn't know that anyone else was dying. So you've got to remember what it was like before we had a viral agent that we were sure of. We were assuming that gay men would randomly die and the only lead-up to it was being gay. That was pretty weird. That did feel like an act of God. We were fearful because we didn't know what we were dealing with.[19]

Alongside this uncertainty, people were realising the devastating impact AIDS could have on the lives of all gay people, even those not infected. In the early 1980s, homosexuality had been illegal in Australia for many more years than it had been legal. In fact, in many States it was still on the criminal code. There was certainly a feeling among gay men that law reform was tenuous and that AIDS had the potential to inspire not only re-criminalisation of homosexuality, but also increased restrictions on the freedoms of gay men and, by association, lesbians. Moreover, there were fears that individual acts of discrimination— gay bashing, workplace harassment, withdrawal of services and so forth— would become more frequent and more socially acceptable under the premise of avoiding AIDS.

Blood Politics: Beginnings of the AIDS movement

AIDS screamed into mainstream public consciousness 1984 when it became known that people could acquire the virus through blood transfusions or donated blood products.[20] The media aired fears that the blood supply in

---

19   Ken Davis, Interview with the author, 5 November 2004. This particular quotation was in response to my question about what, in Davis's view, mobilised the gay community around AIDS.
20   This occurred before the antigen for HIV was identified—although at the time there was a general medical consensus that AIDS must be a blood-borne virus due to the number of people who appeared to have

Australia could already be infected, sparking a realisation among the general public that AIDS could, and likely would, spread beyond populations of gay men and 'junkies'. Heterosexual adults and children were also vulnerable.

I think as young gay men we often didn't understand...We came to [activism] with an arrogance, that we couldn't believe we didn't have rights for a whole lot of things—other disease or disability groups were putting up with a whole lot of suffering that young gay men didn't think they had to put up with—particularly young, rich gay men, suddenly impoverished. But we demanded...often we demanded... entitlements with no conscience that other people didn't have those things. And a lot of the agitation around pensions and housing support and so forth worked because gay men didn't realise that that was the deal—this is what another impoverished or ill person is putting up with. We demanded all this special treatment. The end result was that it improved services for a lot of people. And it allowed other people to follow a bit of a path of taking on the medical providers or the social providers, and saying the nature of the relationship with the customer is different. And that's a good product of the activism. But we didn't strategise that, we just did that because we didn't know any better.

— Ken Davis (2004)

The first newspaper report on the possibility that the Australian blood supply could be infected appeared in *The Australian* on 2 May 1983, with an article discussing concerns of the British Health Authority that blood being imported from the United States might contain AIDS. As Australia did not rely on imported blood products, this article did not receive much reaction.[21] A short while later, however, Dr Gordon Archer, Director of the Sydney Blood Transfusion Service (BTS), put out a public call for 'promiscuous' homosexual men to voluntarily stop donating blood, declaring in a television interview that it was a 'virtual certainty' that the blood supply in Australia was already infected with AIDS.[22] Archer's call made front-page news across the country.[23]

---

acquired AIDS through intravenous drug use.

21   Cook, Sue 1983, 'Disease Fear Leads Red Cross to Ban Gays as Donors', *The Australian*, 10 May, pp. 1–2; Ballard, John 1989, 'The Politics of AIDS', in Heather Gardner (ed.), *The Politics of Health: The Australian Experience*, Churchill Livingstone, Melbourne; Sendziuk, Paul 2001, 'Bad Blood: The Contamination of Australia's Blood Supply and the Emergence of Gay Activism in the Age of AIDS', in Elizabeth Ruinard and Elspeth Tilley (eds), *Fresh Cuts: New Talents 2001*, API Network and University of Queensland Press, Sydney.

22   Archer's call came before there were any identified cases of blood-product transmission in Australia although such transmission was known to have occurred in the United States and there was a realistic probability that Australia would face a similar problem (Sendziuk, 2001, p. 78).

23   Some within the BTS did not support Archer in his assertions. For example, the chair of the National Blood Transfusion Service (NBTS), David Penington, publicly responded that there was no risk of Australia's blood supply being infected with HIV because blood donation in Australia had always been entirely voluntary (apart from a short-lived experiment with a professional donor panel in 1938). Ballard, John 1999, 'HIV Contaminated Blood and Australian Policy', in Eric Feldman and Ronald Bayer (eds), *AIDS, Blood and the*

Archer made his call at a time when there was no test available to screen blood for HIV; indeed, HIV had not yet been identified as a virus. The only step authorities could take to prevent infection was to stop people who might be at higher risk of having AIDS from donating. Despite this, many members of the Sydney gay community were angered by Archer's announcement—not because they opposed having a policy on restricting blood donation, but because they felt those most affected by such a policy should be consulted about its terms and potential impact.[24] In 1983, homosexuality was still on the criminal code in New South Wales. The actions of the BTS seemed to offer further political fuel to those who opposed civil rights for gay men and lesbians. A member of a community organisation called the Gay Solidarity Group contacted Archer to request a meeting to discuss BTS policies. One option they wanted to investigate was whether Archer would be amendable to investigating the feasibility of introducing 'surrogate screening' for hepatitis B, rather than maintaining a policy that singled out particular groups. The Blood Bank had, for some time, been testing all blood donations for the hepatitis B virus—the antigen for which had been identified in the late 1960s. Ironically, this meant that in the 1980s there were large numbers of gay men who regularly donated blood, as they had been encouraged to do so as a means of being tested, anonymously and without cost, for hepatitis B and syphilis. The logic of surrogate testing was that if a person had been exposed to hepatitis B, there was a reasonable chance they had also been exposed to AIDS.[25]

According to activist Ken Davis:

> [The] trouble with the blood ban stuff was that we said as soon as you say that you can't donate if you are a 'promiscuous homosexual', you're really missing the point of how to screen blood and that no one thinks of themselves as a promiscuous homosexual...If you want to formulate something that will exclude, let's talk about it. And the truth is that after that exclusion of promiscuous homosexuals, infection rates went up. And I don't think that was deliberate at all. I think people genuinely didn't understand and wanted to make a contribution and that gay men had been specifically targeted for blood donation for a decade before. So it was a real mess. [26]

Archer refused to meet with the Gay Solidarity Group. In response to this, participants at a Gay Rights Lobby (GRL) meeting organised a picket of the

Politics of Medical Disaster, Oxford University Press, New York, p. 245. Penington was obviously making the assumption that the type of people who would be inclined to sell their blood for cash would be drug users or other people at greater risk of HIV.

24 Don Baxter, Interview with James Waites, 26 November 1993, Oral History Project: The Australian Response to AIDS, TRC 2815/75, NLA.

25 Ballard, 1999.

26 Ken Davis, Interview with the author, 5 November 2004.

offices of the Sydney Blood Bank.[27] The picket was held on 13 May 1983. Placards and leaflets demanding 'Ban the Bigots, Not the Blood' were handed out, stating that the ban on gay donors could be counterproductive as 'closeted' gay men might feel the need to donate blood to prove their heterosexuality, particularly in a situation where they were donating with work colleagues, as was a common practice.[28] Unfortunately for activists, the picket turned out to be largely counterproductive as gay men were portrayed as putting their own interests above public health.

David Lowe says:

> From a public relations point of view for the gay community, [the picket] didn't seem to me to be a sensible course of action. I suspect quite a lot of people must have shared those views and the picket didn't attract that many people, really. There were some people who had been politically active. But it certainly didn't seem to attract a broad consensus…I think it was a little bit unfortunate in a sense also because then it gave the people who wanted to call themselves 'innocent victims' the opportunity to blame the community: 'They have these pickets and want to donate blood'…It probably fuelled fears that some people were deliberately donating blood, which I don't think was the case.[29]

While not necessarily a successful event in its own right, the picket did lead to a number of other actions that proved more constructive. A number of individuals and groups met on 15 May 1983 to discuss the next steps in the 'AIDS campaign'. These groups included the Gay Rights Lobby, the Gay Counselling Service, the Gay Solidarity Group, the Metropolitan Community Church[30] and the Gay Business Association. From this meeting, the NSW AIDS Action Committee (AAC) was established.[31] The first success of the Sydney AAC was convincing the NSW Minister for Health to establish a ministerial advisory committee: the AIDS Consultative Committee. Membership of this committee included NSW Department of Health staff, medical specialists and representatives of the Sydney AAC.[32]

---

27 The Melbourne Blood Bank did agree to a meeting with gay community activists. There were no similar protests to those that took place in Sydney. Phil Carswell, Personal communication, 25 October 2006, Melbourne.

28 Sendziuk, Paul 2003, *Learning to Trust: Australian Responses to AIDS*, UNSW Press, Sydney.

29 David Lowe, Interview with the author, 12 July 2005.

30 Metropolitan Community Church (MCC) Sydney is a Christian church that operates specifically to reach people excluded by established religious groups on the basis of sexuality. The MCC was an active part of the gay and lesbian community in the 1980s (and still is today) and participated in AIDS-movement initiatives.

31 Don Baxter, TRC 2815/75, NLA; Sendziuk, 2003.

32 Sendziuk, 2003.

As Ken Davis recalls: 'that was the genesis of AIDS activism, that small (inappropriate) picket of the blood bank that I wasn't at...that precipitated the State Government having to have a meeting between government, medical people and gay men.'[33]

Prejudice and Queensland Babies

A few weeks after the Sydney Blood Bank picket, the National Blood Transfusion Service (NBTS) released a statement urging sexually active homosexual men, intravenous drug users and sexual partners of these people to abstain from donating. The NBTS had been careful to avoid a community reaction similar to that in Sydney by expanding the groups being asked not to donate beyond homosexual men and using the term 'sexually active' rather than 'promiscuous'. The blood transfusion services in other States also began to ask donors to sign declarations stating that they did not belong to the risk groups identified by the NBTS.[34]

The actions of the NBTS did little, however, to resolve the tension around HIV and blood donation, and the issue dominated headlines again in July 1984 when the first Australian case of AIDS known to have been acquired through a blood transfusion was diagnosed. In this case the blood donor, who was tracked by the Blood Transfusion Service, was a gay man who acknowledged that he was aware of the call for 'promiscuous' gay men not to donate but had not considered himself to be promiscuous. A short while later, the media reported that the same donor's blood had also been used in the preparation of Factor 8[35] and a number of people with haemophilia were being tested for AIDS.[36]

It was a few months after this, in November 1984, when the Queensland Government announced that three babies had died after receiving AIDS-infected blood, and that a donor known to be homosexual was to blame.[37] Probably not coincidentally, the announcement came in the middle of a federal election campaign and it quickly became a highly politicised issue. Public figures and

---

33 Ken Davis, Interview with the author, 4 November 2004.
34 Ballard, 1999.
35 In Australia, 172 cases of HIV acquired through blood transfusions had been identified by the end of 1995 and some 264 people had been infected through blood products used to treat haemophilia (Ballard, 1999, p. 256). This represents approximately 30 per cent of Australians with haemophilia who treated their condition with blood products between 1980 and 1984. People with haemophilia were, in the 1980s, at particularly high risk of HIV infection as Factor 8—the product used to treat haemophilia—was made using the blood of a large number of donors. Hence, people using Factor 8 came into contact with the blood of many more donors than those who had a blood transfusion or received organ donations (Sendziuk, 2001, p. 82).
36 Sendziuk, 2001.
37 Langley, George and Rice, Margaret 1984, 'Three Babies Die of Suspected AIDS: QLD Acts Against Donors', *The Australian*, 16 November, p. 1.

political leaders started to weigh in on the debate about how to deal with AIDS, much of which focused on determining appropriate means by which to control or punish the actions of homosexual men who donated blood. In his speech at the opening of the National Party's federal election campaign, the then leader, Ian Sinclair, publicly declared that '[i]f it wasn't for the promotion of homosexuality as a norm by Labor, I am quite confident that the deaths of these three poor babies would not have occurred'.[38] The ultra-conservative Queensland Premier at the time, Sir Joh Bjelke-Petersen, also blamed the Federal Labor Government's stance on homosexuality, commenting that '[t]he Labor party is as much to blame with their acceptance of that type of low and disgusting lifestyle. And Mr Hawke is to blame by promising equal government support for homosexual marriages.'[39] 'Sir Joh' was backed by his Health Minister, Brian Austin, who, in discussing what punishment should be delivered to members of known 'AIDS risk groups' who donated blood, stated: 'You can't legislate to stop murder. You can put up signs telling people it's illegal to murder someone but that won't stop it.'[40]

The Blood Transfusion Service attempted to allay the blame being placed on the individual whose blood donation had infected the 'Queensland babies' by describing the donor as 'a person with a civic conscience' who had not realised they were an 'AIDS carrier'. A BTS official was reported as saying: 'He [the donor] had been very upset by the revelation and was now suffering extreme regret.'[41] Nevertheless, the Queensland Government, fuelled by sensationalist media, vitriolically continued to pursue punishment for the donor and introduce a punitive approach to protecting the blood supply.

Twenty-four hours after the babies' deaths had been reported, the Queensland Government passed legislation imposing criminal sanctions for false declarations by blood donors. If someone were to lie about their history of homosexuality or drug use when donating blood, they could now be held criminally liable.[42] Despite the reluctance of other State health ministers to impose legal regulations on blood donation, they agreed that all States needed to offer the same blood protection as Queensland. The legislation was adopted by other States a month later at the State Health Ministers' Conference. Australia was the only country in the world to have introduced such laws.[43]

There are two ways to look at this legislation. The first is that it was a pragmatic response to the need to protect the blood supply in the absence of any other

---

38   Davis, Ian and Birnbauer, Bill 1984, 'Sinclair Links Labor with Deaths of Three Babies', *The Age*, 17 November, p. 1; Ballard, 1999.

39   'QLD Considers Manslaughter Charges: Sir Joh Cites ALP on AIDS', *The Canberra Times*, 4 December 1984, p. 1.

40   Ibid.; 'Now Labor Party Blamed for AIDS', *Northern Territory Times*, 4 December 1984, p. 1.

41   Langley and Rice, 1984.

42   Ibid.

43   Ballard, 1999.

means to screen for AIDS. But, while this was certainly the case, the legislation also suggests that authorities felt that the identified risk groups (gay men and intravenous drug users) needed to be controlled. The legislation was introduced amid a politically charged public debate within which prejudice towards gay men was overt. In effect, the moral discourse around homosexuality was translated into legal terms.[44] Furthermore, homosexual discrimination no doubt made it more politically risky for the State ministers to *not* introduce punitive action than it was to introduce it, and certainly State governments—particularly in Queensland—wanted to be seen to be taking decisive action around AIDS.

The media played a major role in directing public debate on this legislation, with commentaries in most major press outlets revealing a mistrust of gay men and their capacity to act responsibly in the face of AIDS. Adding fuel to this fire, newspaper headlines also ran with wholly unsubstantiated allegations that gay people were deliberately and maliciously infecting the blood supply, such as: 'Gays Accused of Giving Blood out of Spite.'[45] Editorials also engaged in this speculation. The broadsheet *The Australian*, for instance, ran a piece on 17 November 1984 that stated:

> The chief medical officer of the NSW Health Department, Dr Tony Adams, believes that there may be a minority of homosexuals who are donating blood to rebel against society. It is hard to accept that anyone could be so vindictive as to take such action but when added to the revelation by a Sydney gay activist that some homosexuals who have recently given blood are now refusing to identify it for fear of persecution, it can only add fuel to the fire.[46]

An editorial in Brisbane's *The Courier-Mail* on the same date suggested that gay men were being irresponsible or selfish in their appeal for civil rights in the face of what could amount to a life or death situation for many people:

> Clearly the medical authorities, both here and in other states, are doing everything possible to limit the spread of AIDS…Sadly, however, the actions of some members of the homosexual community have lacked responsibility and concern…Blood banks have appealed to male homosexuals not to give blood. Yet it seems for a number of reasons, these appeals have been ignored…It was not so long ago in our history that patients suffering other socially-unacceptable, contagious diseases, such as tuberculosis and leprosy, were locked away for what was considered the community good. No one is suggesting that this should happen to

---

44   Hall, Ananda 1998, A Risky Business: Criminalising the Transmission of HIV, Faculty of Law Thesis, The Australian National University, Canberra, <http://law.anu.edu/criminet/ananda's_thesis.html>
45   *Daily Telegraph*, 17 November 1984, quoted in Ballard, 1999.
46   Editorial, 'The New Plague', *The Australian*, 17 November 1984, p. 24.

homosexuals, but the aggressive activists in the movement should not be surprised if there is a violent community reaction to their cause as a result of this serious public health problem.[47]

Common to much of the media commentary at the time was the assertion that calls to punish gay men who donated blood were not based on homophobia, but were the sensible actions of public health authorities. People's moral opinions about gay men were ever present, but consistently denied. This was evident in a piece published by *The Australian* by high-profile conservative commentator Bob Santamaria, in which he claimed that the intention of his column was 'not to pass moral judgment on homosexual acts'. Rather, he writes: 'The sole question with which this column is concerned…is that of public health.' The piece goes on to argue that by claiming the right to privacy and confidentiality in order to ensure protection from discrimination, gay men were asking for extraordinary privileges. He writes that '[w]here public health is concerned, the infringement of the privacy of individuals is rightly held to be secondary to the threatened ravages of epidemic disease'. Gay men, he argues, should not have the right to demand civil freedoms if this contravenes public health priorities.[48]

While it is likely commentators such as Santamaria were genuine in their claims that they did not wish to pass moral judgment on gay men, they were asserting that gay men did not have a right to question or complain about the introduction of restrictions on their freedoms, rights or privacy. Activists who raised concerns about these infringements were heavily criticised for being selfish and irresponsible. The implicit suggestion in this was that if gay men were more 'responsible' there would be no need for such restriction of liberties. But gay men were not trusted with such responsibility and to some extent it seemed that the belief that gay men were to blame for AIDS drove much opinion on public health legislation.

On 8 December 1985, the front-page headline 'Die You Deviate' appeared in Melbourne's *Midweek Truth*. The father of one of the 'Queensland babies' who had died following a blood transfusion had made a public call for the donor—a gay man in his early twenties—to commit suicide or face capital punishment. The article reported the baby's father as saying: 'As the parents of this baby, we feel that the only honorable thing for the murderer of our son to do is to commit suicide.'[49]

Articles such as this depicted AIDS as a murder weapon rather than an illness, suggesting that gay men, not an indiscriminate virus, should be seen as the

47   Editorial, 'AIDS and Responsibilities', *The Courier-Mail*, 17 November 1984, p. 4.
48   Santamaria, B. A. 1984, 'AIDS: Public Reaction and the Gay Community', *The Australian*, 27 November, p. 11.
49   'Die, You Deviate', *Midweek Truth*, 8 December 1985, p. 1.

'killers' of these babies. Even where there was no overt homophobic rhetoric, never was it suggested that those gay men who had been infected with AIDS also deserved sympathy or that they themselves were 'victims' of the disease. The standard practice was to present gay men as inflicting the illness on others, through intention or carelessness. In this way, beliefs about homosexual immorality and deviance played into the construction of AIDS in the public's imagination. HIV prevention was used to justify the curtailment of rights for gay men and lesbians, obscuring the moral opinion embedded in these calls. Activists who demanded a right to privacy and protection from discrimination were portrayed as acting against public health interests.

I was [a member of] the ALSO [Alternative Lifestyles Organisation] Foundation. I was on there as sort of the token leftie…So when they heard news in 1982 of this new thing happening in America, we got a health subcommittee together of four people: myself, the late Ian Dunstan, the late Chris Carter and the late Peter Knight. The four of us sat down together and said what are we going to do about this? Let's call a public meeting. What we decided to do, without any advertising, we booked the Dental Hospital in Melbourne, which was a bold move—we were a gay organisation booking a straight venue. We got a panel of doctors on stage, most of them gay, one straight, and through word-of-mouth filled the auditorium—700 people. Up to that stage, it was the largest political crowd of gay people I had ever seen in my life. I mean we had warehouse parties where we had 1000 people dancing and stuff, but it was the first time I had seen 700 people sitting down paying attention and being well behaved…It was really interesting how that word got through the party scene before it got through the gay press and through the gay political scene. The Drag Queens and the Leather Queens and the Qantas Queens all knew about it, and they knew something was going on that was going to be bad and they were all there in the audience, along with your established left-wing gay acts. That was the irony of the night. It was an amazing cross-section of people who had come there all through word-of-mouth. The networks already were established. That strength of community that was there was nascent—or latent. But it was still quite readily and easily tapped, and once it was tapped it was like a sleeping tiger. It wasn't going to sit down. At that meeting, I'll never forget it was two hours of absolute terror for me because every question we asked the doctors, they said: 'No, we don't know.' They said: 'This is what we do know, we've seen guys coming in and they're gone like that. They're dying within six months.'

This was before we knew about HIV or AIDS. It was just like they're getting sick, body covered in splotches, they were coughing, they were losing weight, they had night sweats, diarrhoea, they had enormous fatigue...So that meeting with 700 people, I'll never forget it, a lesbian activist by the name of Alison Thorne,* who is well known in gay history and so she should be—there was really a feeling of hopelessness through the whole room, people were thinking: 'Oh my god, what's going to happen to us, we're all going to die'—and Alison grabbed the microphone and did the classic Lenin thing, 'what is to be done?'. She said: 'Look at us. We've got to do something about this. I vote we have another meeting in one month's time at another venue and people can volunteer to take on various organising roles', or words to that effect. It was a stirring sort of 'man the battlements' (oh no, she'd never say that, it was 'staff the battlements'!) speech. It was amazing, it was the perfect line at the right time and it instantly galvanised the room. People said yes we can do this, we've got talented people here—we've got doctors, we've got lawyers, we've got policy people. So a month later we had a meeting at the Laird Hotel in Melbourne, a little pub in Collingwood. Ron, the owner, bless his heart (there are so many unsung heroes in this epidemic), gave us a room for free that night. So we crammed in about 35 to 40 people, which is more than we expected. We thought after a month it would die down and people would go back to their little holes. But in that room was the most amazing cross-section of people. It was like the big meeting shrunk down. You had your drag queens, your leather-boys, your political activists, then the sort of ALSO people and people who didn't do political things before but thought this was something they could possibly help with—like nurses and that sort of stuff. And because a lot of them were party people I knew most of them, so when they asked me to chair the meeting I got shoved into the fortuitous position of being the first chair of the first meeting of the Organising Committee on AIDS in Victoria. And I think Sydney had a similar meeting about a month earlier—we were very close. We'd been to Mardi Gras and things together, plus I had political allies in Sydney...So there was already stuff happening up there, so it was logical that we should do the same.

— Phil Carswell (2005a)

---

* While in this text I make only passing reference to the role of lesbians, there were a number of lesbian women actively involved in the AIDS movement and in the subsequent establishment of AIDS organisations. The role that lesbians and heterosexual women played in AIDS activism could be the topic of an interesting thesis in itself. While this was not a topic that could be addressed with any depth in this text due to time and resource constraints, it is worth noting the role of lesbians as it shows that people within the gay community were motivated to take action around AIDS even if they did not feel personally at risk from the virus (lesbians were never identified as a 'risk group' for AIDS, even if they did become implicated to some extent in AIDS hysteria).

Community and Organisation: The movement develops

By the time the 'Queensland babies' crisis erupted, the AIDS movement was well organised, operating through several State-based collectives: the Victorian AIDS Action Committee (VAAC), the NSW AIDS Action Committee (NSW AAC) and similar activists groups in other States.[50]

The first meeting of the VAAC had taken place at the Laird Hotel in Collingwood in July 1983.[51] Following this, on 4 December 1984, the VAAC held its first major public forum since this inaugural meeting. About 600 people attended. At this meeting, a decision was made to transform VAAC into what is now known as the Victorian AIDS Council (VAC). The VAC operated under a more formalised, incorporated structure—the change enabling the organisation to receive government grants (the Victorian State Government was unwilling and unable to fund an informal volunteer organisation).[52] Funding from the Victorian State Government was made available to VAC from 1985 through a grant from the State and Federal Governments' joint-funding initiative.[53]

Phil Carswell recalls:

> A telegram arrives for me as VAC President announcing a $50,000 Commonwealth grant. We all cheer and wet our pants at the same time.

---

50   This analysis focuses predominantly on Sydney and Melbourne as ACON and the VAC were the largest AIDS organisations and both provide a clear example of the strategies undertaken by the AIDS movement. There were, however, organisations similar to VAC and ACON that received government funding in Perth, Adelaide and Canberra. The Queensland story is a little different as this State was subject to the reign of ultra-conservative Premier Joh Bjelke-Petersen throughout much of the 1980s. The Queensland Government for many years actively campaigned against the involvement of the gay community in the AIDS response. Homosexuality remained on the criminal code in that State until 1990. Nonetheless, there was a community response to AIDS in Queensland. The Federal Government was able to override Bjelke-Petersen to some extent by funnelling money to the Queensland AIDS Council through a religious charity. Phil Carswell, Interview with the author, 23 July 2005.

51   Phil Carswell, Interview with the author, 23 July 2005. From this date, the VAAC began organising educational initiatives, producing 'safe sex' information and campaign materials. Volunteers were recruited for care, support and general assistance even before VAAC had any clients (the official AIDS case load in Australia at the end of 1983 was only seven, though this number increased significantly throughout the following year). The first fundraising efforts focused on improving patient facilities at Melbourne's Fairfield Hospital, which was the main hospital for people with AIDS, starting with the rundown patient lounge at the end of the Ward Four corridor. Ibid.; Tobias, Sandy 1988, AIDSLINE—A Profile, Unpublished paper, Victorian AIDS Council, Melbourne; Altman, Dennis 1990, 'Introduction', in Richard Clayton (ed.), Gay Now, Play Safe, Victorian AIDS Council/Gay Men's Community Health Centre, Melbourne.

52   Phil Carswell, Interview with the author, 23 July 2005; Phil Carswell, Excerpt from personal notes made for a presentation on the history of the AIDS epidemic at Sydney University, 2005c; Altman, 1990.

53   Funding was tied to specific projects, with clear anticipated outcomes and a limited time frame. VAC was able to secure funds for administration of the organisation in 1986. Morcos, Monica 1968, 'Money Matters', Annual Report, Victorian AIDS Council, Melbourne, p. 13. The same year, VAC negotiated with the State and Federal ministries of housing to secure a property in which to accommodate people living with AIDS. VAC would provide nursing, 24-hour care and support for residents. Carr, Adam 1987, 'President's Report', Annual Report, Victorian AIDS Council, Melbourne.

This is the largest amount of money anyone of us had thought possible… This also saw the formation of the Gay Men's Health Resources Project, which later became the Gay Men's Health Centre [GMHC] and the recipient of most of the money…The original idea was to establish a user-friendly clinic and health service that could also focus on broader gay health issues such as alcoholism and drug use, STIs [sexually transmitted infections] and the impact of discrimination.[54]

A similar process occurred in Sydney with the NSW AAC being reformed into the AIDS Council of New South Wales (ACON) in February 1985.[55] ACON's foundation meeting was held at the Teachers' Federation Hall in Sussex Street in the city and was attended by more than 500 people.[56] ACON was an amalgamation of several organisations that had been set up in response to HIV/AIDS, including the AAC, the Bobby Goldsmith Foundation,[57] the Community Support Network (CSN)[58] and Ankali support service.[59] By 1989, ACON and the CSN had about 700 members in New South Wales. This included branches in

---

54 Phil Carswell, Excerpt from personal notes made for a presentation on the history of the AIDS epidemic at Sydney University, 2002.

55 Sendziuk, 2003.

56 Don Baxter, TRC 2815/75, NLA.

57 Bobby Goldsmith was a gay man who died in June 1984 of medical complications caused by AIDS. Bobby was active in Sydney's gay scene and community activities (particularly sporting activities) and had a wide range of friends. When Bobby became ill, a group of his friends arranged care and support for him at his home so he was able to avoid hospital. When medical equipment was needed to assist his care, Bobby's friends raised funds for things such as a wheelchair, commode and special support mattress. When Bobby died, the Bobby Goldsmith Foundation Incorporated (BGF) was established in his name. BGF is a fund that supports people with AIDS-related illnesses to be cared for in their homes. Bobby Goldsmith Foundation 1999, *Who Was Bobby Goldsmith?*, Bobby Goldsmith Foundation web site, viewed 24 April 2004, <http://www.bgf.org>

58 Community Services Network Incorporated (CSN) is a volunteer-based community group that provides in-home care for people with AIDS-related illnesses. AIDS Council of NSW (ACON) 2006, *Community Support Network*, ACON web site, viewed 20 May 2006, <http://www.acon.org.au> CSN developed from the AIDS Support Group and AIDS Home Support, which were established by Terry Goulden, a founding member of the Gay Counselling Service. These support services ran alongside the AAC, but were kept separate from political activities as Goulden was concerned that the politics might alienate potential allies. When the AAC was reformed into ACON in February 1985, however, these care and support services were integrated with the other functions of ACON. As an example of the extent of volunteer labour coordinated by CSN, throughout the 1990–91 financial year, CSN staff and volunteers did 11 874 shifts for their 173 clients. This amounted to more than 72 000 hours. The majority of these hours were dedicated to direct care of clients in their homes. Malcom, Anne 1991, 'Community Services Report', *Annual Report*, AIDS Council of NSW, Sydney.

59 'Ankali' is an Aboriginal word meaning 'friend'. The Ankali project was established in 1985 in Sydney. The project trains volunteers to provide one-on-one support to people with AIDS as well as their partners, families and friends. Ankali is now linked to the Albion Street Centre, an HIV/AIDS service and medical clinic funded by the NSW Government. South-East Sydney Area Health Service (SESAHS) 2006, *Ankali*, SESAHS web site, viewed 21 November 2005, <http://www.sesahs.nsw.gov.au/albionstcentre/Ankali/index.asp> Don Baxter, Interview with James Waites, 26 November 1993, Oral History Project: The Australian Response to AIDS, TRC 2815/75, NLA; Ariss, Robert 1993, 'Performing Anger: Emotion in Strategic Responses to AIDS', *Australian Journal of Anthropology*, 4(1), pp. 18–30.

Sydney, Newcastle and on the North Coast. ACON's governing council included 12 elected committee members (unpaid) and the organisation had 25 full-time staff.[60]

In 1985, representatives from AIDS committees and councils from across the country, who had been attending the First National AIDS Conference, passed a vote to establish a national federation of AIDS organisations, to be named the Australian Federation of AIDS Organisations (AFAO).[61]

AFAO, VAC, ACON and other community-run HIV/AIDS organisations across the country, such as the AIDS Action Council of the Australian Capital Territory and the WA AIDS Council, formalised and centralised the base from which activists worked. As Graham Willett writes:

> The work was transforming the activists as much as they were transforming the world. It is not an accident that a shift from 'action committee' to 'AIDS Council' took place in late 1984 and early 1985 as the government and gay activists started to work more closely together. The shift in nomenclature marked a shift in outlook by the organisations and those running them. Adam Carr, who first proposed the change, saw 'council' as evoking respectability and authority, a gathering of experts and their expertise, appealing more to governments, bureaucracies and medical professionals than action committees.[62]

In the early 1980s, the AIDS movement quickly and strategically established a dialogue with the Federal Government. For example, in September 1983, a meeting was organised between the Federal Health Minister, medical researchers and members of the NSW and Victorian AIDS Action Committees. At this meeting, the Health Minister, Neal Blewett, made it clear that the Federal Government was prepared to denote a formal role for the community sector in the AIDS response if they were willing and capable to undertake this.[63] With the relationship already established, activists were later given an opportunity to meet with Blewett and his advisor, Bill Bowtell, to advocate their position on the 'Queensland babies' scandal in 1984.[64]

---

60   Don Baxter, TRC 2815/75, NLA; AIDS Council of NSW (ACON) 1989, *Future Directions for the AIDS Council of NSW: A Strategic Planning Document*, ACON, Sydney.
61   Carswell notes that the Queensland AIDS Committee (QuAC) had some initial reservations as their membership was broader than the gay community and they were concerned that AFAO was primarily gay oriented. Phil Carswell, Interview with the author, 23 July 2005.
62   Willett, Graham 2000, *Living Out Loud: A History of Gay and Lesbian Activism in Australia*, Allen & Unwin, Sydney.
63   Although, as Carswell notes, because the AACs were still in their infancy at the time and not highly organised, the community did not follow up on this meeting as effectively as they could have. Phil Carswell, Interview with the author, 23 July 2005.
64   Phil Carswell, Interviews with the author, 23 July and 17 December 2005.

On the back of this, in late 1984, representatives from the Victorian and NSW AIDS Action Committees, Phil Carswell and Lex Watson, were invited to join the new National Advisory Committee on AIDS (NACAIDS). The committee was set up to advise the Federal Government on human and social aspects of AIDS. It was chaired by prominent Australian media personality Ita Buttrose. Other appointees to NACAIDS included Jennifer Ross from the Haemophilia Foundation, Anne Kern from the Commonwealth Health Department, representatives from the NSW and Victorian Health Departments, the Australian Medical Association and the Royal Australian Nursing Federation.[65]

The appointment of Carswell and Watson to NACAIDS gave the AIDS movement a legitimate place in AIDS policy making. As Carswell points out, the fact that the AIDS movement had two people on the committee meant they were able to both move and second motions, giving them a reasonable amount of power around the committee table.[66] Although they certainly adapted to their new situation, the level of authority afforded to the AIDS movement through their role on NACAIDS was unanticipated by many activists. A number of people had previous experience in political lobbying, but to actually sit on a government advisory body and develop personal relationships with high-level decision makers, including a Federal Government minister, was a new experience.

According to Ian Rankin:

> Over time, the community sector has become more confident that it is entitled to be funded. Certainly in the early-to-mid 1990s I still had a sense that people were surprised that we were allowed to sit around ministerial advisory tables or comment on research programs, etc. We'd come out and boldly claim it. But everyone would still be a bit surprised when it actually happened. I think during the course of the '90s people became more comfortable with the idea that the community sector was valid, should be represented, did have something to say and something to contribute.[67]

Building a working relationship with the Federal Government proved to be an extremely important tactic of the AIDS movement in terms of gaining access to funding and political power, and establishing the public profile of

---

65 Now the Australian Nursing Federation. Altman, Dennis 1992, 'The Most Political of Diseases', in Eric Timewell, Victor Minichiello and David Plummer (eds), *AIDS in Australia*, Prentice Hall, Sydney; Phil Carswell, Interview with the author, 23 July 2005.
66 Phil Carswell, Interview with the author, 23 July 2005.
67 Ian Rankin, Interview with the author, 26 July 2004.

activists.[68] Despite the formalised status of the AIDS councils, there was no doubt, however, that it was the strong base of community support that gave them their political strength in the 1980s and early 1990s. The AIDS movement continued to attract a much broader constituency than those involved directly with the formal organisations. Large numbers of non-aligned activists took part in volunteer community work, and traditional protest strategies such as street demonstrations and lobbying continued to be a feature of AIDS-movement activity.

Bill Whittaker explains:

> What happened is in Australia a number of people came forward, mainly gay men but a couple of exceptions—Margaret Duckett, for example, who just emerged and had skills in lobbying. But a number of gay men who had the skills because of what they had done in the past—lobbying, policy, people who knew how government worked came forward and had skills and were effective. But also there were groups of gay men who…didn't have any of those skills. They were not particularly sophisticated but were brave enough to speak out, turn up and that was very important.[69]

---

68 Despite the political authority afforded by the AIDS movement's relationship with the Federal Government, questions began to be raised about the limitations imposed on the movement once they were operating with government funds and had activists sitting on official advisory boards. There were fears that the movement had become 'coopted' by government and therefore less able to advocate independently the interests of the gay community. Although I do not discuss these issues further in this text, they are important considerations in terms of studying movement building in the longer term. In Australia, concerns that government funding had the potential to demobilise collective action were, to some degree, justified when the Liberal Party won the federal election in 1996, under the leadership of John Howard. The Howard regime began a program of cutting funds to non-governmental organisations. Organisations that publicly criticised the Government, or were actively campaigning against government initiatives, began to feel that their funding was under threat. Many argue that the political efficacy of non-governmental agencies was significantly hampered in this political climate in a way that it was not under the Labor Governments of the 1980s and early 1990s. As AIDS organisations were still partially funded by the Federal Government, some argued that the capacity of the AIDS movement was undermined by the reliance of these organisations on government funds. Even if activists not affiliated with a formal AIDS organisation were to take action against the Government around AIDS, it arguably could threaten the funds of organisations such as ACON and VAC. Staples, Joan 2006, *NGOs Out in the Cold: The Howard Government Policy Toward NGOs in Democratic Audit of Australia*, Discussion Paper 19/06, Faculty of Law, University of New South Wales, Sydney, viewed 3 June 2006, <http://democratic.audit.anu.edu.au/papers/20060615_staples_ngos.pdf>, p. 2; Tabone, Joey 2004, Australia's Response to HIV/AIDS at Risk Through Lack of Leadership from the Commonwealth Government, Media release, 18 May, AIDS Action Council of the ACT, Canberra, viewed 20 November 2005, <http://www. AIDSaction.org.au/content/media/2004/responsetohivAIDS.php> That said, most people interviewed for this text who were involved with ACON and VAC in the early 1980s acknowledged that the partnership with the Labor Federal Government in the 1980s was politically advantageous and progressive—even radical—for its time. Ken Davis, Interview with the author, 4 November 2004.
69 Bill Whittaker, Interview with the author, 6 November 2004.

If you're talking about what caused people to act from a compassionate side of it then I think two things happened. One was again, within an organised gay community, people acted philanthropically and compassionately because they were being actively discriminated against by the broader community. So, for example, it should never have been the case that there was a need to develop an organisation such as CSN [Community Support Network].* It was the case, it was definitely the case, that people were dying in their homes because home care wouldn't come and look after them. [People were] scared of catching [HIV] and that being manifest, even if they didn't say they were scared, into hostility toward people with HIV. Yeah, a downright, flat-out refusal to go and care for people! I'm talking about a time in the early '80s where you had people in hospital in Prince Henry where nursing staff were having to feed patients, if there were nursing staff that were prepared to be working there (nursing staff numbers were quite small). Loved-ones had to come in and feed their patients because the catering staff refused to do anything but leave trays at the front steps of the ward. Now in an environment like that you have to act. It is wrong that you have to act, it is wrong that you have to establish a parallel process. But there is a period of time in which you do have to do that. When I say people were acting benevolently…if you think in the very early '80s with the first fundraising activity that was put on by a group of gay men in Sydney which was to raise money for a guy called Bobby Goldsmith so he could remain at home and die at home rather than have to be hospitalised. And we're talking about a situation where if there wasn't money made then his rent wouldn't be paid and he wouldn't have anywhere to live. So you put those sorts of things together…the reason BGF [Bobby Goldsmith Foundation] sprung up at the time was because that man could not stay at home without being assisted by groups of peers and friends and that group, BGF, worked very closely with CSN to provide them with the necessary goods they require to keep someone at home.

— Levinia Crooks (2005)

* The Community Support Network (CSN) was one of the first home-care and support services set up for people with AIDS. It was westablished at a grassroots level by people within the gay community and was entirely volunteer run. CSN still exists today. Now it has some paid staff and is linked to the AIDS Council of NSW.

AIDS and Gay Politics

The AIDS councils were very much integrated with the gay community. They had a broad support base and many community members were involved. The gay press also ensured that the community was consistently made aware of what the AIDS councils were doing. Moreover, HIV/AIDS was an issue that drew the gay community into political action in a way that other issues never had. Literally hundreds more people were politically active around HIV/AIDS than had ever been around issues such as law reform, and there was a high level of awareness among gay men about the politics of HIV/AIDS, even those with no direct connection to AIDS activism. Indeed, throughout the 1980s gay politics became enmeshed with the politics of AIDS. Lex Watson, a founding member of ACON, once wrote:

> [AIDS] has affected all gay men in a way in which law reform, nice idea though it was (and much though I spent years doing it), did not really do. Many gay people thought anti-discrimination was wonderful, many people felt more confident because of it, many people were very glad they had it. But it didn't, very often, directly and immediately change their lives. AIDS has. And AIDS has consequently rewritten the gay male script in a way that nothing else has. Perhaps one could argue that the Mardi Gras in Sydney, as a gay community event, has come the closest to this far-reaching impact, but AIDS has a very particular resonance.[70]

The AIDS councils became a major organising body for the gay community. Although the government funding they received was primarily directed towards HIV-prevention initiatives, the AACs and the AIDS councils did not lose focus on their objective of protecting the rights and freedoms of gay men and lesbians.[71] Their political intent in this respect was clear from the beginning.[72] For example, when the Sydney AAC was established, they announced their formation in a letter to Neal Blewett, stating that the AAC aimed to, among other things, 'monitor available information on AIDS and provide non-alarmist information to both the gay community and the wider media in order to counter the political attacks on homosexuals that had become adjunct to the AIDS debate'.[73] In Melbourne, a media report in *The Age*, titled 'Gays Form AIDS Group', stated:

---

70 Bill Whittaker, Interview with the author, 6 November 2004.
71 This is not to say that the AIDS action councils, VAC or ACON were against working with other groups or did not see the importance of approaching HIV/AIDS more broadly than the gay community. Over time, the VAC and ACON began to work with other groups affected by HIV, including women, heterosexual men and Indigenous people. Historically, however, it was the gay community that developed these organisations and a large part of their *raison d'être* was the protection of gay rights.
72 Michael, Dean 1987, 'The Political Action Working Group', *Annual Report*, Victorian AIDS Council, Melbourne.
73 Cited in Sendziuk, 2003, p. 74. The AIDS action councils were also given a mandate from the gay community to speak on their behalf. Public meetings took votes allowing the councils to formally represent the gay community, which helped to sideline those who professed to be spokespeople without any community backing (such as Paul Dexter, who claimed to be head of an organisation called the 'Gay Army' although he was the only recruit). Carswell, Phil, Unpublished speaking notes for presentation at conference Retrospectives: HIV/AIDS in Australia, Historical Perspectives on an Epidemic, 27 May 2002, University of New South Wales, Unpublished notes and personal communication with Jennifer Power, 23 July 2005.

Melbourne's homosexuals yesterday announced the formation of a special group to combat what it regards as ignorance and hysteria about acquired immune deficiency syndrome, AIDS. A spokesperson for the Victorian AIDS Action Committee, Mr Adam Carr, said that the group has been set up to speak for the homosexuals in any working groups studying AIDS, to counter incorrect information being spread about the disease and to resist any attacks on homosexual people prompted by the disease. 'We reject any suggestions that AIDS is in any way a gay plague or other similar phrases used out of ignorance or malice,' Mr Carr said. 'We reject any suggestions that homosexuals or any other minority group are responsible for the outbreak of this disease. We will defend the gay community from these attacks.'[74]

The AIDS councils ensured that the media published information about their initiatives, and, amidst the articles that expressed concerns that gay men were spreading AIDS, more positive stories began to appear. For example, on 31 May 1983, the *Launceston Examiner* ran the headline 'Homosexuals to Fight Lethal AIDS'. The article stated that 'Sydney's homosexual community has called for a national seminar to find how best to combat the mysterious AIDS disease that has killed at least 600 people in the US'.[75] The *West Australian* newspaper in the same year reported on actions being taken by the Campaign Against Moral Persecution (CAMP) to inform gay men about AIDS. The article noted that medical specialists had commended a bulletin prepared for gay men by CAMP.[76] In 1985, the *Sydney Morning Herald* ran a headline that read 'Gays Want Govt Help to Prevent AIDS'. The story went on to explain why the AIDS movement was calling for government funding for community AIDS initiatives. It also mentioned that 60 000 brochures about AIDS were already being distributed by the AIDS councils.

The formation of AIDS councils, and the subsequent funding of these councils by the Federal and State Governments, meant two things for gay and lesbian rights. First, for the first time in Australia's history, groups advocating gay and lesbian rights received significant levels of government funding. Second, the political influence of these groups gave them the capacity to establish a strong media profile.

The fear of AIDS was as much a product of the social history and social position of gay men and lesbians as it was about the terror of this unknown, fatal disease. People reacted to the felt experience of injustice that had long been part of life for gay men and lesbians. But also, within the gay community, there was

---

74   'Gays Form AIDS Group', *The Age*, 8 August 1983, p. 5.
75   Needham, Paul 1983, 'Homosexuals to Fight Lethal AIDS', *Launceston Examiner*, 31 May, p. 6.
76   'WA's Homosexuals Warned on AIDS', *West Australian*, 21 May 1983, p. 23.

a collective sense that people needed to protect themselves from the social/political ramifications of AIDS. In the beginning, this was not necessarily a clearly articulated political position so much as an undercurrent of knowledge about gay history that circulated within the community, compelling people to take action. As activist Ken Davis put it: 'My generation...I don't know what we thought we were going to achieve. But we didn't have a choice because we thought we were going to be locked up or dead.'[77]

But as the AIDS movement developed, so did a growing sense of political self-assurance among movement actors. This could be seen in the increasing expectation among activists that the gay community should be consulted by the media on matters concerning HIV/AIDS and that AIDS organisations could, and should, be given funding for their work. Activists gained confidence in their right to be publicly and politically recognised for their work in the AIDS sector and the AIDS movement grew stronger as a result.

> [In] the gay community there was a capacity to behave in an organised, political way because if you consider the timing of when HIV came along, it came along at a time when the gay community (gay male community, although there was a lesbian community it wasn't ever as illegalised nor at the time as organised)... so the gay boys were fighting for political rights, they were out and about and outspoken, they were forming organisations. So we're talking about a group who were skilled, articulate and organised. And on that foundation came HIV...[In] Melbourne they had gone down the path of developing an organisation called ALSO [Alternative Lifestyles Organisation]. At the time that HIV came along ALSO had been raising funds in order to establish a gay and lesbian retirement village, or some sort of aged care facility. That money got diverted into the AIDS Council to put up a mechanism to respond to AIDS. In Sydney, the people who had been involved in the gay rights movement immediately became the people who were involved in HIV. So politically what drove people to action was the fact that they had a nascent community, and [an] incredible amount of political will and intellect drawn into that and they saw that they stood to lose everything if they didn't act. There was a potential there to lose any of the benefits.
>
> — Levinia Crooks (2005)

---

77   Ken Davis, Interview with the author, 4 November 2004.

HIV and the Australian State

The role of the Australian state is an important part of the history of HIV/AIDS in Australia. While the focus of this text is community action, the role of the Australian Federal Government in the response to AIDS provides an important backdrop to this discussion that deserves some space here.

Health in Australia is traditionally the responsibility of State governments. When AIDS arrived, however, it was the Federal Government that took charge of developing and implementing policy. There were several reasons for this. First, the nature of the epidemic meant it was politically unsavoury and risky territory for politicians. They did not want to deal with issues relating to illegal drug use, prostitution or gay men. Cost was another concern. In the mid-1980s, there were estimates of an epidemic far more widespread than that which eventuated in Australia, and State health ministers were keen to ensure that the Federal Government took major financial responsibility for it.[78]

After a long period in opposition, the Australian Labor Party came to power under the leadership of Bob Hawke in 1983. When the Cabinet was appointed, former Rhodes Scholar Neal Blewett took up the position of Health Minister. Blewett recalls that in his first briefing as minister there was some mention of an illness that was affecting gay men, but the issue was not given high priority. At the time, the matter at the top of his agenda was the reintroduction of a universal health insurance system: Medicare. He also planned to institute changes to the Pharmaceutical Benefits Scheme and revive former Prime Minister Gough Whitlam's system of community health programs. AIDS, however, became a core priority of Blewett's period as Health Minister over the course of the 1980s.[79]

Blewett is broadly credited with being central to the 'successful' Australian response to AIDS. It was under his leadership that what came to be known as the community/government 'partnership' approach to AIDS was forged. This model involved provision of funds to non-governmental groups, such as the gay community-run AIDS councils, to enable them to organise prevention and education initiatives at a grassroots level. The model was also applied to other community groups, with funding, for example, being provided to the Australian Prostitutes' Collective and injecting drug user advocacy groups.[80]

---

78   Blewett, Neal 2003, *AIDS in Australia: The Primitive Years, Reflections on Australia's Policy Response to the AIDS Epidemic*, Australian Health Policy Institute Commissioned Paper Series 7, University of Sydney, NSW, viewed 5 May 2006, <http://www.ahpi.health.usyd.edu.au/pdfs/colloquia2003/AIDSpaper.pdf>
79   Ibid.
80   This partnership model had actually first been established in Victoria, when the Victorian Government agreed to fund the development of the Gay Men's Community Health Centre run by the Victorian AIDS Council. Ballard, John 1998, 'The Constitution of AIDS in Australia: Taking Government at a Distance Seriously', in Mitchell Dean and Barry Hindess (eds), *Governing Australia: Studies in Contemporary Rationalities of Government*, Cambridge University Press, Melbourne.

Establishing a working relationship with affected communities was no doubt a feature of Blewett's personal political style. He was also, however, strongly influenced by his senior advisor, Bill Bowtell, who was personally involved with gay community activism. There were also some political precedents that supported Blewett's approach. In 1972, when the Labor Party had briefly been in power under the stewardship of Whitlam, they introduced a series of community health programs that aimed to improve the accessibility of health care. A NSW consortium called Consumer Health Involvement was established, with several subgroups that looked at issues of improving information to consumers and enhancing consumer involvement in policy decision making.[81] This program was scrapped when the Liberal Party took over government in 1975. In 1983, however, when Hawke was elected Prime Minister, there was an expectation—flowing from Whitlam's influence—that there would be a renewed emphasis on community involvement in health.[82] The Commonwealth Department for Health was also about to be thoroughly restructured under a new Secretary, Bernie McKay. The changes were to include greater emphasis on preventative health through a new Health Advancement Division.[83] Also in Australia, the Women's Health Movement had established some models for community involvement and leadership in health and provided an example of the process by which community advocates were able to gain influence within the government bureaucracy.[84] Despite the existence of these precedents to support Blewett's approach to HIV/AIDS, it was still a brave move for a government minister to publicly declare his faith in the capacity of stigmatised groups such as gay men and sex workers to take the lead in preventing a major epidemic.

As well as funding community groups, the Blewett ministry established a structure for consulting the community on AIDS. The National Advisory Committee on AIDS (NACAIDS) first began meeting in 1984, chaired by Ita Buttrose, and included two representatives from the gay community. Representation on NACAIDS was an important political opportunity for the AIDS movement. As one of the community representatives, Don Baxter, recalls:

> The other thing [NACAIDS] did was give those of us who were on there the direct access, personal access to people who were making the decisions. So, while the meetings themselves might have been messy, we always had informal direct links—or even formal ones. I mean you could

---

81 Altman, 1992.
82 Crichton, Anne 1990, *Slowly Taking Control? Australian Governments and Health Care Provision, 1788–1988*, Allen & Unwin, Sydney; Ariss, Robert 1997, *Against Death: The Practice of Living with AIDS*, Gordon and Breach, Amsterdam.
83 Ballard, 1989.
84 Ballard, John 1997, 'Australia: Participation and Innovation in a Federal System', in David Kirp and Ronald Bayer (eds), *AIDS in the Industrialised Democracies: Passions, Politics and Policies*, Rutgers University Press, New Brunswick, NJ; Ariss, 1997.

write to people quite easily and all of that. So, it actually facilitated community sector communications to chief decision makers in a way that never happened in the US or UK or lots of other places.[85]

The community model was politically risky for the Federal Government. At the time there was no precedent for such a model and it involved giving large sums of money to widely mistrusted and stigmatised groups. Many authors note, however, that the model provided political benefits as well. John Ballard, for instance, argues that the community-funding model adopted by the Australian Government could be considered an effective method of governing 'at a distance'.[86] It allowed the Government to claim credit for successes in HIV prevention, while distancing themselves from any materials or initiatives that attracted political or public protest, such as explicit posters produced by the AIDS councils in their HIV-prevention work. This fitted with the longstanding Australian tradition of the use of statutory authorities and royal commissions—autonomous from government—to undertake work that might create political threats.[87] Dennis Altman similarly notes that the willingness of the Federal Government to fund AIDS councils was a reflection both of 'political pressure and of a cynical recognition of the usefulness to governments of groups able to perform certain services either more cheaply…or at arm's length'.[88] Many people who were involved in the AIDS sector at the time also acknowledge, however, that it simply made sense for the Government to consult with the community. At that stage, the Government was desperate for information about AIDS and the gay community in Australia, whose media had been reporting on AIDS since 1981, held most of that knowledge.[89] Moreover, the partnership that developed between the community and the Federal Government in response to HIV/AIDS was unique, and a testament to the capacity of the gay community to organise their response. As community activist Lou McCallum writes: 'The word "partnership" has been used in many areas of national health policy since the relative success of the AIDS partnership, but the partnerships that are developed rarely contain the sort of power and resource sharing that was seen in the response to AIDS'.[90]

It is not the intention of this text to divert the historical focus from the importance of the decisions made by Neal Blewett and his advisors in response to HIV/AIDS. Indeed, the impact of HIV/AIDS would likely have been significantly

---

85   Don Baxter, TRC 2815/75, NLA.
86   Ballard, 1998.
87   Ballard, 1989.
88   Altman, 1992, p. 63.
89   David Plummer, Interview with the author, 30 August 2004; Bill Bowtell, Interview with the author, 28 May 2005; Bill Whittaker, Interview with the author, 6 November 2004.
90   McCallum, Lou 2003, *Review of Paper by Neal Blewett*, Australian Health Policy Institute Commissioned Paper Series 7, University of Sydney, NSW, viewed 5 May 2006, <http://www.ahpi.health.usyd.edu.au/pdfs/colloquia2003/AIDSpaper.pdf>, p. 33.

more devastating in Australia if the Government of the day had pursued a more conservative approach to disease prevention. Strategies implemented under Blewett's stewardship—including the involvement of affected communities and implementation of programs such as the needle/syringe exchange (where injecting drug users were given free access to clean syringes)—have proven in the longer term to be extremely effective HIV/AIDS prevention measures.[91] A supportive Federal Government also represented an important 'political opportunity' for the AIDS movement in that they were afforded a legitimate role in the policy response to HIV/AIDS and funding was provided for community-run education and prevention initiatives.

---

91 See, for example: Blewett, 2003; Drummond, Michael, Health Outcomes International and the National Centre for HIV Epidemiology and Clinical Research 2002, *Return on Investment in Needle and Syringe Programs in Australia*, Department of Health and Ageing, Canberra; Feachem, Richard 1995, *Valuing the Past—Investing in the Future: Evaluation of the National HIV/AIDS Strategy 1993–94 to 1995–96*, Department of Human Services and Health, Canberra.

2. Innocent Identities

Once you could find an innocent victim with HIV through blood then there was a great deal of concern. But I think it became quite apparent that if there was an innocent victim there had to be a guilty one—someone had to be blamed, to be guilty.

— Bill Bowtell[1]

Despite the increasing public profile of the AIDS councils across the country, the capacity of the AIDS movement to challenge anti-gay sentiment that surfaced in response to AIDS was continually tested throughout the course of the 1980s and 1990s. As increasing numbers of heterosexual people acquired the virus, the way in which images about people with AIDS were constructed in public dialogue became an issue that threatened to entrench further the view that gay men were to be blamed for HIV/AIDS. People who had acquired the virus through the blood supply or blood products (a condition generally referred to as 'medically acquired AIDS') or the wives or children of bisexual men who had passed on HIV/AIDS were generally depicted as the 'innocent victims' of the virus. A sharp division emerged between depictions of these 'innocents' and those who were presented as having 'chosen' to bring HIV/AIDS into their life through moral lapses: sex or drug use.

At the Third National Conference on HIV/AIDS held in 1988, Wilson Tuckey, the then Opposition spokesman on health, said in his address: 'AIDS is very much a disease that results from deliberate and possibly unnatural activity. You don't catch AIDS, you let someone give it to you.'[2]

This statement captured a strong media response that gave free rein to homophobic talkback on radio and in letters to the press.[3] While this soon led to Tuckey being replaced in the shadow health portfolio, the issue continued to burn in the media. The view that gay men and drug users were somehow at fault for their illness was continually reiterated—most clearly by conservative media commentators and radio 'shock-jocks', such as Perth-based radio announcer Howard Sattler, who wrote in a *Sunday Times* opinion piece:

---

1   Bill Bowtell, Interview with the author, 28 May 2005.
2   Tuckey, Wilson 1988, Address to Living With AIDS Toward the Year 2000: Third National Conference on AIDS, Department of Community Services and Health, Hobart, 4-6 August.
3   Ironically, the sentiment that 'you don't catch AIDS, you let someone give it to you' was later adopted by AIDS organisations, although obviously the intention was quite different. In the hands of the AIDS councils, the idea that 'you don't catch AIDS, you let someone give it to you' is intended to remind people that they can take measures such as safer sex to prevent HIV/AIDS. In this context, it is meant to empower individuals to take responsibly for their health.

> It is a case of, if the implication fits wear it. AIDS 'victims'…who acquired the disease through homosexuality or intravenous drug use, are guilty of a dangerous act which they could have prevented. They also suffer from their own mistakes, unlike their medically acquired counterparts who were fatally misled by a health service they believed was beyond reproach.[4]

The question of 'choice' became the basis for distinction between the innocent and non-innocent with regards to AIDS. Those who acquired HIV through sex or drug use were routinely represented as having some level of choice about their infection with HIV/AIDS (or at least choice over the actions they took that led to the infection), even in cases where such choices were made before HIV was known of.[5] Of course, a moral assessment about the nature of such choices was an ever-present subtext.

By the mid-1980s, there were moves to seek compensation for people who had acquired HIV through the blood supply. Early in 1986, the Federal Government advisory committee on AIDS, NACAIDS, supported a proposal to allow no-fault compensation to be given to people with medically acquired AIDS. The proposal did not go far, however, meeting with resistance from the Health Minister, who saw it as a dangerous precedent and feared people with other illnesses would follow suit. The move was also resisted by AIDS activists who opposed establishing a system where people's eligibility to gain compensation for illness was assessed on the basis of how HIV was acquired, rather than on the basis of need.[6] Continued lobbying by the Haemophilia Foundation of Australia (HFA) eventually led to a partial resolution of this issue, with the Federal Government providing a seeding grant for the HFA to establish a trust fund to which people with medically acquired HIV could apply for financial assistance.[7]

The issue of compensation continued, however, as people with haemophilia took legal action against several medical institutions: the Commonwealth Serum Laboratories (CSL), Blood Transfusion Services and hospitals.[8] It was a tough

4 Sattler, Howard 1991, 'Silence Is Not So Golden', *Sunday Times*, 24 March, p. 39.
5 Lupton, Deborah 1993, Moral Threats, Sexual Punishment: Discourses on AIDS in the Australian Press, Unpublished PhD Thesis, University of Sydney, NSW.
6 Ballard, John 1999, 'HIV Contaminated Blood and Australian Policy', in Eric Feldman and Ronald Bayer (eds), *AIDS, Blood and the Politics of Medical Disaster*, Oxford University Press, New York.
7 AIDS organisations were not necessarily opposed to the idea of compensation. They were in fact supportive of a campaign push by the Haemophilia Foundation of Australia to hasten the process of setting up a trust fund. They rejected, however, the implication that some people were more deserving of care and compensation than others. AIDS organisations argued that compensation should be administered on the basis of need, not according to the means by which an individual acquired the virus. The general political and public consensus had always tended towards the view that gay men who had acquired HIV through sex should not be eligible for any form of compensation. Ballard, 1999, p. 257; Sendziuk, Paul 2003, *Learning to Trust: Australian Responses to AIDS*, UNSW Press, Sydney.
8 Executive Director of the Haemophilia Foundation in the early 1990s, Jenny Ross, makes it clear that the foundation was only ever seeking compensation for a medical procedure that caused harm and further

case to prove as people had to show they acquired HIV at a time when medical providers had reasonable knowledge of the possibility of contamination, but had failed to take action. In other words, they had to establish that medical negligence had occurred. The first case of a man with haemophilia successfully suing a hospital came in December 1990 when the Alfred Hospital in Melbourne was ordered to pay $870 000 damages, plus more than $10 million in legal fees. This led to a massive push by the HFA and the mainstream press for governments to provide compensation rather than force people to endure such excessively expensive and traumatic legal proceedings. In May 1991, the WA Government negotiated a package with 22 claimants, each of whom received up to $301 000. South Australia and Victoria negotiated similar settlements later that year.[9] The NSW Government was less forthcoming, ordering the Government Senate Standing Committee on Social Issues to open an inquiry into the issue of compensation.[10] The terms of the review were 'to investigate and report on, as a matter of urgency' the following:

1. whether patients who have contracted HIV infection through blood, or blood product, transfusion or via artificial insemination from a donor are receiving adequate and comprehensive health and welfare services

2. whether compensation should be paid by the Government to patients who have contracted HIV infection through blood, or blood product, transfusion or via artificial insemination from a donor

3. whether the decision regarding the suitability of blood and semen donors made by health authorities in 1983–84 was appropriate in light of the information available at the time regarding HIV infection.[11]

The terms of reference for this inquiry reinforced conservative discourse around guilty versus innocent victims by maintaining the 'mode of transmission' as the central epidemiological category by which decisions would be made about whether compensation was appropriate. In his analysis of this inquiry, Michael Hurley argues that by differentiating between modes of HIV transmission the whole basis of the inquiry rested on the presumption that some people had greater knowledge, awareness or choice than others in the means by which they acquired AIDS. It also immediately created two categories of people with HIV:

illness. They never sought to demonstrate that people with haemophilia were 'innocent' victims of AIDS or that any other groups were 'guilty'. The media might have adopted such language, but this was not at the encouragement of the Haemophilia Foundation. Jennifer Ross, Executive Director, Haemophilia Foundation of Australia, Interview with Heather Rusden, 11 February 1993, Oral History Project: The Australian Response to AIDS, TRC 2815/18, National Library of Australia, Canberra [hereinafter NLA].

9 Sendziuk, 2003.

10 Hurley, Michael 1992, 'AIDS Narratives, Gay Sex and the Hygenics of Innocence', *Southern Review*, 25(2), pp. 141–59, at p. 412.

11 Parliament of New South Wales 1991, *Legislative Council Notices of Motions and Orders of The Day First Session of The Fiftieth Parliament Wednesday 3 July*, Parliament of New South Wales, Sydney.

those who may 'blame' others for their HIV infection and those who may 'blame' only themselves.[12] Throughout the inquiry, numerous submissions implied that gay men and injecting drug users had an awareness of the possible health risks involved in their activities (even if they did not know about HIV) and could have withdrawn from them, whereas people who had acquired HIV through medically based procedures had no choice about the activity that resulted in their infection. For instance, Hurley refers to a submission that states: 'Those people who were engaging in careless sexual activity and who were using intravenous drugs knew there were health hazards associated with that and freedom of choice was exercised in engaging in these activities.'[13] According to this logic, although most HIV-positive people in New South Wales at the time had acquired the virus before its existence was known, the fact that their actions posed potential health risks with regards to other diseases or complications meant they willingly placed themselves at greater risk of acquiring HIV.

The media beat-up that occurred around the inquiry tended to reinforce notions that gay men's 'choices' contributed to AIDS and that their guilt and selfishness were further exacerbated by AIDS activists' resistance to paying compensation to 'innocent' victims.

In early August 1991, as the inquiry was being heard, a member of the NSW Government Standing Committee on Social Issues, MLC Franca Arena, called a press conference to respond to allegations that AIDS activists were planning to publicly 'out' her two sons as gay using a poster campaign. A journalist had warned Arena about the alleged poster campaign so she attempted to undermine it with a public assertion that AIDS activists were malicious and intent on harming the reputations of her and her family. As it turned out, there was no evidence that a poster campaign had been planned and it never occurred.[14] But the outcome of her press conference was a front-page headline in the *Sydney MorningHerald* slamming AIDS activists: 'Vicious Gay Campaign Against Franca Arena.'[15] The paper also ran a feature article titled 'Gay Guerillas Come Out to Prey', discussing the political tactic—adopted at various times by some gay groups—of publicly 'outing' high-profile individuals. The article argued that gay groups deliberately destroyed the lives and careers of public figures for their own selfish political agenda.[16] The ethics of 'outing' is a topic of debate within the gay community and is by no means something all gay activists condone. But regardless of opinion on this matter, the media portrayal

---

12 Hurley, 1992.

13 Ibid., p. 150.

14 A poster campaign labelling Arena a 'homophobe' did later take place. AIDS activists accused her of homophobic conduct for arguing publicly that only 'innocent victims' deserved compensation. Hurley, 1992; McClelland, Jim 1991, 'Both Sides Wrong in Outing Case', *Sydney Morning Herald*, 14 August, p. 12.

15 Hurley, 1992.

16 Stapleton, John and McCarthy, Phillip 1991, 'Gay Guerillas Come Out to Prey', *Sydney Morning Herald*, 10 August, p. 36.

of AIDS activists in relation to the Franca Arena controversy contributed to the construction of an image of gay men as morally questionable, selfish and potentially dangerous.

The outcome of the NSW Government inquiry appeared to be dissatisfaction on all sides. AIDS activists were frustrated with the outcome, arguing that the $10 million allocated to compensating people who had acquired HIV though medical procedures should be used to assist all people with HIV/AIDS, or at least those most in need. Yet advocates for those with medically acquired AIDS were also upset about the relatively small individual payouts (which ranged from $5000 to $50 000).[17]

Innocence and Discrimination

The notions of 'innocence' and innocent victims of AIDS meant people with medically acquired HIV/AIDS were distanced, to some extent, from the stigma associated with gay men or drug use. The general fear of AIDS at the time, however, certainly did not allow for 'innocent victims' to avoid prejudice altogether. Indeed, analysis of the way in which non-homosexual people with HIV/AIDS were treated by the mainstream community is a useful way to assess how much of the stigma associated with HIV/AIDS was related to homophobia and how much was fear of contagious disease.

Executive Director of the Haemophilia Foundation in the early 1990s, Jennifer Ross, recalls that many of her members requested that information from the foundation be sent to them in unmarked envelopes. People feared that if others knew of their haemophilia they would assume they also had AIDS. As Ross describes: 'The fear is incredible.'[18] Regardless of the fact that most people with haemophilia who acquired HIV would have done so through blood products, discrimination was still a major issue. This is perhaps most marked in the case of children. By the late 1980s, there were several well-publicised cases from the United States of HIV-positive young people being persecuted or banned from school.[19] But the case that received the highest profile in Australia was that of NSW toddler Eve Van Grafhorst.

---

17   Hole, Jacquelyn 1991, 'HIV Sufferers United in Condemning Report', *Sydney Morning Herald*, 5 October, p. 2.

18   Jennifer Ross, TRC 2815/18, NLA.

19   There were some high-profile cases in the United States where communities demanded that HIV-positive children be removed from schools. In 1985, the Centers for Disease Control (CDC) published guidelines advocating school-aged children with HIV/AIDS be allowed to attend public schools. Parents across the country reacted with anger, fearing the risk to their children. The issue became most heated in the case of Ryan White, a thirteen-year-old boy who was infected with HIV/AIDS and had haemophilia, who was barred from school in Kokomo, Indiana, in 1985. In another case, parents organised a boycott of schools in New York because the Board of Education had made a decision to admit one unnamed student with HIV/AIDS to an

Eve van Grafhorst was born prematurely in July 1982. She underwent 11 blood transfusions to save her life. One of these transfusions infected her with HIV.[20] When she was three years old, in 1985, Eve was banned from her kindergarten in the Kincumber area, north of Sydney, for supposedly presenting a risk to other children by being a 'biter'. Eve had been banned from the centre once before this, but was allowed to return on the advice of a psychologist that she no longer presented a 'biting' risk. Parents of the centre, however, mounted a vocal protest and 40 of the 58 children who attended were withdrawn on the day Eve was scheduled to return.[21] It was only two weeks later that Eve was banned again for biting.[22] Fears that Eve would spread HIV/AIDS to other children ignited what has been described as a 'wave of media-fuelled public persecution' against Eve and her family.[23] People would spit at Eve in the street and some neighbours moved house to get further away from her.[24] Eventually, following years of harassment, Eve and her family moved to New Zealand, where she died from AIDS-related illnesses in 1993.

On Eve's death, the Mayor of Gosford, who was responsible for governing the Kincumber area, said: 'We should never treat anyone like pariahs or lepers but we found it pretty difficult for a while. She was a victim of a time, of a very sad time.'[25] As this quotation suggests, AIDS-related discrimination was a product of 'AIDS hysteria' and was by no means directed exclusively towards gay men. Unlike the discourse on AIDS and gay men, the persecution of Eve was, however, followed by a sense of shame after the event. Press reports refer to Eve as a 'teacher'—as someone who taught people to be more compassionate towards those living with HIV/AIDS. When Eve died, the media focused on the guilt and sorrow felt by people involved in the persecution. A biography of Eve printed in the *Sydney Morning Herald* after she died stated:

> Eve, who in her quiet way shamed Australia into admitting its ignorance and prejudice towards AIDS sufferers, was mourned by family and friends, politicians, and the community that chased her from her home eight years ago...Councillor Dirk O'Connor, the Mayor of Gosford, the

---

unnamed public school. On 9 September 1985, 11 000 New York children did not attend school. Brier, Jennifer 2002, Infectious Ideas: AIDS and Conservatism in America 1980–1992, Unpublished PhD Thesis, Rutgers University, New Brunswick, NJ. In Alabama in 1987, the house of a family who had three sons, each of whom had haemophilia and was HIV positive, was torched following threats against the family warning them to keep their sons out of school. AVERT 2006, *The History of AIDS 1987–1992*, AVERT web site, viewed 18 April 2006, <http://www.avert.org/his87_92.htm>

20 Bagwell, Sheryle 1985, 'The Van Grafhosts Learn How to Cope', *The Australian*, 18 November, p. 8.

21 Editorial, '7 Children Lend Their Support', *Newcastle Herald*, 1 October 1985, p. 1.

22 Editorial, 'AIDS Girl Banned on Biting Count', *Newcastle Herald*, 14 October 1985, p. 6.

23 Steven Mark, Lawyer and President of NSW Anti-Discrimination Board, Interview with Diana Ritch, 12 August 1993, Oral History Project: The Australian Response to AIDS, TRC 2815/52, NLA.

24 Whelan, Judith 1990, 'The AIDS Baby Who Made it', [Agenda Section], *The Sunday Age*, 15 July, p. 2.

25 'Shame and Grief Mark the Death of a Small Teacher', *Sydney Morning Herald*, 22 November 1993, p. 3.

town which rejected Eve and later apologised for the way it treated her, said he was glad the Australian community had made its peace with Eve before she died.[26]

By 1993, however, the Australian public had certainly not accepted that ignorance and prejudice had been features of the community's response towards all 'AIDS sufferers'. In the same year of Eve's death, Bill Mandle wrote an opinion piece for *The Canberra Times* that stated:

> We may rightly have sympathy for the miniscule number who suffer from accidental AIDS, the transfusion victims and those with inherited AIDS. One may have some, but less, sympathy for those heterosexuals who have had normal intercourse with ones who turn out to have been infected bisexuals. But why we should be persuaded to have any more than the normal meed of sympathy one has for the sick or criminal is beyond all reason—particularly if the sickness is self-inflicted and the criminality is a deliberately unlawful act taken with full cognisance of its illegality.[27]

In the case of Eve—and the many other tragic stories of HIV-positive children being persecuted—the central issue was that the community feared these individual children would unintentionally pass on AIDS to their peers. In contrast, gay men as a group—regardless of their HIV status—were constructed as untrustworthy, deviant and blameworthy in the face of AIDS. The notion of 'irresponsibility' was extended beyond individual sexual practices to encompass 'gay lifestyles'. The entire gay community was seen to be at fault for the spread of HIV and no gay man was considered innocent.[28]

Media Moves: Refiguring AIDS, refiguring gay

It is difficult to make any firm conclusions about how successful the AIDS movement was in challenging the social construction of 'innocent' versus 'guilty' people with AIDS. But campaigns around this issue provide perhaps the most interesting examples of the way in which the AIDS movement consciously engaged with a 'politics of knowledge' around HIV/AIDS—deliberately seeking to break down the association between AIDS and deviance and the perception that some were more innocent than others.

---

26   Ibid.
27   Mandle, Bill 1993, 'AIDS Gets Too Much Unjustified Attention', *The Canberra Times*, 17 January, p. 26.
28   Gould, Deborah 2000, *Sex, Death and the Politics of Anger*, Unpublished PhD Thesis, University of Chicago, Ill.

[In] ACON, I was always wanting to do outward-looking activities that assumed most of the people we needed to talk to weren't part of the inner city gay community. So we put up the [HIV-positive] Speakers' Bureau and that was as much for us as it was for them. Because it meant that we had to keep 'retailing' what we were thinking to these groups in the public...So that was funny because it meant that people with HIV and gay men and other people that were volunteers had to negotiate all these immensely political questions on a daily basis with groups of the public—schools, Rotary clubs, workplaces. And it meant that we had this 'reality therapy' all the time...it got us out of that AIDS Council building...'Retailing' the story of AIDS to the public face-to-face, with feedback, was extremely useful. So we had a daily feel for what was in people's heads. Of course it was all a lot messier than anyone imagined. Of course there were people who had extremely hostile views and were very dismissive and were like: 'it's a gay plot' and 'why should they be treated specially' and 'the Government is conspiring with the gays to get a special deal'. But by and large that wasn't true, and as people more and more (personally) knew people with AIDS that really turned around. So by the end of the time we were doing that, I don't know when that was, '93 or something, you'd go to a school and a girl would get up and say: 'look, my friend is on a combination of AZT [medication] and other drugs, or whatever, do you reckon it's worthwhile?'

— Ken Davis (2005)

According to Ian Rankin:

> Embedded in the philosophy of inclusion and respect was an adverse reaction to media stereotyping. So people put work into doing things like media guides and that sort of thing. So there has been an acute awareness that the way the media was reporting was accentuating stigma and limiting people's quality of life.[29]

As Rankin suggests in the above quotation, activists were acutely aware of the potential for media stereotyping of gay men and people with AIDS, and took action to reorient the language used by media outlets in regard to people with AIDS. Most notably, they lobbied for the media to cease using the terms 'innocent' in relation to HIV/AIDS, encouraging them to either not make any reference at all to how a person acquired the virus or use terms such as 'medically acquired AIDS' or other less morally charged terms. Activists also worked to change media use of the expressions 'victim' or 'sufferer' of AIDS— terms that were seen as disempowering for people living with AIDS. The media strategy involved building relationships with particular journalists who were

---

29 Ian Rankin, Interview with the author, 26 July 2004.

sympathetic to their position, making sure they had priority access to the AIDS councils' press releases and ensuring they had regular contact with AIDS council representatives. Activists also created media guides and contact information, gradually 'training' the media to both anticipate and seek commentary from AIDS organisations.

David Plummer says:

> We also did things like set up media awards for best reporting... Reporters who were known for being homophobic in the past would get the press releases late—after their deadline. Reporters who had been good would get it early so they could write it up before others got to it. So we did all that sort of stuff. We got Adam Carr to formalise that and write up a media briefing kit. That was designed as an A4 series of graphs and charts and contact people that would go to journalists, so they could pull it out and see who to talk to, and only the people we wanted would be on that list. So it was comprehensive and clearly thought through response.[30]

AIDS organisations also provided regular and consistent information to the media about HIV/AIDS itself—the scientific and medical as well as the social aspects. This was a highly successful strategy as journalists came to expect, and seek out, information from the AIDS councils. Thus, a large amount of information about AIDS being fed to the media came to be marked with the particular language and ideology of the AIDS movement.

David Plummer recalls:

> I clearly remember those debates around the board table at the Victorian AIDS Council. The propaganda battle...wasn't so much propaganda, but we had to manage through the media the potential for homophobia to severely get out of control. For example, when I was president of AFAO, every morning I would get into work at 8.30...and we'd go through all the newspapers looking for stories and by 9.30 we'd have a press release out. We didn't have email then, we only had a fax machine, but we had this new system of polling the faxes out to a number of outlets. We couldn't afford to go through a press agency, so we just polled it out to a number of major newspapers. We revamped the *National AIDS Bulletin*, so it was a much more glossy magazine. Adam Carr was writing the gay health update, every week or two weeks, [which] put out the latest epidemiological update of AIDS around the world. That was incredibly informative. At that stage, I was working at Fairfield

---

30   David Plummer, Interview with the author, 30 August 2004.

Hospital in Melbourne and it was standard for Fairfield staff to read the *Gay Health Update* to find out what was going on. That was their source of medical information.[31]

As a result of its strong media campaigning, the AIDS movement developed the capacity to command media attention. As early as 1986, Phil Carswell, then President of the VAC, noted: 'You don't often see AIDS talked about in the papers without a quote from someone in VAC. The media attitude has changed. We've tried to talk to the reporters and get them to understand the complexities of what they're working on.'[32]

Whether or not this media publicity led directly to a reduction in the innocent/guilty divide is not clear. Activist Ken Davis recalls that other factors also contributed to shaking this division. In particular, there was some questioning of what it meant to be 'innocent' when groups of heterosexual women, who had contracted the virus through sex with their husbands, came out and publicly questioned whether they were more 'innocent' than gay men given they had also acquired the virus through sex.[33] In an analysis of media reporting on HIV/AIDS conducted in 1993, Deborah Lupton found that the media slowly came to demonstrate greater sympathy towards some gay men living with HIV/AIDS. She notes that since the early days of AIDS there had been an increasing number of articles in which stories of individual gay men with AIDS were told and explicit expressions of prejudice started to lessen. The focus of such stories, however, was often on how HIV-positive gay men were atoning for their 'sins' through educating others about HIV/AIDS or caring for people who were ill. In contrast, people who had acquired HIV though blood transfusions or blood products were presented as deserving of sympathy and compensation. Lupton concludes that the fundamental division between people who had caught the virus through sex and those who had caught it through blood products retained its presence in the media. Even where the term 'innocent' was not used explicitly, reports about individuals living with HIV/AIDS invariably included how the subject of the story had acquired the virus.[34]

Engaging the Public

In April 1987, the infamous 'Grim Reaper' television campaign hit Australian screens. The commercial depicted a cloaked 'Grim Reaper' pacing ominously in

31   Ibid.
32   Carswell, Phil 1986, 'President's Report: Where We've Been, Where We're Going', *Annual Report*, Victorian AIDS Council, Melbourne.
33   Ken Davis, Interview with the author, 4 November 2004.
34   Lupton, 1993.

a 10-pin bowling alley, set to bowl down a group of men, women and children. These images were so striking that nearly 20 years after the campaign ended, and despite the fact that the advertisements screened for less than three weeks, they can still be recalled in detail by wide sections of the population. The image of the Grim Reaper is still often drawn on as a symbol of Australia's response to AIDS in the 1980s.[35]

The campaign had been initiated by NACAIDS, its main goal being to broadcast to the heterosexual community the message that everyone was vulnerable to HIV/AIDS, not just gay men.[36] Many AIDS activists, however, were disappointed with the content of the Grim Reaper campaign (which had been approved by a subcommittee of NACAIDS that did not include the VAC or ACON representative), arguing that it negatively represented gay men. It was feared that people would see the 'Grim Reaper' as symbolising gay men rather than HIV/AIDS, thus reinforcing the notion that it was gay men and not a virus who were responsible for AIDS deaths. Also, information about HIV prevention was not included in the television commercial. Despite these misgivings, AIDS activists did recognise that the publicity around HIV/AIDS generated by the Grim Reaper campaign was an invaluable resource for them in terms of attracting public attention. Being the first large-scale television promotion about HIV/AIDS, and the first major publicity campaign to suggest that heterosexual people were also at risk of catching the virus, it ignited a flurry of media and public hysteria. For AIDS organisations, it became an opportunity to increase their public profile, as the VAC President recalls:

> I didn't see that ad before it came on television. It was a special subcommittee of NACAIDS who finally approved it. I remember Bill [Bowtell]…told me that they were fighting over it until the last minute because of the opening words which were, I think: 'At first we thought it was just homosexuals…' Bill objected to 'just'. It made it sound like it was OK if it was homosexuals. But now it's for 'you', which implied that there was some sort of hierarchy of pain. And he recalls he actually spent a lot of time arguing that point, but got out-voted in the end. And it was a very tough decision, it was ministerial level and prime-ministerial. I regret that in the ad. But I don't regret what the ad provided for us in terms of an open door to every school in the country, and [an] open door into every bowls club and social organisation and Rotary [club] in the country, every doctor, GP and health professional who tried to ignore it in the past now couldn't.[37]

---

35   Sendziuk, 2003.
36   Vittelone, Nicole 2001, 'Watching AIDS, Condoms and Serial Killers in the Australian "Grim Reaper" TV Campaign', *Continuum: Journal of Media and Cultural Studies*, 15(1), pp. 33–48.
37   Phil Carswell, Interview with the author, 23 July 2005.

To challenge the negative portrayal of gay men in the Grim Reaper commercial, and to take advantage of the intense upswing in public attention to AIDS, the VAC organised a counter-campaign that involved running an advertisement on 10 000 milk cartons highlighting VAC initiatives and HIV/AIDS information.[38] They also produced a free HIV/AIDS information booklet.[39]

In other States, the AIDS councils were inundated with inquiries from the general public. For example, the AIDS Action Council (AAC) of the ACT took more than 500 calls in the weeks following the Grim Reaper campaign, as its former coordinator recalls:

> Most of the 537 calls we took were from the worried-well. This group is clearly not at risk, or is at low risk, but are concerned with some minor aspect of the AIDS phenomenon—hairdressers, mosquitoes, or more commonly, teenage daughters coming of sexual and independent age. They take a lot of time and patience to deal with, and it is tempting to leave them to their worries. But they are of course the landlords, business people, service providers, or simply colleagues, parents, children or siblings of people at risk. They are people who can provide— or withhold—services to our client groups—and like you they are potential AIDS educators.[40]

AIDS activists also made face-to-face contact with many members of the broader, heterosexual community through care and support work. In the early 1980s, community volunteers provided virtually all home-care services for people who were ill with AIDS-related illnesses (mainstream services were reluctant to cater for people with AIDS). As most of these volunteers were gay men or lesbians, the volunteering side of the AIDS movement created many opportunities for gay people to connect with the mainstream public. Volunteer carers regularly met, and interacted with, the extended families of people ill with AIDS as well as their friends and neighbours. Also, as community-run volunteer services such as CSN and Ankali became more established, increasing numbers of heterosexual people volunteered, often because they had friends or associates who were connected in some way to the HIV/AIDS sector or because they had known someone with AIDS. While these networks began within the gay community, they gradually expanded to bring increasing numbers of heterosexuals into personal contact with gay people and AIDS activists.

---

38   Phil Carswell adds: 'imagine the impact of those milk cartons around the family breakfast table.' This is one example of the 'reach' that the AIDS movement had—influencing public consciousness way beyond the borders of the gay community. Phil Carswell, Personal communication, 25 October 2006, Melbourne.

39   Grant, Peter 1987, 'The Education Working Group', *Annual Report*, Victorian AIDS Council, Melbourne.

40   Westlund, John 2006, 'Address to Public Meeting by Co-ordinator of the AIDS Action Council of the ACT, 23 June 1987, Canberra', in Ian Rankin (ed.), *AIDS Action: A History of the AIDS Action Council of the ACT*, AIDS Action Council of the ACT, Canberra.

[People volunteered who were not part of the gay community] but there was normally a connection. I mean there had to be a connection…But the connection was knowing someone who had been cared for, having a person who had been cared for, and then caring for others. So there were a lot of relatives involved, whether it be the odd straight brother or cousin or sister, mother, father, grandmothers, great aunt, nextdoor neighbour, it would often be that network. And that may even go into, or domino out, to that person's network. There were people who got involved because they were somebody's friend…I trained up a group of people in Wollongong and we advertised for people to come and do this and I think there were two people who did the training who were not gay, both of them were involved in the Health Department, both of them knew me (not hugely well). Both of them had been involved in drug rehab work during their training and one of their closest friends was a gay man—he didn't have AIDS, but he also did the training. So, yes, there were other people involved, but the agency would not have survived [if it relied on] non-gay men.

— Levinia Crooks (2005)

What I found was that as more and more cases were diagnosed and more and more people needed support—actual physical care teams—that there was this real osmotic effect out into the 'burbs and the bush. Families got to meet their first openly gay people. There was a real tectonic shift or movement of understanding. For the first time, I think, families got to meet functioning, reasonable, nice gay men and women…That helped break a lot of stereotypes. In the early days, we used to have AIDS funerals where the biological family were out the front with the priest not knowing what on earth he's going to say because he doesn't know the person he is burying, and these rows and rows up the back of wailing queens. And the biological family would look at the 'family of choice' and say: 'Well, who are you?' And we'd say: 'Well, who are you? We knew him better than you did.' At some of these services, they were all cleaned up and it would be: 'What are you talking about? That's not the guy I knew'…Eventually, over time, they became one. It took a while, and is still obviously not in all cases. I've never really heard it explored a lot, but I think that's a really important theme—that we actually went out there into the 'burbs and into the homes and into people's lounge rooms and nursed their sons in front of them—changed their nappies and cleaned up the vomit… And actually provided a lot of emotional support for the family, too. And I think that changed a lot of hearts in a lot of ways that is really unquantifiable, but was definitely there because from then on…that was the precursor to the whole notion of why we suddenly have gay characters all over the TV screen, why we have *Queer Eye for the Straight Guy*. There was that cultural shift that happened…I don't think any of us saw the silver lining that this big black cloud had and that's the fact that many, many, many more people have now met a homosexual person.

— Phil Carswell (2005a)

HIV/AIDS also led to the creation of the first positions within the State and federal bureaucracies that were to be occupied by openly gay men. Most State governments adopted the Federal Government's commitment to community involvement in the HIV/AIDS response. Working within this framework, roles for gay community members were created within the new HIV/AIDS divisions or groups within some State health departments. Although gay people had certainly been employed by government agencies before this—and many had probably been quite open about their sexuality at work—this was the first time the State and Federal Governments deliberately and consciously hired gay people. The Victorian Health Department even ran a specialised training course for their staff to prepare them for a new 'gay recruit'—something that seems laughable by today's norms, but is indicative of the lack of gay visibility within the Public Service in the early 1980s. Phil Carswell was among the first group of people employed by the Victorian Health Department in its new AIDS branch. He recalls:

> When I went to the Health Department in 1980 (whenever it was), I was told they had actually had a group set up for people who were working with me who had never known what a gay person did...They seriously had a class...They were very cautious and on reflection I can see why they were. It was a cultural experience for them too and you can't underestimate the fundamental nature of that change that took place. I think that was the most important part of the AIDS epidemic that has so far been undocumented...With all that going on, I think it sowed the seeds for a much deeper acceptance than there had been in the past. I think there's been a tolerance in the past, but I think that there is now more acceptance.[41]

Personalising AIDS

Along with introducing more of the heterosexual public to gay men and lesbians, the AIDS movement was successful in publicly presenting a 'personal face' to HIV/AIDS. That is, rather than allowing information about HIV/AIDS to be presented to the public only in the form of statistics or 'faceless' information, activists ensured people living with HIV/AIDS had a public profile. This became a powerful political strategy, not only in terms of lobbying for political change, but with regards to reducing AIDS-related stigma. HIV-positive activists visibly challenged stereotypes about what people with AIDS were like.

---

41   Phil Carswell, Interview with the author, 23 July 2005.

The People Living With AIDS (PLWA)[42] movement began organising in the late 1980s. PLWA activists were a dynamic part of the broader AIDS movement and campaigned alongside other activists on a number of fronts. For example, in the mid-1980s, they were heavily involved in a campaign to increase the number of beds allotted to HIV/AIDS patients in St Vincent's Hospital in Sydney.[43] But PLWA also played a distinct role within the AIDS movement by creating visibility for, and challenging negative stereotypes about, people with AIDS. As the former convener of PLWA New South Wales, Robert Ariss, writes:

> All I can say is that such [media] work is essential if the debilitating image of 'AIDS victim' is to be challenged and our self-determination established and accepted, by ourselves and others. PLWA has a major role to play here, and I believe we have been very successful in increasing public understanding of PLWAs in this state.[44]

Having people willing to publicly disclose their HIV status was at the heart of the PLWA strategy. While for many people this was personally an incredibly confronting thing to do, it was a powerful strategy for the movement in terms of eliciting empathy and creating a personal, compassionate connection between the general public and people with AIDS—humanising the virus.

According to Levinia Crooks:

> The shift [in public attitudes towards people with AIDS] happens early on when people are prepared to stand up and say they're people with HIV. So for me the shift actually occurs about 1987 with the beginning of the PLWA movement, as a movement of people standing up saying we've got HIV, whether that's a gay man, whether that's a positive woman—being openly known to be positive. That doesn't mean there's not discrimination, but that marks the turning point…In a way, it's that kinda thing where you can't 'out' somebody if they're already out. That doesn't mean I say everybody needs to be out, and there's a whole heap of reasons why you may not want to be out.[45]

PLWA developed a network of HIV-positive people who were willing to speak publicly about their experiences. People from this network began to be invited to speak in schools and to community groups.[46] Creating opportunities for people to actually meet someone with AIDS was a strategy designed to reduce

---

42 Later to become People Living With HIV/AIDS (PLWHA).
43 Ariss, Robert 1989, 'Convener's Report, PLWHA NSW', *Annual Report*, People Living with HIV/AIDS NSW, Sydney.
44 Ibid.
45 Levinia Crooks, Interview with the author, 28 January 2005.
46 In New South Wales, the Positive Speakers Bureau was established as a formal organisation in 1994. It still operates today (<http://www.plwha.org.au/PSB/>). It was preceded in 1988 by a Speakers' Bureau which

the tendency for people to associate AIDS only with a particular 'type of person' (someone with whom they would never interact) rather than a person who had a name and individual identity.

> In terms of barriers, and this may just be my personal take on it, there seemed to be a huge personal cost in becoming a public AIDS activist. It usually meant disclosing your sexuality in a confronting way: often also disclosing your viral status in a confronting way. And even if this didn't seem of great consequence to an individual if they were living in 2010 in Prahran or wherever, it did have the ability to shock and confront the nation at large. People still took exception and were surprised in those days. So when you work that through the networks of families and all those networks that we exist in, the idea of doing that for the whole of your future, because you get marked out as a significant voice in a controversial issue…People tend to remember, or people perceive that they are making lifelong commitments to that identity. I think we've seen during the '80s and '90s significant changes in the way people's sexual identity is understood, lived and practised. Stuff we would have taken for granted as gay identity being a certain thing of a certain shape in the '80s is perhaps in the 2000s different.
>
> — Ian Rankin (2004)

Cultural Space to be Gay

While gay identities in general began to find a more prominent place in public life due to the AIDS movement, the nature of HIV/AIDS also gave activists an opportunity to direct public attention toward expressions of (homo)sexuality that previously had been very clandestine. This came about because HIV/AIDS created an imperative to initiate sexual health programs with groups or individuals that lacked visibility, even within the gay community itself. The Gay and Married Men's Association (GAMMA) project is one such example.

In Melbourne, GAMMA had been operating as a small social support group for married gay men since the mid-1970s. In the mid-1980s, 'bisexual men' had been identified by the Federal Government as a key group to be targeted for HIV-prevention education. This was for both epidemiological and political reasons as bisexual men, along with injecting drug users, were seen to be the 'link' by which HIV/AIDS could pass from the gay community to heterosexual people. An organisation such as GAMMA, which had existing networks with bisexual

included self-identifying positive speakers, and by speakers with HIV helping educate Commonwealth Public Services staff from 1985. In Victoria, a similar organisation exists: the PLWHA Victorian Speakers Bureau (<http://www.plwhavictoria.org.au/speakers.htm>).

men, was an obvious group for the Government to target. In 1986, GAMMA received a grant from NACAIDS to be used for HIV/AIDS education and research into the sexual practices of bisexual men, particularly those married to women who regularly engaged in sex with other men. The NACAIDS grant was the beginning of a much larger 'GAMMA project' that was also extended to New South Wales.[47] Funding was then expanded and a national project involving a telephone counselling service was established.[48] Clearly, without the imperative of HIV prevention, the Federal Government would have been unlikely to support, or provide any recognition to, a group for men married to women who chose to have sex with other men outside their marriage. HIV/AIDS changed the scope of what was acknowledged publicly with regards to sexuality.

Gay and lesbian youth were another group who gained greater public recognition in the wake of HIV/AIDS. Adolescence is often considered to be a time when people are developing their identities. Young people are seen to be in flux, moving towards their fully formed adult self. It is a common view that sexuality develops over the teenage years, and that young people are yet to reach full sexual understanding or maturity. As such, homosexuality is often not acknowledged among young people. It is frequently assumed that people cannot be capable of defining themselves as gay or lesbian when they are still young, and if they do it is assumed to be a 'phase'. Moreover, social norms generally maintain the view that young people need to be safeguarded from sex or any sense of their sexuality. Assertion of their homosexuality by a young person is associated with a loss of innocence.[49]

HIV/AIDS brought with it a threat to the health and lives of young people who were engaging in homosexual sex. Community AIDS organisations responded to this by initiating campaigns and projects directly targeting young gay men. When such programs first began, they incited widespread controversy. For instance, in 1990 the Victorian Government banned a poster and print campaign that had been produced by the VAC's Youth Project Team. The poster targeted young men who were considering having sex with another man. The poster's slogan, written prominently across the bottom of an image of two young men kissing, was 'When You Say Yes, Say Yes to Safe Sex'. The poster also stated that homosexuality was natural and it encouraged young men to seek out support groups and people to talk to. Initially, *TV Week* magazine refused to publish a print-media version of the poster on the basis that it would offend

---

47   Gamma Project Victoria n.d., GAMMA Project: AIDS Bisexual Men and Their Female Partners, Undated publicity flyer, Gamma Project Victoria; Gamma Project Victoria 1986, GAMMA Melbourne AIDS Public Education and Awareness Project, Media release, Gamma Project Victoria.
48   Tsitas, Evelyn 1988, 'Married and Having a Gay Old Time', *Australasian Post*, 2 July.
49   Griffin, Christine 1993, *Representations of Youth: The Study of Youth and Adolescence in Britain and America*, Polity Press, Cambridge; Irvine, Janice 1994, 'Sexual Cultures and the Construction of Adolescent Identities', in Janice Irvine (ed.), *Sexual Cultures and the Construction of Adolescent Identities*, Temple University Press, Philadelphia.

their readership. The then Victorian Shadow Health Minister, Marie Tehan, followed suit, calling for a ban on the ad and the withdrawal of funding to the VAC.[50] In a media statement, Tehan stated that '[i]t is scandalous that state or commonwealth money should be spent on advertisements encouraging young people to engage in homosexual activity, with statements such as: "it's natural and if you're safe you'll have a great time"'.[51]

The Advertising Standards Council went on to recommend that no media outlets allow publication of the poster. In protest, a 'kiss-in' was staged in Melbourne's Bourke Street Mall on World AIDS Day, 1 December 1990. Organised and advertised by several AIDS groups, including the VAC and the AIDS Coalition to Unleash Power (ACT UP), the campaign message was 'Kissing Doesn't Kill: Greed and Indifference Do'.[52] The AIDS councils adopted the stance that social support and self-esteem were key factors in ensuring young people make informed choices about their sexual activities and sexual health. They pressed ahead with youth-oriented 'safe sex' promotions despite public criticism.

Further controversy emerged in 1997 around two programs launched by the WA AIDS Council (WACAIDS). The first was an anti-homophobia education package for high schools. The second was a public campaign titled 'Trust Your Feelings'. Targeting young gay men and lesbians, the 'Trust Your Feelings' campaign was aimed at suicide prevention. Its central strategy was public dissemination of a poster that had images of young lesbian and gay couples kissing on the cheek. Following media controversy, the 'Trust Your Feelings' campaign was rejected for funding by the then Commonwealth Family Services Minister, Judi Moylan. The basis of Moylan's argument was that it was 'more of a recruitment campaign for lifestyle preferences' than a message for suicide prevention.[53] The issue was controversial because people believed that adult homosexuals were deliberately seeking to influence the sexuality of youth, to 'recruit' them to the gay lifestyle. Arguments were run in the newspapers, such as the following: 'It is of great concern to our community when these types of organisations actively promote their homosexual behaviour as an acceptable or alternative lifestyle to all impressionable teenagers in our schools.'[54]

> I am concerned because it is a joint project for the WA AIDS Council and the Gay and Lesbian Counselling Service. They are not in a position to give a balanced view of behaviour toward homosexuality because both

50   McKenzie, James 1992, *When You Say Yes*, Young People from the Victorian AIDS Council and the Gay Men's Community Health Centre, Melbourne.
51   Tehan, cited in Heath, Sally 1990, 'AIDS Poster Starts a Row Over Safe-Sex Campaign', *The Age*, 26 July, p. 6.
52   AIDS Coalition to Unleash Power (ACTUP) 1990a, Campaign Poster for 'Kiss In', AIDS Coalition to Unleash Power, Victorian Chapter, Melbourne.
53   Macdonald, Janine 1997, 'Anti-Suicide Program "Had Gay Message"', *West Australian*, 15 August, p. 11.
54   Croft, David 1997, 'Homosexuals in Schools', Letter to the Editor, *West Australian*, 6 August, p. 14.

organisations endorse homosexual behaviour as an acceptable lifestyle for teenagers. They could make young, impressionable students quite vulnerable.[55]

Although many of the AIDS councils' youth campaigns became cloaked in negative publicity such as this, the debates that were held on these issues also created public space in which ideas about the nature of both adult homosexuality and youth sexuality were discussed. By asserting the need for programs to protect young people from HIV, the AIDS movement introduced a new perception of gay and lesbian youth as mature, capable and above all likely to be sexually active. Moreover, AIDS activists had an opportunity to openly discuss and publicly refute the notion that gay men were interested in 'recruiting' young people to homosexuality. For instance, WACAIDS issued open statements arguing that it is not possible to 'turn' heterosexuals into homosexuals.

> No parent or teacher should ever assume their child or student is heterosexual. Statistics show that at least five per cent of the population will develop a gay or lesbian identity. No amount of 'promoting, encouraging or teaching' can influence sexual orientation. There is, however, a separate need for responsible education, support and counselling for young homosexuals.[56]

In many ways the evidence of rising HIV rates eventually muted public criticism of youth-oriented HIV-prevention campaigns. The very possibility that young people could be at risk of HIV/AIDS became a legitimate argument for creating services that aimed to protect gay youth. Through such services, AIDS organisations began to craft a new public space for youth to express a gay and lesbian identity. They gave greater acknowledgment and visibility to gay and lesbian young people, as well as introducing discourse that was affirming of youth homosexuality. Additionally, HIV/AIDS forced health and welfare professionals working with young people, as well as schools, to address homosexuality. This has led to a significant increase in support and services for gay youth over the past two decades.[57] Increasingly, public dialogue around young gay men and lesbians is couched in positive terms, rather than panic about sexual corruption or loss of innocence. For example, in 1998 the WA Health Department released a report aimed at reducing the suicide rate in gay and lesbian youth. The report stated: 'The existence of gay, lesbian and bisexual

---

55   Dawson, Jim and Dawson, Lyn 1997, 'Dangers of Indifference', Letter to the Editor, *West Australian*, p. 14.

56   Pratt, L. 1997, 'They Deserve a Future', Letter to the Editor, *West Australian*, 7 August, p. 13.

57   Griffin, 1993; Rumesberg, Don 2002, 'The Early Years of Gay Youth', *The Advocate* [Los Angeles], 25 (June), p. 26.

young people is often denied, ignored or treated with contempt by society, especially the media and the education system, so that there is little opportunity for them to recognise, take pride and act on their sexual identity.'[58]

By opening a door for recognition of forms of sexuality that do not necessarily sit easily in mainstream Australia, HIV/AIDS raised a challenge to existing knowledge about, and attitudes towards, sexuality. The changing status of gay and lesbian youth, demonstrated by evident shifts in public discourse on youth and homosexuality over the course of the AIDS epidemic, is evidence of this. Such shifts resulted from the organised action of the AIDS movement.

According to David Plummer:

> Certainly [public acceptance of homosexuality] was the aim, and... this was quite clear at the beginning. If we're going to deal with AIDS properly we have to destigmatise the groups. As long as they remain marginalised, no access to services, no recognition for partnerships and things like that, then that sort of ghettoisation is exactly what favours the spread of disease and a whole range of other public health problems. So that was the aim and, yes, I think that did happen a bit. I think hopefully it made it easier for some younger people who found that there were ways of discussing things that were not possible to speak about prior to this.[59]

From Fear to Change

In Australia since the 1980s, HIV/AIDS has become inextricably linked with homosexuality. As activist Adam Carr states: 'Since the early 1980s, the gay experience has had AIDS as its cornerstone, a daily reference point, written indelibly into the culture. Everything gay men do is tangled up in AIDS.'[60]

When AIDS activists first began to campaign, there were claims that they were untrustworthy or selfish—reflected in ideas such as the notion that gay men were likely to conspire to deliberately infect the blood supply with HIV. This reaction followed the historical trajectory of discrimination and negative attitudes towards gay men. HIVAIDS did not create these ideas; they were old notions applied to a new situation. But paradoxically, this new situation also carried with it opportunities for gay activists to challenge and change long-held public attitudes towards homosexuality.

---

58 Kendell, Christopher and Walker, Sonia 1998, 'Teen Suicide, Sexuality and Silence', *Alternative Law Journal*, 23(5), pp. 216–21.
59 David Plummer, Interview with the author, 30 August 2004.
60 Cited in Wilmoth, Peter 1990, 'Keeping AIDS in the News', *The Age*, 13 October, pp. 8–9.

The formation of AIDS councils, and the subsequent funding of these councils by the Federal and State Governments, meant two things for gay and lesbian rights. First, for the first time in Australia's history, groups advocating gay and lesbian rights received significant levels of government funding. Second, the political influence of these groups gave them the capacity to establish a strong media profile.

Through debates such as that around 'innocent victims', as well as those generated by controversy over gay youth and blood donation, ideas about the nature of homosexuality and the characters of gay men were publicly contested. AIDS created an opportunity for gay men to regularly appear in the media with intelligent, articulate arguments both supporting their perspective on HIV/AIDS and advocating the rights of gay men and lesbians. Activists presented a 'personal face' to both gay men and the AIDS crisis and there were many opportunities for gay activists to interact face-to-face with the general public. AIDS activists also fought for increased visibility of gay identities. Gay youth, for instance, gained greater acknowledgment and recognition within Australian society as a result of youth-oriented HIV-prevention campaigns. The range of activities undertaken by the AIDS movement effectively turned around a situation that appeared to threaten the rights of gay men and lesbians into one in which new opportunities for social inclusion were founded. Arguably, through the HIV/AIDS crisis, gay men and women came to know unprecedented levels of community acceptance and public visibility. As Bill Bowtell put it:

> It was remarkable…The one thing I thought would happen in '83–84 would be the end of the gay stuff. I thought that whatever happened, you were basically fighting a retreat from Moscow. My view was…that we might as well go down on the attack, we might as well just do the right thing, get the money—I could use all the politics I had to force the issue at the top, and get the money and go down…particularly when you had Reagan and the beginning of this fundamentalist reaction that's become so catastrophic in the United States over 20 years. I won't even say it's right wing because that does a lot of unnecessary damage to people who are genuinely right wing…And that was the beginning of it in the '80s. And you could see this happening and you could say well this is going to sweep us from power. And I just thought the power of it would be so strong that we would just go under…The fear, the homophobia, the reaction. I've always thought there would be a reaction to the '60s. And I thought in the '80s it would come. But it didn't…we said 'well we'll just fight'. 'We'll just do the right thing.' But I would never have thought in fact the result of the fighting back, or the fight about this, things would become so dramatically different…[Because] of HIV I think gay people

and other marginalised groups in and around them staked a place in the sun and they won't be tossed [aside]…The question you can ask is well, was it worth having HIV to have that happen? The answer is no, it's not…It's a bit like World War II: it greatly advantaged the position of women—the war. But given the choice between oppression of women and World War II, what would you have had? It's a terrible question to ask. But social upheaval and these things have a habit of busting up very conservative social structures. So I think you can make that point. You never get a chance to choose between the liberation of women and World War II, you just make the point that it reconfigures things and power and visibility. And HIV and AIDS did that around the world.[61]

New social-movement theorists focus on the cultural significance of social movements, positioning movements as struggling for symbolic capital, and claiming cultural space to express new forms of social identity or space to articulate new ideals.[62] Perhaps one of the most significant achievements of the AIDS movement was not its contribution to tangible outcomes such as policy change, but its influence on changing the cultural environment. The AIDS movement was able to introduce into mainstream consciousness new ideas about the nature of homosexuality and the role that gay people play within society.

61   Bill Bowtell, Interview with the author, 28 May 2005.
62   Canel, Eduardo 1997, 'New Social Movement Theory and Resource Mobilization Theory: The Need for Integration', in M. Kaufman and H. Dilla Alfonso (eds), *Community Power and Grassroots Democracy: The Transformation of Social Life*, International Development Research Centre, Ottawa, <http://www.idrc.ca>; Fraser, Nancy 1998, 'Heterosexism, Misrecognition and Capitalism', *New Left Review*, 228, pp. 140–50.

Part Two: (Mis)trust and Medicine

3. Public Health and AIDS Activism

A lot of the work of the AIDS movement in the 1980s was about the way in which HIV/AIDS and the people most affected by it were defined and the steps that needed to be taken to address AIDS. This work was done in conjunction with a range of other individuals and organisations with an interest in HIV/AIDS—most notably from within the Government and the medical profession. Kevin White and Evan Willis argue that there were three core groups competing to 'enforce their definition of the (HIV/AIDS) situation'.[1] The first of these groups was the 'inner circle' of doctors, scientists and medical researchers working in the HIV/AIDS sector. White and Willis describe the second as the 'dissenting enclave'—those non-governmental groups such as the AIDS movement who worked in parallel with the inner circle, but also challenged their scientific autonomy. The third group is the 'exoteric' body of lay-people surrounding both the inner circle and the dissenting enclave. This 'exoteric body' tends to support the knowledge and values of the inner circle, and seeks to minimise the impact of the dissenting enclave. In the case of HIV/AIDS, the exoteric body was usually people with an anti-gay, pro–nuclear-family agenda—often religious organisations or conservative public commentators. Borrowing from White and Willis, the following chapters explore the relationship between these three groups in the production of knowledge about HIV/AIDS, and in defining Australia's social and public health response to HIV/AIDS. I focus predominantly on the relationship between the medical profession (the inner circle) and the AIDS movement (the dissenting enclave), although those forming the 'exoteric body' (such as conservative churches and various journalists) also influenced the direction of discussion about HIV/AIDS at various times. The way in which HIV/AIDS came to be perceived and dealt with in Australia was largely a product of both the contest and the collaboration that occurred between these different social groups and the work of individuals who sat within both groups, such as gay men who were doctors.

As AIDS activists had attained a more credible and legitimised position within the Federal Government's response to HIV/AIDS, there was pressure on the 'inner circle' to negotiate with them. The tension this created was evident in one of the first major debates in Australia about public health responses to AIDS: the issue of HIV antibody testing.

---

1   White, Kevin and Willis, Evan 1992, 'The Languages of AIDS', *New Zealand Sociology*, 7(2), pp. 127–49, at p. 127.

To Test or Not to Test?: HIV antibody testing

The first HIV antibody test—the ELISA[2] test—began to be used in Australia in April 1985. As this was some years before any effective antiviral treatments were available,[3] the arrival of the ELISA test meant that people could be diagnosed as HIV positive but were not treated for the virus. For individuals who tested positive, doctors could do little besides advising on healthy lifestyle and nutrition choices and providing ongoing surveillance of related illnesses. Doctors could try to manage the physical symptoms of AIDS-related infections when they appeared, but an early diagnosis of HIV was not likely to change an individual's long-term prognosis. Despite this, medical authorities and many individual doctors strongly advocated the HIV test, with the Albion Street Clinic in Sydney (a prominent HIV/AIDS and sexual health clinic) releasing a pamphlet that proclaimed 'A Simple Blood Test Could Save Your Life'.[4] From a medical research perspective, the ELISA test created the capacity for wide-scale monitoring of the virus. There was also a general view held by many medical professionals that knowing one's HIV status was a good thing in terms of self-care and accessing appropriate clinical services as early as possible.

For many people in the gay community, however, the reasons *not* to submit to an HIV test far outweighed the reasons for testing. As well as unease about the stress and emotional trauma that would likely be associated with a positive diagnosis, people were concerned about the discrimination they might face if they were known to have HIV. Studies conducted by the Queensland and WA AIDS councils at the time also showed that gay men were reluctant to take an HIV test because they did not trust government guarantees about the confidentiality of test results. Unsurprisingly, given that homosexuality was still on the criminal code in those States, gay men also feared persecution by authorities if they did test positive.[5] The following extract from the memoirs of an Australian man, David Menadue, describes well the tension brought about by an HIV test:

---

2   ELISA is an abbreviation for 'enzyme-linked immunosorbent assay'.
3   The first breed of HIV medications—a drug known as Zidovudine (or more commonly AZT)—began to be trialled in the United States in 1986 but did not become widely available in Australia until the 1990s. Sendziuk, Paul 2003, *Learning to Trust: Australian Responses to AIDS*, UNSW Press, Sydney.
4   Ibid.
5   Bull, Melissa, Pinto, Susan and Wilson, Paul 1991, 'Homosexual Law Reform in Australia', *Australian Institute of Criminology Trends and Issues in Crime and Criminal Justice*, 29, <http://aic.gov.au>

My doctor, David Bradford,[6] pronounced, 'David, I'm sorry to have to tell you this, but your test is positive.'

So much for my friends who claimed there was no way this virus had reached Melbourne yet. So much for my general practitioner who had said several weeks earlier that the swollen glands in my armpits were probably the result of a transient infection, and that I didn't need a test for this new virus...

The test had only been available in Australia for a few months, and hardly any of my friends had chosen to be tested yet. Some were afraid to find out the result. And others couldn't see the point. As one friend put it, 'What's the value of knowing you're positive? There are no treatments, it's likely to cause you added stress, and who knows, you might suffer discrimination if people find out your status'...

A counsellor at the clinic asked who I wanted to tell the news. I was about to reply that I was sure all my gay friends would support me, when he advised caution. 'Even people in the gay community don't understand much about this virus yet. Some people may harbour real fears about catching it from you, whether that's realistic or not. Think carefully about who you tell and how you handle it.'

It was finally starting to dawn on me. This was not news that would necessarily invite acceptance, understanding or compassion. This was not necessarily the same as revealing my sexuality. Even the gay community, my support base with whom I had developed my sexual identity over the past ten years, might not embrace this news. This was about disease, infection and death. There was no telling how people would react.[7]

The issue of whether or not to encourage gay men to undertake testing became a major debate among AIDS activists—and between activists, governments and researchers. Some felt that the importance to medical research was such that the movement should advocate testing even if the health benefits for individuals were negligible. Lex Watson, President of ACON at the time, wrote in *Outrage* magazine:

---

6 David Bradford was a gay man and physician. He was involved in the political and medical side of the HIV/AIDS response. Phil Carswell describes Bradford as 'a true hero, living legend' for his role in assisting people with HIV/AIDS. Phil Carswell, Personal communication, 25 October 2006, Melbourne.
7 Extract from Menadue, David 2003, *Positive*, Allen & Unwin, Sydney.

There is little dispute that more needs to be known about the natural history of the infection, and that is what is gained through testing. As a community it is clearly in our interests to participate in such research. A strong case would need to be made for non-cooperation in such work and, in my view, subject to satisfactory confidentiality procedures existing, such a case has not been made.[8]

In spite of this, a sense of unease about the security of test results underpinned all debate. It was felt that the risks posed to gay men's social security were greater than the potential research benefits of wide-scale testing. In the same edition of *Outrage*, Phil Carswell, former President of the VAC, wrote:

At the moment, to take the antibody test is to agree to put your name and address on a list of gay men, a list over whose future use or misuse neither you nor your doctor have ultimate control, and to risk being publicly identified as an 'AIDS carrier', which is how the media invariably (and falsely) identify Ab+[9] people. The consequences of being so identified could be unpleasant. Already in the US gay men are being denied insurance, employment and housing on the grounds of an Ab+ finding.[10]

Carswell went on to conclude that '[t]he fact is that this test is simply not a useful diagnostic tool. Its only real uses are for sampling work, to measure the progression of seropositivity in the at-risk groups, and for screening blood products.'

Both Carswell and the VAC went on to review their position on testing when antiviral treatments became available and it was demonstrated that early diagnosis could improve health outcomes for people testing positive to HIV. The line taken against testing at the time, however, was that gay men should be practising safe sex regardless of their antibody status (to protect either themselves or others) and that HIV testing should not form part of an HIV-prevention strategy. It was seen as something individuals might submit to for personal reasons, but not an appropriate basis for public health practice and therefore not something that the AIDS movement should, in principle, advocate.[11]

---

8   Watson, Lex 1985, 'Antibody Testing Unquestionably Has Some Value', *Outrage*, 21 (February), pp. 5 and 7.
9   HIV antibody positive.
10   Carswell, Phil 1985, 'Gay Men Should Ignore This Test', *Outrage*, February, pp. 5–7.
11   Ibid.

Meanwhile in the clinic, I had patients coming in feeling anxious about HIV testing and worried the Government would be collating lists of people with HIV. At this stage, it was thought to be quite a rare infection, and therefore feasible that people could be basically taken out of circulation and quarantined. And during that period there had been calls from respected medical academics for quarantine, even though in other forums it was argued that it wasn't going to be viable nor necessarily the best strategy...But you've got to remember that...at that stage it was less than 10 years since homosexuality had been decriminalised. Prejudices ran very deep...So there was clearly in some people's minds, some patients, this idea that if they got tested there could be... people actually spoke about how the Nazis were able to round up Jews during the war because of information they gave in the census prior to the Second World War. So they were aware that this was a possibility. Even if it was an unlikely possibility, it was something they [thought about].

— David Plummer (2004)

Apprehension about testing was indicative of the climate of fear HIVAIDS had generated among the gay community. Concerns were magnified when, in 1985, the NSW Government proposed legislation that would make it mandatory for doctors to supply the Government with the names of all people testing positive to HIV (commonly referred to as compulsory notification legislation). This raised alarm among gay men, with many people cancelling appointments for testing or demanding their medical records be destroyed.[12] AIDS activists voiced opposition to the proposal, announcing publicly that they did not trust the NSW health authorities to retain the confidentiality of medical records. Presenting the concerns raised at a gay community meeting held in January 1985, Lex Watson stated to the media:

> We are worried about the uses to which the information could be put...It could be passed on to police or employers and we will not be cooperating with the government unless we get iron-clad, water-tight guarantees about confidentiality. If the test results are made notifiable, we will recommend homosexuals do not take them and actively campaign against them.[13]

---

12 McDonnell, Dan 1985, 'Patient Panic on AIDS Law', *The Sun*, 28 September, p. 13; Green, Roger 1985, 'With Compulsion, Victims Go Underground', *The Canberra Times*, 6 September, p. 10.
13 Lex Watson cited in Sanderson, Wayne 1985, 'Gays May Refuse AIDS Test', *Daily Telegraph*, 14 January, p. 5.

Challenging Medical Authorities

The prospect of compulsory notification of HIV test results brought to the surface many of the anxieties HIV/AIDS had raised for gay men. It became a focus for fears that HIV/AIDS would lead to the reintroduction of State-sponsored surveillance of gay lives and new levels of discrimination. Certainly in the early 1980s there was every reason to wonder whether the types of 'HIV/AIDS containment' measures that would be enacted could lead to such a situation.[14]

Anxieties were eased to some extent by the introduction of anonymous testing systems such as name-coding.[15] As Bill Bowtell, advisor to the Federal Health Minister at the time, recalls:

> In Sydney it worked out really well because very quickly people like [Dr] David Cooper and [Dr] Ron Penny established relations of trust with the gay community and were able to build these long-term studies and cohorts and things. And people could know that if they gave their name and they enrolled in these studies that the doctors weren't going to publish them and misuse them—that they were honestly well motivated and that the Government wasn't going to use the names of all these HIV-positive people to detain them or arrest them or remove them from society. So it had an immensely beneficial effect because what happened very quickly was that our approach [brought] trust…trust turned into tests. People got themselves tested because they trusted the system and they could turn up for a universal, free, anonymous HIV test. They could give the name Donald Duck if they wanted to. But in those early years they could turn up and get tested and they would know that they weren't going to get sanctioned.[16]

Also key to increased confidence in testing systems was the presence of gay or gay-friendly doctors and medical clinics. Clinics run by gay doctors, or specifically catering to the gay community, had been established prior to HIV/AIDS, usually specialising in sexual health care for gay men. As such, there was

---

14 Despite the fears expressed by people in the early 1980s, significant breaches of confidentiality with regards to HIV test results never eventuated in Australia and legislation to protect people living with HIV/AIDS from discrimination became part of the Federal *Disability Discrimination Act* in 1992. Cabassi, Julia 2001, *Barriers to Access and Effective Use of Anti-Discrimination Remedies for People Living with HIV and HCV*, Occasional Paper No. 1, Australian National Council on AIDS, Hepatitis C and Related Diseases, p. 6.

15 Bill Bowtell, Interview with the author, 28 May 2005; Ken Davis, Interview with the author, 4 November 2004; David Lowe, Interview with the author, 12 July 2005.

16 Bill Bowtell, Interview with the author, 28 May 2005. The one downside to this decision from an epidemiological point of view is that, in hindsight, it is not possible to measure how many times people were tested so the figures on HIV rates for the time generally have to be adjusted to account for multiple tests. I doubt, however, that many people would argue this downside means anonymous testing was the wrong decision to make at the time. Carswell, Personal communication, 2006.

a network of clinics that members of the gay community did, in general, trust. As former Director of the NSW AIDS Bureau and community activist David Lowe put it:

> In terms of trust in confidential processes…having general practitioners, like the [gay-run] Taylor Square people as an example, meant people did trust the confidentiality of the system…But I think people actually trusted the confidentiality of the results if they had it done in a place like that. Albion Street [Clinic] was anonymous. So I don't think that was a hugely substantial issue in reality. It was right that people had concerns about it, so it was an issue. But I think people generally felt comfortable about being tested in those settings. I think there was a big debate about whether people should be HIV tested or not. And I think that the main [issues] in that debate where whether knowing you were HIV positive had any relevance, what would you do?…[T]he reality was that. I would think that a very large majority living in the inner part of Sydney would have been tested within a year or two of the test becoming available. I don't have any data to back that up. That's based entirely on personal impressions. But most of my friends knew their HIV status and I can't remember many people who didn't…So I think the debate was a bit of a false debate in terms of the reality of people's lives, I suspect. But I think it was probably still a useful debate in terms of what is the most useful approach to HIV.[17]

As Lowe articulates, although there were still concerns about compulsory notification legislation, gay clinics combined with anonymous testing facilities meant that over time many gay men did elect to be tested. This did not mean, however, that the debates about testing and compulsory notification legislation were resolved or became irrelevant. Indeed, the stance taken by AIDS activists in response to the testing issue was highly significant because it established their critical engagement with medical authorities and launched a major discussion about the most effective way to respond to HIV/AIDS. The AIDS movement demonstrated its willingness to campaign against medical interventions it did not consider warranted. The support that AIDS activists received from the gay community as a whole meant that medical professionals could not afford to ignore them. If the AIDS movement was calling for people not to submit for testing then any public health regime that relied on large numbers of the affected population being tested could be undermined. While many individual doctors recognised this,[18] supporting the gay community in their rejection of

---

17 David Lowe, Interview with the author, 12 July 2005.
18 These doctors also feared that compulsory legislation could lead people to avoid any contact with medical authorities, further limiting AIDS research and undermining prevention efforts.

compulsory notification legislation, there were other medical professionals who continued to reject any involvement of the gay community in the medical or public health response to HIV/AIDS.[19]

Tension between the AIDS movement and the medical fraternity had been developing prior to the testing debate. When Federal Health Minister, Neal Blewett, had set up NACAIDS, he had also established a separate committee: the AIDS Task Force. The role of the Task Force was to provide 'objective' medical advice about AIDS to the Government. Its membership included various clinical and scientific researchers and it was chaired by conservative medical academic Professor David Penington. In early 1985, the AIDS Task Force had released a report that projected between 20 000 and 50 000 Australian men were already carrying 'AIDS antibodies'. Headlines appeared in newspapers depicting these projections as reality rather than estimates: '50,000 Sydney Men Now Carry AIDS.'[20] AIDS activists felt that this was a vast overestimation. They accused the Task Force of scaremongering in a cynical gesture aimed at directing government funds away from community organisations and towards scientific research. In protest, gay men began to withdraw their support from a major AIDS research study. Convener of the Sydney AAC, Lex Watson, reported to the media that individuals had decided to pull out of the study because they were angry not only about the most recent actions of the Task Force but also because some leading medical professionals were calling for the closure of homosexual bathhouses and the cancellation of the annual Sydney Gay and Lesbian Mardi Gras.[21] Watson went on to argue that much of the division between AIDS activists and doctors stemmed from a refusal by the AIDS Task Force to allow openly homosexual representation on their board or to consult regularly with gay community representatives. Professor Penington responded to this by stating that the technical side of the AIDS issue should be left to doctors. He argued that '[i]f we are not able to address the scientific and medical problems without addressing the political problems, we won't get anywhere'.[22]

While Penington did not oppose community education about AIDS, his public statements indicated that he did not believe education and community participation should receive funding at the expense of medical and scientific intervention. In essence, Penington's views represented a commitment to a biomedical model of disease prevention that had long been the basis of public health efforts in Australia—a model that had medical testing and immunisation at its core. In the early 1980s, however, there was an emerging body of thought internationally on public health that was beginning to have influence within

19   Green, 1985.
20   Frail, Rod 1985, '50,000 Sydney Men Now Carry AIDS', *Sydney Morning Herald*, 31 January, p. 1.
21   Bagwell, Sheryle and Leser, David 1985, 'Crisis Point in Gay, Doctor Relationship', *The Weekend Australian*, 2 March, p. 3.
22   Professor David Penington cited in ibid.

Australia. Commonly referred to as the 'new public health', this new body of thought lent some support to arguments being made by AIDS activists for a community-led approach to AIDS prevention.

'New Public Health': A political opportunity?

The original foundation of public health did not emerge from biomedicine. Eradication of contagious diseases was in the past more likely to be a matter related to urban infrastructure and social organisation. Improved living conditions, clean water and containment of sewage were key to curbing some of the deadliest epidemics of the eighteenth and nineteenth centuries—namely, cholera and typhoid. Through such measures, the idea that the physical state of humans is determined by the social and environmental world, rather than physiology alone, first gained mainstream credibility.

This perspective, however, came to be overshadowed by the discovery of microbes in the eighteenth century—a discovery that led to greater interest in the way in which germs spread from person to person rather than the social causes of ill health. 'Germ theory' of this type, along with breakthroughs in immunisation, convinced public health practitioners to favour individual-level and biomedically oriented measures, such as testing and the development of vaccines. Public health thus began to emerge as an extension of the medical and pharmaceutical industries.[23]

From the 1960s onward, however, treatment of acute illness had advanced to the point where the most critical issues facing the health system had become management of chronic conditions and disease prevention. To deal with this, governments were beginning to fund a range of alternative healthcare practices such as community-based care, physiotherapy and health promotion. As a result, the base of what was considered 'credible' medical intervention was broadening. The involvement of practitioners other than Western medically trained doctors was becoming more acceptable in the health sector. The orientation towards prevention of chronic disease meant that health was again being seen in terms of social factors. What came to be referred to as the 'new public health' approach was generated in this context.

---

23 Frohlich, Katherine, Corin, Ellen and Potvin, Louise 2001, 'A Theoretical Proposal for the Relationship Between Context and Disease', *Sociology of Health and Illness*, 23(6), pp. 776–97; Lupton, Deborah 1995, *The Imperative of Health*, Sage Publications, London; Brandt, Allan 1997, 'Behaviour, Disease, and Health in the Twentieth Century United States', in Allan Brandt and Paul Rozin (eds), *Morality and Health*, Routledge, New York; White, Kevin 1996, 'The Social Origins of Illness and the Development of the Sociology of Health', in Carol Grbich (ed.), *Health in Australia: Sociological Concepts and Issues*, Prentice Hall, Sydney.

The philosophy of the new public health movement is underpinned by a 'holistic' approach to health, seeking to influence environmental and social barriers to good health as well as factors under an individual's control, such as their eating and exercise habits. The 'social orientation' of the new public health means that the role of doctors is de-emphasised and the involvement of people who are in a position to change or improve social conditions is central. Hence, community participation is a major part of the 'new public health' method.[24]

By the early 1980s, the new public health philosophy was beginning to have influence in international forums, with the World Health Organisation (WHO) adopting its principles in its 'Health for All by 2000' campaign launched at its Alma-Ata conference in 1978.[25] Australia was recruited to a group of countries that would work on developing 'new public health' models. The second International Health Promotion Conference in which these new ideas were the main focus of discussion was held in Adelaide in 1988.[26]

Alongside this growing prominence of new public health theories, a consumer health movement had been developing in Australia throughout the 1970s. During his short reign as Labor Prime Minister in the early part of the decade, Gough Whitlam had introduced a government-funded Community Health Program as well as a Women's Health Program and Medibank (the precursor to Medicare). When the more conservative Coalition came to power, with Malcolm Fraser as its Prime Minister, and all of these programs were dismantled, a number of community groups formed an alliance to lobby for their reinstatement. This collaboration, sponsored by the Victorian Council of Social Services and various philanthropic trusts, established the Health Issues Centre in 1983. The Health Issues Centre generated enough public profile to enable it to contribute regularly to media and other national forums on issues such as access to health services and equity in health care. The centre was a strong advocate for the reintroduction of Medicare and it campaigned around the issue of consumer rights in the health sector. State governments responded to such campaigns by establishing consumer complaints processes, such as the NSW Health Department's Complaints Unit set up in January 1984.[27]

In 1985, after the Labor Party had been returned to power, the Commonwealth Government set up the Better Health Commission (BHC), which was charged with following up the WHO Health for All by 2000 guidelines. The BHC recommended

---

24   Bates, Erica and Linder-Pelz, Susie 1990, *Health Care Issues*, [Second edition], Allen & Unwin, Sydney; Crichton, Anne 1990, *Slowly Taking Control? Australian Governments and Health Care Provision, 1788–1988*, Allen & Unwin, Sydney; Woolcock, Geoffrey 1999, A Vector of Identity Transmission: AIDS Activism and Social Movement Theory, Unpublished PhD Thesis, La Trobe University, Melbourne.

25   Crichton, 1990, p. 111.

26   Ibid.

27   Carter, Meredith and O'Connor, Debra 2003, 'Consumers and Health Policy Reform', in P. Liamputtong and H. Gardner (eds), *Health Social Change and Communities*, Oxford University Press, Melbourne.

that Australia increase spending on disease-prevention programs. This led to the establishment of health promotion divisions within each State health department and increased Federal Government funding for their programs. The Commonwealth Government also founded the Australian Institute for Health (later the Australian Institute for Health and Welfare) and the National Centre for Epidemiology and Population Health (NCEPH), both of which collected data on population health. The National Health and Medical Research Council (NHMRC) convened a public health subcommittee, and a health advancement section was established within the Federal Department of Community Services and Health. Much of the health promotion rhetoric that came out of these new agencies was similar to welfare-state policies—looking at income redistribution, housing policy and education as well as health care—and was consistent with new public health philosophies.[28]

So, concurrently with the appearance of AIDS, there was emerging support—internationally and domestically—for non-biomedical involvement in health care. This was a cultural and political opening for the AIDS movement. Certainly, among health bureaucrats and a number of allied health professionals working in preventative health care there was a growing awareness of the new public health and increasing acceptance of community involvement in health care and disease prevention.[29] Also, the Women's Health Movement, which had grown throughout the 1970s in the United States and Australia, had gone some way towards redefining the boundaries between medical experts and health consumers. Using a critique of patriarchal institutions—of which the medical system was considered one—the Women's Health Movement sought to lessen the knowledge gap between practitioner and client as a means of redressing the power imbalance. A core philosophy of the Women's Health Movement was enabling women to assume a sense of 'control' over their healthcare decision making.[30] Feminist academics also contributed to this. In particular, feminist critiques of science have been at the forefront of challenging concepts of 'truth' and 'fact' in the medical sciences.[31]

In the early 1980s, however, the new public health approach was very new. In hindsight, many people have commented that AIDS was the first real test of these new ideas because there was an organised community seeking to play a role in its prevention.[32] But at that time, neither government nor AIDS activists had

---

28 Crichton, 1990.

29 Ken Davis, Interview with the author, 4 November 2004.

30 Epstein, Steven 1996, *Impure Science: AIDS, Activism and the Politics of Knowledge*, University of California Press, London.

31 Ibid.; Kehoe, Jean 1996, Medicine, Sexuality and Imperialism: British Medical Discourses Surrounding Venereal Disease in New Zealand and Japan: A Socio-Historical and Comparative Study, Unpublished PhD Thesis, Victoria University of Wellington, New Zealand.

32 Altman, Dennis 1994, *Power and Community: Organizational and Cultural Responses to AIDS*, Taylor and Francis, London.

the extensive vocabulary around consumer health and community participation that exists today. The WHO 'Ottawa Charter', which encapsulates a political and community empowerment approach to health promotion, was not published until 1986, long after AIDS activists had initiated their own brand of social/community approach to disease prevention.[33] Moreover, AIDS activists were pushing to be actively included in government and medical decision making. Their vision for community involvement extended far beyond a framework in which they would be considered just 'consumers' of health services.

The tension between activists and medical professionals about the direction of HIV/AIDS policy and practice is indicative of the fact that the new public health approach was far from universally understood or accepted. Australia has a long and successful history of disease eradication through mass immunisation, assisted by the island geography of the country, which allows for stringent quarantine regulation. In Australia, population-wide immunisation of children throughout the 1940s and 1950s meant diseases such as polio and tuberculosis became virtually non-existent by the 1970s.[34] By the time AIDS arrived in the 1980s there certainly was not broad agreement on the idea that patients or lay-people should be involved in health policy making. By initiating such a strong community response, AIDS activists were the public face of a new paradigm of thought in public health, and this presented a challenge to the existing order of the health system.[35]

The divisions between activists and advocates of traditional public health were heightened in the mid-1980s when questions began to be raised about whether HIV/AIDS funding should be directed towards a community education model or a more traditional public health approach combining scientific research and clinical measures.

The Politics of Safer Sex

In the mid-1980s the Federal Government, in a momentous move, agreed to support a community-based model of HIV prevention. This approach was adopted from a strategy paper that the Victorian AAC had devised in 1984 that articulated the need for education materials to be appropriately targeted to the community with which they sought to engage—in this case, gay men.

33   Plummer, David and Irwin, Lyn 2004, Grassroots Activities, National Initiatives and HIV Prevention: Clues to Explain Australia's Dramatic Early Success in Controlling HIV, Paper presented at the TASA Conference, 8–11 December, La Trobe University, Beechworth, Vic.

34   Waldby, Cathy, Kippax, Susan and Crawford, June 1990, 'Theory in the Bedroom: A Report from the Macquarie University AIDS and Heterosexuality Project', Journal of Social Issues, 25(3), pp. 177–85.

35   Wachter, R. 1996, 'AIDS, Activism, and the Politics of Health', in Stella Theodoulou (ed.), AIDS: The Politics and Policy of Disease, Prentice Hall, Upper Saddle River, NJ.

The paper also stated that gay men were likely to be wary of attempts to 'educate' or dictate to them about matters of sex and sexuality from sources outside the community.[36] The Federal Government was aware of this report and accepted its findings, agreeing to fund gay community AIDS organisations to run HIV-prevention education. A cost-sharing agreement was enacted between the Federal and State governments through which the Victorian AIDS Council and the AIDS Council of NSW received establishment grants of $56 000 and $74 000, respectively. This gave the AIDS movement funds with which to create increasingly sophisticated HIV education materials and programs.[37]

The catchcry of 'safe sex'[38] came to define the AIDS era. It was this that formed the basis of community education campaigns rolled out by the AIDS councils in the 1980s, and it was a concept that came to be adopted by health promotion agencies across the world. The notion of safe sex continues to be a familiar, almost ubiquitous, expression in contemporary Western culture.[39]

The idea of safe sex was introduced to the Australian AIDS movement by American activist Michael Callen in a booklet titled 'How to Have Sex in an Epidemic'.[40] The first safe-sex campaigns in Australia were initiated as early as 1982 when the Sisters of Perpetual Indulgence, a mock order of (drag) nuns, distributed a leaflet explaining in detail exactly what safe sex entailed. The leaflet also discussed Karposi's sarcoma, pneumocystis carinii pneumonia (PCP) and other illnesses and symptoms now known to be associated with AIDS.[41]

Following on from this, one of the first activities of the Victorian AIDS Action Committee (VAAC) education team was the Fantom Frangers, a community theatre act in which volunteers dressed in white 'Fantom'[42] suits demonstrated how to use condoms at gay saunas and other venues. VAAC's theatrical act, the *Safe Sex Sisters*, also carried the safe-sex message to the gay community through their 'nurse' drag shows performed at gay nightclubs.[43]

---

36   Ballard, John 1992, 'Australia: Participation and Innovation in a Federal System', in David Kirp and Ronald Bayer (eds), *AIDS in the Industrialised Democracies: Passions, Politics and Policies*, Rutgers University Press, New Brunswick, NJ.

37   Ibid.; Sendziuk, 2003.

38   During the 1990s, health education workers and community groups began to use the term 'safer sex' instead of 'safe sex', acknowledging that there is some risk of STI and HIV transmission involved in all sexual encounters, although this is minimal if safer-sex practices are adopted.

39   Altman, 1994.

40   Prestage, Garrett 2002, Investigating Sexuality: A Personal View of Homosexual Behaviour, Identities and Subcultures in Social Research, Unpublished PhD Thesis, University of New South Wales, Sydney; Ariss, Robert 1997, *Against Death: The Practice of Living with AIDS*, Gordon and Breach, Amsterdam.

41   Australian Federation of AIDS Organisations (AFAO) 1992, *HIV/AIDS and Australia's Community-Based Sector: A Success Story in Prevention*, Paper commissioned by the Commonwealth Department of Health, Housing and Community Services for the National HIV/AIDS Strategy Evaluation, Australian Federation of AIDS Organisations, Canberra.

42   The original Phantom was a comic-book superhero.

43   Victorian AIDS Council 1993, *A Dangerous Decade: Ten Years of AIDS*, Victorian AIDS Council, Melbourne.

The inaugural meeting of the Victorian AIDS Council on 4 December 1984 was also the launch of their first major safe-sex campaign: 'Great Sex, Don't Let AIDS Stop It.' The campaign included the VAC's first brochure on safe sex, the content of which had been modelled on a leaflet produced by the American Sisters of Perpetual Indulgence.[44] This was followed up in 1985 with a promotion developed around the slogan 'You'll Never Forget the Feeling (of safe sex)', a parody of a television commercial for Sheridan bedsheets being run at the time.[45]

> In a situation where people are really fearful and stigmatised and where people don't know what a [test] result means, everyone should assume that they are able to get AIDS...So we were running on 'use condoms'—at least for anal sex. We had [a New York produced] poster at ACON at the time, which said 'don't do rimming, don't do oral sex, don't kiss, limit your partners'. That was their first safe-sex promo. So it actually had nothing about condoms. All four recommendations were wrong and impossible. The gay community wasn't going to give up all kissing or oral sex. And a behaviour change to limit partners is in some way a lot harder to engineer than using condoms. So we were quite lucky, we went for the French line on a viral agent and that it was transmitted through anal sex to both partners...And therefore [by saying 'use condoms', we] were putting forward to Australian gay men an achievable short-term behaviour change.
>
> — Ken Davis (2005)

The approach taken to education by AIDS organisations was—and still is—based on the notion of what has been termed 'sex positive'. They deliberately sought to eroticise safe sex, using visually explicit images and commonly used language: 'fucking' not 'sexual intercourse'.[46] It was on the basis of it being too explicit that the first major safe-sex campaign of the NSW AAC was refused government funding.[47] The campaign, titled 'Rubba Me', run by Garrett Prestage, featured a drawing of two men having sex and used the words 'Rub Cocks', 'Rub Bodies', 'Use Rubbers'. The accompanying text discusses a range of safe-sex practices— jacking off, nipples, thigh fucking, wrestling, tickling, body licking, biting— and concludes with the phrase, 'If you still want to fuck or be fucked then it will be safer if you roll on a rubber'.[48] The NSW Health Commission had originally intended to fund the Rubba Me campaign, but withdrew money in February 1985 when they were shown its content. While the Bobby Goldsmith Foundation and the Gay Counselling Service provided funds that enabled it to

---

44   Phil Carswell, Personal Communication, 25 October 2006.
45   Victorian AIDS Council, 1993.
46   Sendziuk, 2003.
47   Australian National Council on AIDS, Hepatitis C and Related Diseases (ANCAHRD) 1988, *1997 Report to the Minister for Health and Family Services*, ANCAHRD, Canberra; Prestage, 2002.
48   Waldby et al., 1990.

go ahead as planned, it did spark some controversy.[49] Newspapers reported the launch of the 'Rubba Me' campaign with headlines such as: 'X-Rated Posters Mark Gay AIDS War—Homosexuals have officially declared war against the killer disease AIDS: Some homosexual groups are producing "X-rated" posters which tell gays how to have sex without dying.'[50]

AIDS activists, however, continued to develop similar campaigns, buoyed, rather than deterred, by such attention. Over time, State and Federal governments came to accept (or at least overlook) the explicit and erotic imagery of gay-oriented safe-sex materials, and most campaigns since 'Rubba Me' have been, at least indirectly, government funded. But the strong proviso remains that these materials are not to be distributed to 'mainstream' or young audiences. Unambiguous, explicit sexual detail has been deemed permissible only for gay men (who are already considered far from innocent in such matters).[51] The nature of safe-sex campaigns and materials produced by community-based AIDS organisations over the years has ranged from posters, brochures, safe-sex packs and videos to theatre, cartoons, cabarets, dance parties and 'cruising cards'. Gay Dowsett captures the depth of this work, writing:

> [Perhaps] nowhere else is it possible to see the tremendous impact of the engagement of the national HIV/AIDS policy with gay community activism than in their HIV prevention activities...It is this work, its innovation and daring, its libidinous imagery exuding homoerotic desire, that captured gay men's sexual culture and attached it to HIV/AIDS prevention in a way no public health issue has previously achieved.[52]

The community-education model adopted by the AIDS movement advocated the empowerment and support of the affected communities, based on the logic that individuals will have greater capacity to negotiate safe sex and make 'healthy' decisions if their self-esteem is high and they feel safe. Community leadership and positive messages about gay sex were central to this 'safe sex' promotion strategy. Activists used their position on government advisory bodies such as NACAIDS to promote this, while AIDS councils lobbied for funding to employ peer educators to run grassroots safe-sex campaigns.

Bill Whittaker recalls:

> [Community activists] pointed out to government that...we were the ones who knew how to do it. We were the only ones with the remotest possibility of engaging with that community and it had to be the

---

49 ANCAHRD, 1998; AFAO, 1992.
50 Olszewski, Peter 1985, 'X-Rated Posters Mark Gay AIDS War', *Melbourne Truth*, 26 January, p. 13.
51 For more discussion on this topic, see Waldby et al., 1990.
52 Dowsett, Gary 1998, 'Pink Conspiracies: Australia's Gay Communities and National HIV/AIDS Policies, 1983–1996', in Anna Yeatman (ed.), *Activism and the Policy Process*, Allen & Unwin, Sydney.

community itself which was mobilised to be able to do anything effective about this epidemic. Bureaucrats sitting in health departments are not going to know how to engage with specific populations like that.[53]

The success of this community-education strategy and the extent to which gay men have adopted regular safe-sex practices are widely contested issues. Australian studies conducted in the late 1980s indicated that gay men were more likely to use condoms or other methods of safe sex following education campaigns.[54] Sexual health clinics at the time also pointed to decreasing rates of anal gonorrhoea—possibly indicative of more regular use of condoms.[55] Moreover, the incidence of new HIV infection peaked in 1984 and then began to decline. This was a faster rate of decline than was seen in other Western countries and has been cited as evidence of the success of gay-community interventions, as the rate of new HIV transmissions started to drop before government money had been made available.[56]

In the 1980s and early 1990s, however, many members of the medical community (although certainly not all, as I will discuss later) were not convinced that safe sex alone would be an effective HIV-prevention strategy and maintained that a medical model, based on extensive testing of high-risk groups, was the more scientifically valid course of action.[57] 'Safe sex' education as a public health strategy was new and untested. For many, this approach was considered too 'unscientific' to address a major disease epidemic such as HIV.

Of course, as is often the case, such criticism of the community-based education approach to HIV came in the context of limited resources. Many doctors were upset that funds were being diverted from what they considered to be the most scientifically valid approaches to public health. Activists also had their own interests in acquiring government funds. So these two competing perspectives on public health were pitted against each other, not only because they represented different views of disease prevention and medical intervention, but because each approach required money. For both groups, influence over government decision making was critical.

---

53   Bill Whittaker, Interview with the author, 6 November 2004.
54   Margo, Jill 1989, 'Safe Sex Hailed as AIDS Cases Drop', *Sydney Morning Herald*, 5 June, p. 8; Warren, Matthew 1988, 'Gay Men Embrace "Safe Sex" Practices', *The Australian*, 26 December, p. 3; Ariss, 1997.
55   Sendziuk, 2003.
56   Plummer and Irwin, 2004.
57   Ariss, 1997.

> [HIV] is still cited as the [public health] model that you should try. And whilst it's probably not possible to generate the same cohesive community mobilisation [with other issues], what it has led to is understanding that you need to talk to consumers...You see everywhere consumers involved. This is a product of HIV. And this is a tremendous benefit...You tend to just think of what we are doing in terms of numbers of people dying of HIV. But there are broader consequences, which I think [if] one's feeling pretty depressed these days, it's good to reflect on them, it's good to remember them.
>
> — Bill Whittaker (2004)

Through their critical stance towards traditional public health measures, the AIDS movement asserted an alternative moral practice in public health. Activists emphasised the breach of civil rights and potential for discrimination inherent in 'test and contain' public health approaches, implicitly disputing the common assumption that science and medicine are, by nature, 'objective' and apolitical. The AIDS movement also brought an alternative paradigm of knowledge to public health policy. It was successful in 'normalising' an approach to public health that was not based solely on medical knowledge. Instead, HIV prevention and health promotion were reframed as community and political issues, not solely medical and scientific problems. While the AIDS movement gained some support for their actions from emerging ideas about 'new public health', formal 'new public health' models of disease prevention and health promotion, such as the WHO's Ottawa Charter, did not come into being until the latter half of the 1980s. When HIV/AIDS first emerged there was certainly no solid evidence of the efficacy of this approach and political support was tenuous. There was also enormous resistance to the involvement of lay-people from within the health sector. The AIDS movement broke new ground in initiating and demonstrating this new model of public health.

In hindsight, the community-empowerment approach to HIV prevention adopted by Australia came to be recognised internationally, including within the WHO, as a 'best practice' public health model.[58] Despite foreboding criticisms at the time that 'de-medicalising' the AIDS response could be disastrous, AIDS activists are now recognised worldwide for their role in the development of this model.

---

58   AFAO, 1992.

Compulsory Testing?

Some of the more vocal critics of a community-led public health response to HIV/ AIDS sat on the government-appointed AIDS Task Force. The AIDS Task Force was an advisory group established by the Federal Health Minister to prepare advice for the Government on scientific matters relating to HIV/AIDS and to suggest how best to allocate funding for research, prevention and treatment. The committee comprised practising and academic medical professionals and, as noted previously, was chaired by Professor David Penington, a haematologist working in academia and former Chair of the National Blood Transfusion Service (NBTS).

In 1984, the AIDS Task force devised a containment strategy for HIV/AIDS that would involve the establishment of wide-scale HIV-testing programs and a system of compulsory notification to the Health Department of positive results so the epidemic could be monitored.[59] This approach raised two issues. The first was the question of how such a program could be implemented in an environment where people were reluctant to present for testing. The second was what measures would or could be put in place to prevent those identified as HIV positive from further transmitting the virus. Would they be quarantined or have their actions restricted in any way?

Strict observance of clinical symptoms of illness, facilitated by patient monitoring and testing, is fundamental to Western biomedicine. This occurs at the level of individual patient care as well as for monitoring communicable diseases at a population level.[60] Once a test became available for HIV, it was logical for medical professionals to consider how best to use it to monitor and contain the virus. While most doctors considered voluntary testing for individual diagnosis as the only reasonable application of the test, there were many who advocated mandatory testing as a sound basis for a public health strategy.

The idea of mandatory testing was never considered by the Australian Government to be a reasonable public health strategy in the case of HIV/AIDS. Nevertheless, some people did take the idea seriously and it was picked up in media debate with some commentators likening HIV testing to the compulsory chest X-rays used to screen for tuberculosis in the 1950s. It was argued that as Australia had used compulsory medical screening before there could be no claims of discrimination by the gay community if it were once again adopted for

---

59   Sendziuk, 2003.
60   Emke, Ivan 1992, 'Medical Authority and its Discontents: A Case of Organised Non-Compliance', *Critical Sociology*, 19(3), pp. 57–80.

AIDS. As a journalist writing in *The Age* put it: 'Compulsion is never attractive in a "rights" minded society, but we have come to accept it in many areas of public health and safety where the alternatives may be considered worse.'[61]

Some in the medical field, including AIDS Task Force Chair, David Penington, began to investigate methods by which identified 'at risk' populations, such as gay men, injecting drug users and prison inmates, could be compelled to submit for testing.[62]

Although the cost and logistics of such a venture meant the Federal Government remained opposed to the idea, the Health Minister, Neal Blewett, could not ignore the increasing attention being paid to the issue. In July 1986, Blewett invited a range of stakeholders—community activists, medical professionals and government representatives—to attend a summit, with the aim of achieving consensus on the matter. At the summit, it was agreed that testing should remain voluntary and take place only with informed consent and with pre and post-test patient counselling.[63]

The outcomes of this forum did not, however, entirely resolve the issue. In early 1987, the Victorian Government proposed changes to infectious diseases legislation that would have made testing of individuals participating in 'high risk' behaviour mandatory. The Victorian AIDS Council mounted a campaign against this, arguing that the delineation of 'high risk' behaviour was a highly subjective exercise—one that had potential to be an exercise in moral persecution rather than sensible public health. Following an intensive lobbying effort, this section of the legislation was eventually dropped from the draft bill.[64] The issue was raised again in 1988 with the release of a Federal Government discussion paper on the response to HIV/AIDS, which was essentially a draft of the First National AIDS Strategy. In response to the draft strategy, the Federal Opposition Liberal Party published an alternative discussion paper that proposed mandatory HIV testing of all people with sexually transmitted infections and those showing symptoms of AIDS. The paper also recommended diverting AIDS funds away from community education in favour of much broader testing regimes.[65]

The media latched on to this upsurge in attention to compulsory testing and it became the basis of several opinion polls. *The Age*, for example, ran a poll in which 75 per cent of respondents felt that those 'suspected by a government health officer' of being homosexuals should be required to have an HIV test and

61 Barnard, Michael 1985, 'AIDS: A Time to Get Tough?', *The Age*, 19 March, p. 19.
62 Sendziuk, 2003.
63 Ballard, 1992.
64 Carr, Adam 1987, 'President's Report', *Annual Report*, Victorian AIDS Council, Melbourne.
65 McCauley, Carmel 1988, 'Opposition Looks at Mandatory AIDS Test', *The Age*, 1 September, p. 4.

87 per cent felt that all injecting drug users should be tested. A follow-up poll indicated that only 9 per cent of respondents thought that HIV testing should be anonymous.[66]

Public Health: 'Getting tough'?

AIDS activists railed against compulsory testing in any form because of concerns that obligatory testing in itself breached civil rights, but also because they felt that any notion of 'mandatory action' implicitly endorsed some form of forced detainment.[67] By taking this stance, however, activists and their supporters were often depicted as actively impeding public health.[68] The media regularly used the phrase 'get tough' to describe what were perceived as more serious public health measures: 'A Tougher Approach to AIDS Prevention';[69] 'AIDS: A Time to Get Tough?';[70] 'Making It Tougher in War on AIDS';[71] 'Tough Action the Only Way to Fight AIDS';[72] 'AIDS: MPs "Soft" on the Fight'.[73] Community education and support for civil rights were considered a 'soft' approach. 'Getting tough' became a euphemism for what was perceived to be the more objective, scientific approach to public health, focused mainly on wide-scale monitoring and containment of HIV-positive individuals. Perceptions on what

---

66 Carney, Sean 1988, 'Support for Wider Use of AIDS Tests', *The Age*, 5 December, p. 1; Pirrie, Michael 1988, 'AIDS Experts Reject Compulsory Tests', *The Age*, 2 September, p. 10.

67 Historically, containment—or quarantine—had formed the basis of public health policy in Australia. It was a strategy used to counter many of the major infectious disease outbreaks in the early part of the century. In the early 1900s, for example, the impact of the Spanish influenza epidemic was minimised through the quarantining of international naval and passenger ships arriving in Australian waters. Those suspected of harbouring the pathogen were sent to a Commonwealth Quarantine Station. Briscoe, Gordon 1996, Disease, Health and Healing: Aspects of Indigenous Health in Western Australia and Queensland, 1900–1940, PhD Thesis, The Australian National University, Canberra, viewed 22 May 2006, <http://histrsss.anu.edu.au/briscoe/intro.html> A series of sanatoria was established as prophylactic and curative centres for tuberculosis. Smith, F. B. 1996, 'Beating Mortality: Health Transition in Australia', *Eureka Street*, 6(9), p. 55; Crichton, 1990, p. 22. Quarantining HIV-positive people was occasionally raised as an option by some medical figures and conservative commentators. But as it became clear fairly early on that HIV was not transmissible by casual contact, the Federal Government never seriously considered it as an option as a wide-scale strategy. The option of detaining and quarantining HIV-positive individuals who 'act in a malicious manner attempting to infect others' was, however, raised by the Federal Government in its 1988 discussion paper on the national HIV/AIDS strategy. 'AIDS Isolation Might Be Necessary: Church', *The Courier-Mail*, 15 February 1989, p. 16. Cuba was the only country in the world to ever institute mandatory quarantining of people with HIV—in 1986. While compulsory quarantine was lifted in 1994, in 2003, nearly half of the country's HIV-positive population still chose to live in sanatoriums. This might have been because conditions in the country became so poor following the collapse of the Soviet Union—Cuba's key international financial supporter—that sanatoriums provided a better standard of care and living. Hansen, Helena 2003, 'Human Immunodeficiency Virus and Quarantine in Cuba', *JAMA*, 290, p. 2875.

68 Ariss, 1997.

69 *The Age*, Editorial, 10 June 1989, p. 11.

70 Barnard, Michael 1985, *The Age*, 19 March, p. 19.

71 *The Mercury* [Hobart], Editorial, 23 November 1989, p. 8.

72 *Daily Telegraph*, Editorial, 2 August 1989, p. 10.

73 Lawrence, Tess 1989, *Sunday Press*, 25 June, p. 9.

'getting tough' involved invariably contained some form of legislative action, and many journalists tended to demonstrate great support for any form of legal measures introduced in Australia to contain HIV/AIDS.

In a number of States, laws were enacted making it a criminal offence to not warn sexual partners of one's HIV status, if HIV positive.[74] The *NSW Crimes Act* was also amended to make it an offence for 'maliciously causing or attempting to cause another person to contract a grievous bodily disease, which includes HIV/AIDS'.[75] Similar laws were enacted in all States and Territories of Australia. Further, as discussed in the previous chapter, it also became an offence in all States to make false declarations to the Blood Bank about one's eligibility to donate.

While laws such as these on one level appear to make good sense in terms of using available State powers to limit the spread of HIV, they were also enacted within a highly politically charged environment. Governments needed to be seen to be responding to the threat of HIV/AIDS and legal measures were more familiar and more politically 'sellable' than community education for gay men. For politicians in opposition, the need to 'get tough' was an easy criticism to level at the Federal Government.

In his address to the Third National Conference on HIV/AIDS held in 1988, Wilson Tuckey, the then Opposition spokesman on health, argued that in the interest of public health people with HIV should not be afforded any anonymity or freedom. The message was a direct critique of the Federal Government's support for community education, implying that the Government was going soft on AIDS because policy had been captured by AIDS activists.

Tuckey said:

> Now let's just compare that and this demand for public compassion with our attitude to others who put our health and the life of individuals in our community at risk. We have very strict quarantine and isolation laws for contagious diseases. The public has accepted that and you have been very successful politically in isolating AIDS from that point of view. There was no public policy debate that erupted as a result of Julian

---

74 In New South Wales, the *Public Health Act 1991* makes it an offence if 'a person knowing that they are suffering from a sexually transmissible medical condition has sexual intercourse with another person, unless he or she has been informed of the risk in advance and voluntarily agrees to accept it'. Watchirs, Helen 2002, *Reforming the Law to Ensure Appropriate Responses to the Risk of Disease Transmission*, Occasional Papers No. 2, ANCAHRD Position Paper, Australian National Council on AIDS, Hepatitis C and Related Diseases, Canberra, viewed 15 April 2006, <http://www.ancahrd.org/pubs/pdfs/op_2_may02.pdf>

75 Ibid., p. 15.

> Beale's exposure to yellow fever[76]...We have little sympathy for those who maim or kill in acts of violence, no matter how unpremeditated they might be.[77]

While Tuckey's views are known for their extreme conservatism, sometimes bordering on the ridiculous, this quotation is still indicative of the argument circulating in public discourse that an appropriately 'tough' approach to public health had no moral engagement. Concerns raised by AIDS activists about civil or human rights were often met with the contention that measures adopted in the interests of public health were matters of science not morality. Activists were accused of dismissing scientific rationality. The need to 'get tough' was cited as reason enough to ignore the human rights concerns of the gay community.

The resistance was remarkable. There was absolutely [an] institutional resistance from the Department of Health. Quite famously, [a] Chief Medical Officer [in the early 1980s] wrote an assessment of what was going on with this disease, and he wrote: 'whatever else you can be assured of Minister, you can be sure this is not a virus.' They were immensely behind the eight ball and offered very little practical help [institutionally] in the early months of the problem. But the great resistance came from the traditional, orthodox medical and scientific establishment who had their hands on the NHMRC and those things, who believed completely, as a matter of given revelation, that they should take control of the response to the epidemic. When they realised the Government was serious about putting money and resources into it, they took a very traditional, orthodox, clinical/medical view and said we will take control of it. What they really meant was we don't believe in prevention, we believe in taking control of HIV/AIDS after the event—after the infection has occurred. And they were extremely dismissive of the view that the epidemic could be prevented. They were very supportive of the orthodox view of sanction and isolation and quarantine. They were very hostile to the involvement of people like Ita Buttrose, hostile to the idea of effective marketing and they certainly didn't believe that affected groups could or would or should take responsibility for changing and modifying behaviour.

— Bill Bowtell (2005)*

---

* Bill Bowtell, Senior Advisor to the former Australian Minister for Health, Neal Blewett, Interview with the author, 28 May 2005.

---

76 When a bill to amend the *Disability Discrimination Act* to include HIV/AIDS was being tabled in Federal Parliament, Wilson Tuckey explained further this example, stating: 'It is interesting that during the time that I mentioned a shadow Minister, the honourable member for Bruce (Mr Beale), came back to Australia from a yellow fever area. When he got back he was unable to produce evidence that he had been inoculated before he left. The health authorities immediately said to him that he could not travel north of a certain parallel in Australia until he had completed a quarantine period. He did not do that: he ignored their instructions. I do not support him in that because I think he was foolish.' Parliament of Australia 1992, *Disability Discrimination Bill 1992: Second Reading*, 19 August 1992, Parliament of Australia, Canberra, <www.aph.gov.au>

77 Tuckey, Wilson 1988, Address to Living With AIDS Toward the Year 2000: Third National Conference on AIDS, Department of Community Services and Health, 4-6 August, Hobart, p. 740.

Creating the 'Gay Lobby'

Alongside rhetoric about the need to get tough on AIDS, AIDS activists were referred to as the 'gay lobby'. The 'gay lobby' was presented as a powerful group of lobbyists intent on ensuring their own interests above those of the heterosexual public. Doctors argued that the 'gay lobby' was blocking scientifically proven public health measures in order to protect 'homosexual rights'.[78] This view was aired most prominently in the wake of a speech made by prominent eye surgeon Professor Fred Hollows in the early 1990s, in which he stated that he believed the 'gay lobby' had too much authority in HIV/AIDS policy making. Hollows used the word 'hijacked' to explain what he saw as the excessive influence of the gay community over government decisions.[79]

> I'll give you an example: I went into the staffroom at Fairfield Hospital once, around 1986. I was talking to one of the senior physicians there who was involved in treating people with AIDS. They all knew that I was both [a gay man] and a doctor. The Fairfield medical staffroom was really nice; it no longer exists. It was a sitting room with comfortable chairs and an open fire, newspapers, things like that. We'd often discuss issues. One of the senior physicians said to me: 'Don't you think there's a conflict of interest in the gay community being involved in AIDS?' That same theme came out time and time again. It was the theme that being gay compromises public health...It wouldn't happen for a non-stigmatised group. No-one would suggest that if you were doing medical research into diseases of children that liking children would be a conflict of interest.
>
> — David Plummer (2004)

The 'gay lobby' was regularly presented as anti-science, selfishly promoting the rights of gay men over the best interests of the general population and ignoring scientific evidence. This positioned gay men as a group of people whose opinions and actions should not be trusted.[80]

Arguments about the undue influence of the 'gay lobby' clearly hinged on negative stereotypes about gay men. But also, there was a sense that many

---

78   Davis, Ken 1992, 'AIDS: The Right Unveils its Agenda', *Green Left Weekly*, no. 59 (17 June), p. 10.
79   Ibid.; Browning, Bob 1992, *Exploiting Health: Activists and Government Versus the People*, Canobury Press, Melbourne; Editorial, 'Managing the Truth on AIDS', *Sydney Morning Herald*, 8 June 1987, p. 6; Dewsbury, Ruth 1989, 'Doctors Accused of Silence Over AIDS', *Sydney Morning Herald*, 29 April, p. 7; Kent, Simon 1992, 'Fred Wants to Tell AIDS Story Like It Is', *The Sun-Herald*, 22 March, p. 15; Date, Margot 1992, 'Storm Continued Over Hollows AIDS Speech', *Sydney Morning Herald*, 4 March, p. 2.
80   Browning, 1992; Davis, 1992.

people within the medical profession did not trust AIDS activists because they felt that gay men, who had such a personal stake in AIDS policy, could not be objective when it came to public health policy.[81]

De-medicalisation of AIDS

The model of HIV prevention advocated by the AIDS movement came to be seen by some medical professionals as the 'de-medicalisation' of AIDS—a move away from 'real' public health measures. At the Third National Conference on AIDS in 1988, Dr Bryce Phillips, the Federal President of the Australian Medical Association (AMA), addressed the meeting. In his speech, he criticised the separation of the 'medical model' and the 'community education model', expressing concern that this kept medical professionals out of the loop in terms of provision of information and education on HIV/AIDS. He stated:

> The 'demedicalisation' of AIDS in Australia over the past four years must be redressed immediately. AIDS has major social and moral implications, but it is an infectious disease and the medical profession has a central role [to play] in its prevention and management. In carrying out this role the doctor has a responsibility both to the individual and [to] the community.[82]

Phillips campaigned publicly on this issue, informing an article published in *The Bulletin* magazine in April 1989, which stated: 'Australian doctors want a much greater emphasis on testing for the virus. And they want the disease to be notifiable. They see the government's emphasis on counselling and advertising as providing social solutions to medical problems.'[83]

In 1989, the AMA Vice-President, Bruce Shepherd (who went on to become AMA President in May 1990), began to campaign for compulsory HIV testing of all surgical patients. In the interests of protecting healthcare workers, Shepherd argued, doctors should have a right to know the HIV status of all their surgery patients. The debate had been fuelled further by an announcement from the Freemasons Private Hospital in Melbourne that it would refuse admission and

---

81 Ballard, 1992.
82 Phillips, Dr Bryce 1988, The Role of the Australian Medical Association, Presented to Living With AIDS Toward the Year 2000: Third National Conference on AIDS, Department of Community Services and Health, 4–6 August, Hobart, p. 641.
83 Barnett, David 1989, 'Surgeons Alarmed at AIDS Risk', *The Bulletin*, 25 April, pp. 38–41.

treatment to any HIV-positive person.[84] There had also been a few cases in Sydney where people were refused surgery on the basis of HIV risk: in 1988 St Vincent's Hospital in Sydney declared it would not treat a man for heart surgery because he was HIV positive;[85] in 1989 a gay man appealed to the NSW Equal Opportunity Tribunal because his doctor would not perform minor elective surgery unless he agreed to have an HIV test.[86]

Shepherd's concerns, however, were clearly not only the health of medical staff.[87] Shepherd was convinced that HIV/AIDS policy had become captive to the 'gay lobby', leading to an overemphasis on non-medical solutions and the marginalisation of doctors from the AIDS sector. In April 1989, Shepherd announced plans for a conference on HIV/AIDS that would be 'free of politicians and lobbyists'—open only to doctors, dentists and nurses.[88] The *Sydney Morning Herald* reported Shepherd as saying 'the meeting was to redress the imbalance where AIDS was being treated politically and by legislation, but not scientifically'.[89]

Shepherd received support for his position from the President of the Australian Association of Surgeons (AAS), Dr David McNicol. Both were openly critical of the Federal Government's response to HIV/AIDS. The AMA and the AAS clearly wanted HIV/AIDS to be viewed as a biomedical problem that neither politicians nor community activists had the expertise, or right, to be involved with. The strategies of Shepherd were deliberate attempts to reduce the power of non-medical experts (in this case, the AIDS movement leadership) to participate in AIDS policy and to reassert the autonomy and control of the medical profession.

84   Dewsbury, Ruth 1989, 'AIDS Test Urged for Health Workers', *Sydney Morning Herald*, 9 March, p. 10.

85   By 1993, when the case was heard in court, St Vincent's admitted that the decision was made in the context of the ignorance and fear of AIDS that were a reality at the time. Date, Margot 1993, 'Patient With HIV Denied Surgery', *Sydney Morning Herald*, 18 January, p. 5.

86   Heary, Monica 1989, 'Gay Man Fights AIDS Test Demand', *The Australian*, 16 May, p. 7.

87   This issue had also become embroiled in tensions between the AMA and the Federal Government over the reintroduction of Medicare. The AMA vehemently opposed a national health insurance system such as Medicare. Blewett, Neal 2003, *AIDS in Australia: The Primitive Years, Reflections on Australia's Policy Response to the AIDS Epidemic*, Commissioned Paper Series 7, Australian Health Policy Institute, University of Sydney, NSW, viewed 5 May 2006, <http://www.ahpi.health.usyd.edu.au/pdfs/colloquia2003/AIDSpaper.pdf>

88   Bill Bowtell, Interview with the author, 28 May 2005; Ballard, 1992; Misztal, Barbara 1990, 'AIDS in Australia: Diffusion of Power and Making of Policy', in Barbara Misztal and David Moss (eds), *Action on AIDS: National Policies in Comparative Perspective*, Greenwood Press, New York; Dewsbury, Ruth 1989, 'AIDS Test Urged for Health Workers', *Sydney Morning Herald*, 9 March, p. 10; Sendziuk, 2003.

89   Sampson, John 1989, 'Date Set for AIDS Summit', *Sydney Morning Herald*, 10 April, p. 9.

> Blewett had to constantly keep his eye on homophobia. Homophobia profoundly underwrote everything that happened. If you remember, Blewett got into trouble because Bruce Shepherd and the AMA accused him of being gay...and accused him of having a conflict of interest...The issue there was that they didn't need to say that that was good or bad, the implication that was immediately apparent was that therefore he had a conflict of interest and that AIDS would get out of control—rather than saying having someone gay in a position like that would give insights into a difficult problem that they wouldn't have otherwise, which would actually make for better control. In retrospect, we know that that's exactly what happened. But this is what I mean—that Blewett was suffering from homophobic attacks. Homophobia was compromising their ability to do things.
>
> — David Plummer (2004)

Shepherd and McNicol were frustrated by the Federal Government's reluctance to support their call for mandatory testing of surgery patients.[90] The debate led to a very public row between them and Health Minister Blewett. At one point, Blewett instigated defamation proceedings against Shepherd, McNicol and the Australian Broadcasting Corporation (ABC) for broadcasting McNicol's suggestion that Blewett was gay. Insinuating that Blewett's sexuality needed to be questioned, McNicol was reported as saying 'the public had a right to know how AIDS policy was formed' and to know about 'the sort of people involved in administration of policy and funds to ensure there are no conflicts of interest'.[91] The suggestion was, of course, that Blewett might have a conflict of interest, or be unduly influenced by the 'gay lobby', because he was himself homosexual (at the time, Blewett was in a heterosexual marriage).[92]

The debates about HIV testing and the '(de-)medicalisation' of HIV were fundamentally a fight for influence and funding as each side sought a greater share of available government money to shape the HIV/AIDS response in their vision (as is the nature of politics). But these debates were also part of a struggle around who would or should be considered a legitimate 'expert' on HIV/AIDS.[93] As Dennis Altman has written:

---

90   The proposal for compulsory testing of surgical patients was considered in some States (such as Tasmania in June 1990), but it did not come to fruition. Darby, Andrew 1990, 'Tas to Look at AIDS Laws', *Sydney Morning Herald*, 28 June, p. 6; Sendziuk, 2003.

91   Dewsbury, Ruth 1989, 'Blewett Launches Defamation Actions', *Sydney Morning Herald*, 22 July, p. 11.

92   Many years later, following his retirement from political office and some time after the death of his wife, Blewett did allow it to become public knowledge that he had begun a relationship with another man.

93   Misztal, 1990; Ballard, John 1998, 'The Constitution of AIDS in Australia: Taking Government at a Distance Seriously', in Mitchell Dean and Barry Hindess (eds), *Governing Australia: Studies in Contemporary Rationalities of Government*, Cambridge University Press, Melbourne.

In the early developments around AIDS one can see the outlines of a struggle for control, in which medical professionals, government officials, affected communities, and traditional sources of moral authority, particularly churches, vied to be seen as the 'experts' on the new disease. How AIDS was conceptualised was an essential tool in a sometimes very bitter struggle: was it to be understood as a primarily bio-medical problem, in which case its control should be under that of the medical establishment, or was it rather as most community-based groups argued a social and political issue, which required a much greater variety of expertise.[94]

Negative attitudes towards homosexuality became part of this struggle for control—evident in discourse that suggested that the 'gay lobby' could not be trusted to act in the best interests of public health. Conversely, the validity of some medical approaches to HIV prevention—such as wide-scale HIV monitoring and notification—were questioned by activists because they did not trust medical authorities to maintain confidentiality or to protect the civil rights of gay men who tested positive. In effect, it was to some extent because of prejudice against gay people that AIDS activists came to challenge medical authorities and to initiate a method of public health that challenged many biomedically oriented approaches.

Confronting science and medical authorities in this way did not, however, mean that there was a perpetually hostile relationship between AIDS activists and medical professionals. While there were some individual doctors who certainly represented and upheld the traditional authority of Western medicine, there were others who were willing to develop working relationships with activists, and indeed there were many who sat in both groups (gay men who were doctors). Developing relationships between activists and doctors was not, however, necessarily an easy process. Prior to HIV/AIDS, there had been few situations where groups of medical doctors were forced to form working partnerships, or negotiate, with the gay community and vice versa. Both groups came from vastly different social and ideological locations and there was little history of trust between them. Nevertheless, relationships between AIDS activists and the medical profession were necessary given the approach the Federal Government had decided to pursue in response to AIDS. These relationships became even more complex, however, as new medical treatments for HIV became available towards the end of the 1980s and into the 1990s.

---

94   Altman, 1994, p. 26.

4. Treatment Action

The first hope of a possible course of treatment for HIV came in the second half of the 1980s. Azidothymidine or Zidovudine (AZT) was originally developed in the 1960s for the treatment of cancer. In 1986, however, US researchers announced that it would begin to be trialled as a potential antiviral medication for HIV. This was the first clinical therapy to be developed for HIV. Before this, the only available treatment had been for AIDS-related conditions, such as antibiotics for infections. Nothing until this point had promised the possibility of forestalling the damage caused by HIV to the body's immune system. People were excited about the potential for this to be a 'miracle drug'.[1]

Large-scale clinical trials had been set up in the United States to test for the efficacy and safety of AZT. In 1987, the Australian National Health and Medical Research Council (NHMRC) funded an Australian arm of the trial. It was not long after this that US trials were terminated so that people in the 'control group' of the trial, who had been receiving placebo pills, could be offered AZT. The drug was proving to be effective.[2] This move did not, however, translate into wide availability of the drug in Australia. Australian authorities were not prepared to approve the drug on the back of US research. AZT trials continued.

For those who had been diagnosed HIV positive in the 1980s, AZT was the first hope of a lifeline and, although people were cautious, there was much hype about the possibilities. Knowing that the drug was attainable in the United States but not Australia was immensely frustrating for some people with HIV/AIDS.[3]

When it became clear that it could be a long time before AZT would be widely available in Australia, frustration and anger became driving forces for the AIDS movement. Activists agitated for AZT to be immediately approved for wide distribution in Australia. At the time, only those enrolled in the Australian trial had access to the drug, and limited government funds meant this number was small. The high cost of AZT was also proving prohibitive. Even if the drug was more widely available, it was estimated that a year's supply would cost an individual about $10 000.[4]

1   Sendziuk, Paul 2003, *Learning to Trust: Australian Responses to AIDS*, UNSW Press, Sydney.
2   Ariss, Robert 1997, *Against Death: The Practice of Living with AIDS*, Gordon and Breach, Amsterdam.
3   Ibid.
4   Ibid.

The issues raised by the AZT trial marked the beginning of the AIDS movement's engagement with the pharmaceutical and medical systems in Australia. Activists in Canberra began to campaign for AZT to be added to the Federal Pharmaceutical Benefits Scheme (PBS) as well as for its immediate approval by the Therapeutic Goods Administration (TGA).[5] At the State level, ACON organised a rally in November 1987 to demand that the NSW State Government provide extra funding for the immediate expansion of the existing AZT trial.[6]

According to Don Baxter:

> A key moment in ACON's history, and in the history of the epidemic really, was the demonstration that ACON organised in November '87 for the provision of AZT, outside Parliament House when [Peter] Anderson was still the [NSW Health] Minister. They were trying to get away with limiting provision of treatments because they were too expensive. I think we demonstrated then that they were not going to get away with those sorts of decisions.[7]

We were hearing reports of AZT, a new drug that was being trialed in the States, and these refocused [his] thoughts on America, regenerating in him the old illusion that if only he were in a different place he might somehow discover himself to be a different person...AZT sounded more promising than the do-it-yourself cures of the AIDS underground: but the more he thought about it, the more both AZT and America itself receded into an unattainable dream...We could hardly afford the airfare, let alone the obscene price that Burroughs Wellcome found it proper to charge for their new drug. And even if we made it to New York, there was no apartment, no family, no medical insurance to come home to. At the end of the road there would be at best a public hospice. That prospect shattered the fantasy.

— John Foster*

* Extract from Foster, John 1993, *Take Me to Paris, Johnny*, Black Inc., Melbourne—a memoir by John Foster of his lover's life and death from AIDS.

Medical Dominance and Treatment Action

When Talcott Parsons coined the term the 'sick role' he was making the point that in modern society being sick is a socio-cultural experience as much as it is a

---

5   Ariss, 1997.
6   Ibid.
7   Don Baxter, Interview with James Waites, 26 November 1993, Oral History Project: The Australian Response to AIDS, TRC 2815/75, National Library of Australia, Canberra [hereinafter NLA].

physiological one. According to Parsons, once a person is diagnosed as 'sick' they are ordained with a particular set of expectations, including passive acceptance of their doctor's advice. The sick role implies that patients are required to be compliant and cooperative in the service of getting well.[8] Those who do not adhere to such a role risk acquiring labels of 'deviancy' or 'insanity'.

The modern medical system has only limited room for the active involvement of lay-people. Western-trained doctors have an official mandate to define the nature of health issues and determine treatment regimes. This is supported by the state through licensing structures that regulate who may and may not identify themselves as a legitimate health professional. There is a common acceptance that those who are not trained within the discipline of Western medicine are not eligible to contribute to medical knowledge. That is, those who are not qualified according to orthodox Western medical tradition—or are not compliant with it—are given little authority to comment on 'health issues' considered by the medical profession to sit within its domain.

Evan Willis describes the history of the Australian health system as one of competing tensions between occupational groups—the dominant group being medical doctors.[9] Midwives, for example, were once considered the primary 'experts' in relation to pregnancy and childbirth. In more recent history, however, their role has been marginalised by obstetricians. The medical profession increasingly dictates the role that midwives may legally play in child-birthing. This shift has not occurred because midwives are less capable than obstetricians of successfully delivering a child in the majority of circumstances. Rather it has been a process of one more powerful profession (in terms of financial and ideological power) staking a claim over the occupational territory of another. The knowledge and experience of midwives are positioned as a less sophisticated and reliable form of knowledge than that of Western medicine; patients are directed away from midwifery services towards GPs and obstetricians.[10]

The point being made by Willis is that the dominant role of doctors in matters pertaining to the body, health and illness is historically grounded. Medical knowledge is not innately more appropriate for understanding issues such as childbirth than that which informs other healing occupations. Nor is it the only way of assessing such issues. Indeed, childbirth was never considered a medical issue before it was framed as such by Western medicine.[11] This is not to say that

---

8   Crossley, Michele 1998, '"Sick Role" or "Empowerment"? The Ambiguities of Life with an HIV Positive Diagnosis', *Sociology of Health and Illness*, 20(4), pp. 507–31.

9   Willis, Evan 1989, *Medical Dominance: The Division of Labour in Australian Health Care*, Allen & Unwin, Sydney.

10   Ibid.

11   I do not intend in this discussion to argue that obstetrics and modern medicine have not contributed to improving the safety of childbirth for both mother and infant. The point, rather, is that it is relatively

medical knowledge is irrelevant to health or that medical advances have not improved the physical condition, and extended the lives, of many individuals. But medical doctors gained the authority and autonomy that they currently have through the political and socioeconomic history of the medical profession in relation to other groups and the dominant position that science and medicine have acquired in the modern West.[12]

In the 1980s, the concept of 'consumer participation' or 'community involvement' in the medical system was very new. Recalling her impression of the medical system in the 1980s, a former advisor to Federal Health Minister Neal Blewett, Kate Moore, writes:

> In my early experience of the health system, I saw it as a fortress surrounded by a moat—with all the drawbridges drawn up to prevent outside influence or scrutiny. The only way in or out of the edifice was over a drawbridge marked 'patient', where the role was ascribed as being passive and compliant. Any attempt to cross the drawbridge in other ways was met with outright hostility. Participation by consumers through the more conventional means we are now used to was just not possible then—so it was necessary to bring down the drawbridges through noisier and perhaps more confrontational methods.[13]

In terms of the extent to which they 'drew down the drawbridges' of the medical establishment, the AIDS movement has been one of the most successful community health movements in Australia. This is especially so in relation to the role the AIDS movement played in instigating systematic changes to the structures by which pharmaceuticals are trialled and approved for distribution in Australia, and in increasing the involvement of lay-people within the health sector as a whole.

As 'treatment action' around AZT began to expand, the AIDS movement made demands on both the Government and the medical profession in several key areas. First, activists wanted the Government to fund trials of new HIV therapies and to put more money into existing trials.[14] Second, they wanted the time it

---

recently that childbirth has come to be considered a medical process rather than a natural stage of human development. The high degree of medicalisation has excluded midwives from the process. In the majority of circumstances, midwives would be just as capable as a medical doctor of seeing through a safe pregnancy and delivery. Wearing, Michael 2004, 'Medical Dominance and the Division of Labour in the Health Professions', in Carol Grbich (ed.), *Health in Australia: Sociological Concepts and Issues*, Pearson, Sydney, p. 276.

12   Ibid.; Willis, 1989.

13   Moore, Kate 2006, 'Consumer Participation: A Personal Reflection', *Health Issues*, No. 89, pp. 14–17, at p. 15.

14   For example, in early 1990, ACON began lobbying the Government for greater commitment to testing DDI, a drug that was showing promising results in US trials—particularly for people who were intolerant of AZT (which could produce intense side effects) or for whom AZT was no longer working. Whittaker, Bill 1990, Treatment Issues—Updates on AZT and DDI, Letter to members of the Australian Federation of AIDS Organisations from the National President, 25 June.

took for drug therapies to be approved for use in Australia to be drastically shortened. On these two points, the major targets of treatment activism were the Therapeutic Goods Administration (TGA) and the Federal Health Minister. Alongside this, activists also made demands of medical research institutions and individual doctors involved in the trialling of new HIV medications. They wanted greater accountability to people living with HIV/AIDS—and to the community in general—in terms of the way in which they conducted their research. Activists argued that the complex legal and ethical issues raised by HIV/AIDS and the processes of clinical trials necessitated the participation of a wide range of stakeholders, particularly people who were most affected personally by the outcomes of such trials. Activists also took charge of accessing their own knowledge and information about HIV medicine.

AIDS Knowledge, AIDS Action

Although the AZT trials brought 'treatment action' to the forefront of AIDS activism, it was not the first time the AIDS movement had challenged medical dominance. The willingness of activists to question medical intervention was evident throughout earlier debates about HIV testing. But also, from the beginning of the 1980s, activists had regularly disseminated detailed medical information about AIDS to the gay community through the gay press and community-produced brochures. As such, activists had a high level of medical knowledge and were accustomed to controlling the flow of medical information to the gay community. Rather than waiting for health information to be provided to them from medical authorities, activists researched, produced and disseminated clinical reports about HIV/AIDS. Activists did not see 'medical knowledge' as an area outside their domain. Nor did they view medical authorities as having an inherent right to control such knowledge and information.[15]

In July 1981, the gay community newspaper the *Sydney Star Observer* published a short article about cases of pneumonia that had been detected among gay men in the United States.[16] Following this, the local gay media released new information about the virus as it emerged from the United States. The first lengthy article was published in *Campaign* magazine in April 1983, just after the first AIDS case

15   Adam Carr was a journalist who, from the early 1980s, began to write articles on HIV/AIDS for the gay press. Carr read all the medical literature he could find on HIV/AIDS and followed all information being published through US sources, translating this into language that would be easily understood by the general public. Carr is regularly cited as one of the key sources of information about HIV/AIDS for the gay community throughout the 1980s and 1990s. Many of these articles can still be viewed on Carr's personal web site: <http://www.adam-carr.net/>
16   Ariss, 1997.

had been detected in Australia. As information in the mainstream media in the first few years of the 1980s was minimal, AIDS reporting in the gay press was the primary source of information about the disease for many people.[17]

We had people that had respect for evidence early on—epidemiology. And the trouble was our level of epidemiology at that stage was pretty much gossip. But we managed to make it so that it was more reliable gossip. When you can't do double-blind clinical trials, but what you've got is a network of gay GPs who have seen guys every day and have talked to each other and are talking to you, that intelligence has to be treated, I think, the same way as the classic Cochrane type study—in context. If we had waited for the real hard evidence to come by, we would have all become infected, if not dead. We had to make certain judgments at times based on what we knew and what we felt. It was intuitive stuff but a lot of it was gut right—the evidence backs [it] up in some cases rather than the other way around. But I think it's understandable at the first stages of the epidemic where there is panic—not only panic personally and psychologically but socially.

— Phil Carswell (2005a)

In the very early 1980s, AIDS activist also found themselves supplying information to general practitioners. At this point, there were only a small number of scientific publications on AIDS worldwide.[18] Virtually the only AIDS reporting read by some members of the medical profession came from the gay-community media and AIDS activists. The absence of alternative sources also meant the Government relied on information from AIDS activists. This provided activists with an opportunity to play a formal role in the AIDS response.[19]

When AZT and the first antiviral medications became available, AIDS information published in the gay press became much more detailed and focused on providing information about treatment options. A number of treatment-specific publications came into being. In 1988, activist Terry Bell established the *AIDS Advocate*, a treatment information and advocacy newsletter. Bell's philosophy was one of empowerment through education. His objective was to ensure people with HIV had enough knowledge to be able to ask questions of doctors and determine their own course of treatment. In part, this was a strategy

---

17   David Plummer, Interview with the author, 30 August 2004; Ariss, 1997; Misztal, Barbara 1990, 'AIDS in Australia: Diffusion of Power and Making of Policy', in Barbara Misztal and David Moss (eds), *Action on AIDS: National Policies in Comparative Perspective*, Greenwood Press, New York; Ballard, John 1989, 'The Politics of AIDS', in Heather Gardner (ed.), *The Politics of Health: The Australian Experience*, Churchill Livingstone, Melbourne.

18   See, for example, Marx, Jean L. 1982, 'New Disease Baffles Medical Community: "AIDS" is a Serious Public Health Hazard, but May Also Provide Insights into the Workings of the Immune System and the Origin of Cancer', *Science*, 217 (13 August), pp. 618–22.

19   David Plummer, Interview with the author, 30 August 2004.

of shifting the power imbalance between doctors and patients. But also, Bell was aware that, at the time, many GPs did not have a great deal of knowledge about HIV treatment themselves, so patients simply had to do their own research.[20] Alongside this, another treatment information magazine, *Talkabout*, began to be published in 1988 by the organisation People Living With HIV/AIDS (PLWHA) in New South Wales. Then, in the early 1990s, the national peak body, AFAO, established a treatment information program with assistance from Federal Government funding. The project produced a regular publication, the *HIV Herald*, which was distributed nationally. The *HIV Herald* provided information about available treatments as well as continuing and upcoming drug trials. AFAO also began work with the National Association of People With AIDS (NAPWA) to produce *Positive Living*, a publication that was first released in 1995 and quickly became one of the major sources of information about HIV treatments in Australia. Publishing treatment information such as this was intended to endow people with enough knowledge to determine their own course of HIV treatment. It also encouraged people to adopt an inquisitive and critical approach to medicine and science, and to the advice of their doctors. While it might seem like an obvious initiative for activists to take in hindsight, there was no real precedent in Australia at the time for patient groups taking charge of medical advice. Certainly, the notion that patients should be encouraged to take a critical approach to their doctor's advice was uncommon.[21] As activist Ian Rankin observed: 'Some issues such [as] how a patient should go about choosing a GP or their right to have a say in their own treatment had never been [debated] before in Australia.'[22]

Coordinating Treatment Action

Late in 1990, the then Federal Minister for Health and Community Services, Brian Howe,[23] agreed to make AZT more widely available through clinical trials. Previously in Australia people had been permitted to enter trials for AZT only if their T-cell/CD4[24] cell count was less than two hundred. Following an ongoing campaign by activists, Howe changed the regulations to enable people with a

---

20 Ariss, 1997.

21 Hurley, Michael 2001, *Strategic and Conceptual Issues for Community Based, HIV/AIDS Treatments Media*, Researchers in Residence Program, Working Paper 3, Australian Federation of AIDS Organisations, Newtown, NSW, and Australian Research Centre in Sex, Health and Society, La Trobe University, Melbourne; Ariss, 1997.

22 Ian Rankin, Interview with the author, 26 July 2004.

23 Brian Howe replaced Neal Blewett as Federal Health Minister following the federal election in February 1990 in which the Australian Labor Party retained government.

24 HIV infects cells in the immune system and the central nervous system. The main cell HIV infects is called a T helper lymphocyte (T-cells). The T-cell is a crucial part of the immune system as it coordinates the actions of other immune system cells. A large reduction in the number of T-cells seriously weakens the immune system. Progression of HIV can be monitored by measuring the number of T-cells in a person's blood.

cell count of less than 500 to access AZT trials, bringing Australia into line with the model being used in America at the time.[25] This allowed many more people to access AZT, but only if they were part of the trial.

> Government even back then was reactive largely. And the non-government actors set the agenda. What you found in the Health Department and among politicians was an openness to doing the right thing. But they were looking for ideas and they went to the non-government sector for suggestions. You've got to realise that there was almost no research or information either on the social class of people affected or the epidemic. In those early days we didn't even know a virus caused it. It was all speculation. So the research was lacking, in that formal scientific sense. But certainly there were very clear sources of information from the communities themselves. They knew how it worked. That's something that's different now. Now government tends to think they know it all. They can just do a literature search. Whereas back then they didn't claim to know it all and they listened. They wanted to know the 'street talk', how it all worked.
>
> — David Plummer (2005)

In terms of making AZT available to people outside clinical trials, there were two major delays. First, the company that produced AZT, Wellcome, needed more information than it had available at the time for its submission to the TGA. Also, the TGA committee that made the final assessment, the Australian Drug Evaluation Committee (ADEC), met infrequently and lacked mechanisms to respond quickly to new evidence. So even after submissions were received by ADEC there were no guarantees about the time the committee would take to process them. Wellcome finally delivered their submission with new data to ADEC on 31 May 1990. The AFAO met with the Health Minister, Brian Howe, in the same month to ask him to push ADEC to consider the Wellcome application as a priority issue. At the ADEC meeting on 26 June 1990, however, the submission was not even discussed.[26]

This angered people within the AIDS movement and the issue came to a head in 1990 when, at the National AIDS Conference, demonstrators stormed the stage while Howe was delivering the opening address. Activists demanded Howe set in motion a system to 'fast-track' experimental HIV drugs; they then pre-empted the rest of his speech by officially declaring the conference open before he was

---

People are considered asymptomatic if their T-cell/CD4 count is greater than or equal to 500 cells/mL. AVERT 2005, *The Different Stages of HIV Infection*, AVERT web site, viewed 20 March 2006, <http://www.avert.org/hivstages.htm>

25   Sendziuk, 2003; Whittaker, 1990.
26   Whittaker, 1990.

able to.[27] As Robert Ariss writes: 'Media coverage of the event presented images of a new Federal Minister of Health, Brian Howe, humbled before a crowd of shouting men and women sporting T-shirts demanding, "Cut the Red Tape".'[28]

Alongside this, a coalition of community AIDS organisations was established. Calling itself the AIDS Treatment Action Committee (ATAC), the committee was an alliance of, among others, ACON, VAC, People Living With AIDS (PLWA) Victoria, the AIDS Action Council of the ACT, PLWA ACT, National People Living With AIDS Coalition (NPLWAC), AFAO and the AIDS Coalition to Unleash Power (ACT UP).

Members of ATAC were politically astute lobbyists. They used very simple but striking and consistent messages in their media statements. The cover page of all their media kits included a cartoon depicting a man watching television, a look of enlightenment across his face. The caption reads: 'It suddenly dawned on him, lives could be saved if he approves HIV treatment faster.'[29] They campaigned on a number of fronts, organising community protests as well as engaging at a bureaucratic level. For example, ATAC prepared a cost–benefit analysis arguing the case for early provision of HIV treatment in economic terms. The report, which they presented to the Federal Government, concluded that 'early access to available treatments combined with vigorous investment in treatment research will lead to a significant lessening of the direct and indirect monetary costs and the human and ethical costs of HIV/AIDS'.[30] ATAC also conducted street demonstrations and grassroots campaigns. At the 1991 Sydney Gay and Lesbian Mardi Gras parade, ATAC led a contingent of more than 100 people dressed in black T-shirts adorned with a pair of red lips ingesting an AZT capsule.[31] ATAC was good at integrating their political lobbying with gay-community education. They produced a community information kit about AIDS treatments and organised regular public forums at community, social and sporting events.[32] The various organisations involved in ATAC also contributed their own resources to the campaign. For instance, the VAAC produced the first guidelines on ethical standards in HIV/AIDS clinical research, articulating the changes they wanted to introduce.[33] Also, in 1991, ACON established an AIDS Treatment Importing Scheme. This scheme exploited a 1990 amendment to

---

27   Woolcock, Geoffrey 1999, *A Vector of Identity Transmission: AIDS Activism and Social Movement Theory*, Unpublished PhD Thesis, La Trobe University, Melbourne.

28   Ariss, 1997, p. 186.

29   AIDS Treatment Action Committee (ATAC) 1991a, National Media Kit, July, ATAC, Sydney.

30   AIDS Treatment Action Committee (ATAC) 1991b, *The Economic, Social and Ethical Costs of HIV/AIDS, Adapted from AIDS Council of NSW 1990 'The Trialing, approval and marketing of treatments and therapies for HIV/AIDS and related diseases: a policy document'* ACON, Sydney, ATAC, Sydney.

31   Ariss, 1997.

32   Andrews, Dean 1991, 'HIV and AIDS Treatments: Action Campaign Gears Up', *Sydney Star Observer*, 28 June, p. 1.

33   Phil Carswell, Personal Communication, 25 October 2006.

the *Australian Therapeutic Goods Act* that allowed individuals to import, for their personal use, pharmaceuticals not yet approved in Australia provided they obtained a doctor's prescription. ACON's scheme assisted GPs to write appropriate scripts, and instructed people with HIV how to order drugs from overseas suppliers. The scheme also arranged bulk postage of drugs to reduce postage costs (which were often very high).[34]

Treatment activism began to broaden beyond AZT to encompass research related to all HIV treatment. For example, in late 1988, news from the United States indicated a derivative of egg lipids could be effective as an HIV antiviral therapy. In the United States, the treatment—called AL721[35]—was accessible because it fell under the 'alternative' therapy banner. Following a campaign by US activists, the American Food and Drug Administration (FDA) had made AL721 available as a food supplement rather than a pharmaceutical. The Albion Street Clinic in Sydney announced that it would undertake a trial of AL721 early in 1989, and put out a public notice to people warning them not to purchase the drug from overseas until it had been tested in Australia. Before the trial had commenced, however, the director of the Albion Street Clinic, Dr Julian Gold, announced that due to new evidence indicating the inefficacy of AL721 the trial would probably be cancelled. AIDS activists were angry that this decision was made without their notice, leading them to organise a more focused campaign around medical institutions' unwillingness to incorporate community interests into their decision making.[36]

The media campaigning that accompanied this was not, however, always successful. For example, a press release put out by the organisation People Living With AIDS (PLWA) NSW in May 1989 asserted that clinics had a moral obligation to base their research priorities on community need and social responsibility.[37] The media did not respond to the press release as activists had hoped. Instead, the angle taken was that PLWA was foolishly, or desperately, clinging to ineffective treatments and should listen to the experts. The press quoted researchers who argued clinical trials were the fastest means to evaluate the efficacy and safety of drugs and that weakening restrictions placed on drug trials could allow unsafe drugs onto the market, with potentially disastrous outcomes.[38] Such criticism, however, did not deter activists. In fact, media attention such as this was indicative of the level of debate the AIDS movement generated around the issue.

---

34   Sendziuk, 2003.
35   For more information on AL721, see Antonian, L., Shinitzky, M., Samuel, D. and Lippa, A. 1987, 'AL721, A Novel Membrane Fluidizer', *Neuroscience and Biobehavioral Reviews*, 11(4), pp. 399–413.
36   Ariss, 1997.
37   Ibid.
38   Ibid.; Epstein, Steven 1996, *Impure Science: AIDS, Activism and the Politics of Knowledge*, University of California Press, London.

ACT UP Australia: Action = life

One of the more radical activist groups that formed part of the Australian AIDS movement was the AIDS Coalition to Unleash Power (ACT UP). American activist and playwright Larry Kramer first started ACT UP in New York in 1987. Following this, chapters of ACT UP were established throughout the world. Although ACT UP chapters generally maintained ties with each other, the organisation always remained resolutely 'grassroots' and informal with no centralised body and only limited formal structures. ACT UP was characterised by its distinctive form of cultural activism and use of symbols—the most prominent being the pink triangle, a symbol used internationally by the gay liberation movement reminiscent of the patch homosexuals were forced to wear by the Nazis during World War II, accompanied by the slogan 'SILENCE = DEATH'.[39]

> At that time we were giving about one major demonstration a month, and the way it was handled was there would be an issue chosen and we'd plan the demonstration for three or four weeks and then we'd give the demonstration. It was happening about once a month. The first one was the one at Kent Street about AZT availability. The next demonstration in May was at Parramatta Gaol about prisons and condoms and...[NSW Minister for Corrective Services Michael] Yabsley's mandatory testing bill, and there was a big crisis in prisons happening at that time and all that sort of stuff.
>
> — Bruce Brown (1991)

The first Australian chapter of ACT UP formed in Sydney in April 1990. Many people involved in this first group were already participants in the AIDS movement. But ACT UP also attracted people who sought a new, more militant direction to their activism. ACT UP created opportunities for people who had not been integrated into the structures of the AIDS councils or other organisations to participate in the AIDS movement.[40]

ACT UP's first Australian street demonstration took place in April 1990. The protest was held outside the Commonwealth Health Department in Canberra where the offices of the TGA were located. Protestors demanded ADEC release AZT for use in the early stages of HIV, rather than when T-cell counts were lower.[41] The demonstration received extensive television coverage, particularly

---

39   Epstein, 1996; Woolcock, 1999.
40   Ariss, 1997.
41   Brown, Bruce 1991, Acting Up Down Under (ACT UP Campaign Sheet), AIDS Coalition to Unleash Power, Sydney, [paper held at the Noel Butlin Archives, Ref. H3N/12, No. 174/8].

its street performance of deathly Grim Reapers wearing 'ADEC' labels, theatrically refusing to give AZT capsules to people with AIDS. A protest 'die-in' was also staged on the pavement and there was an attempt to storm the ADEC offices.[42]

As Bruce Brown recalls:

> The repercussions of that first demonstration were that ACT UP gained this tremendous self-esteem…I think ACT UP's breakthrough is that, whether or not ACT UP and AIDS issues are gay rights issues per se, they are often perceived as such, for any organisation which…was gay driven, had never received that kind of publicity in Australia. And we had this breakthrough in that ACT UP was getting regular mainstream publicity, and this was something new to a lot of activists to have that sort of success.[43]

ACT UP played an important role in the overall landscape of AIDS 'treatment action', largely because of its skill in attracting media attention. The dramatic use of theatre and imagery, along with confrontational actions, worked well with the mass media and most ACT UP events received coverage.[44]

One of the larger ACT UP protests was staged in Sydney in 1990 to coincide with the Sixth International Conference on AIDS. The conference was being held in San Francisco and American chapters of ACT UP had organised a 'takeover' of the main meeting hall.[45] Anticipating that there would be wide-scale international media attention on HIV/AIDS because of the conference takeover, Australian chapters of ACT UP staged a concurrent protest outside the American Consulate in Sydney. This achieved high-profile media attention.

According to Bruce Brown:

> [Like] many other ACT UPs in the world [we planned] to protest at the American Consulate concurrent with the march in San Francisco, to protest the HIV travel restrictions that the American INS [Immigration and Naturalization Service] enforces…[This] was really ACT UP's watershed, it was a kind of galvanizing thing where we really gained our reputation and our visibility.[46]

The confrontational, anger-driven tactics of ACT UP often generated tension between it and other sections of the AIDS movement. Many people felt ACT UP was simply unnecessary in Australia where activists were already included in

---

42   Ariss, 1997.
43   Bruce Brown, Interview with Martyn Goddard, 7 June 1992, Oral History Project: The Australian Response to AIDS, TRC 2815/6, NLA.
44   Woolcock, 1999.
45   Ariss, 1997.
46   Bruce Brown, TRC 2815/6, NLA.

government decision-making structures. There was a belief that ACT UP was an American import—a militancy that was necessary in the era of Reaganism but counterproductive in the context of Australian politics. They also criticised ACT UP for attacking some individuals within government or other agencies who were generally supportive of the AIDS movement. The tension, however, came from both sides. ACT UP's position was that the AIDS councils were an extension of government bureaucracy and not adequately reflective of the needs of people with AIDS. ACT UP activists felt that the non-confrontational politics of the broader AIDS movement kowtowed to government interests. They wanted to harness feelings of anger around HIV/AIDS, creating a more direct-action style of political demonstration.[47] In hindsight, it is probably fair to say that the two styles complemented each other well despite tension at times, and indeed there were many activists who were members of both the AIDS Councils and ACT UP.

ACT UP—FIGHT BACK—STOP AIDS was our chant for all occasions at full voice with whistles blaring. ACT UP is a direct action group that grew out of anger and inaction. We were not silent. But we were not an educational unit. We didn't see ourselves addressing safe sex education campaigns ('keeping negatives negative' as some of us saw it). We did not write reports or ask for funding costs. We used language that was provocative and often controversial. 'Murder' for example, was oft [sic] used. We targeted individuals. We also tried to re-claim some of that language, calling ourselves militant queers, taking back power and pride when we could. We sought and encouraged press coverage. We were loud. We were also an 'issue based' organisation in that we held actions or zapped offices and government departments in relation to a particular issue or target. We planned immediate and topical action and reactions. Identify. Do. Then on to the next one. Bang. We didn't always fully regard the feelings and reactions of those around us, to say the least, or always plan too many steps into the future, and we got a lot of criticism over the [effects] we caused for some people. This was quite legitimate criticism in many cases, but was something we saw as a necessary, a legitimate part of our Modus Operandi.

— Ken Basham*

---

* Basham, Kenn 2006, 'Speech given at the "Reflections" Exhibition at the Canberra Museum and Gallery 8 December 2004', in Ian Rankin (ed.), *AIDS Action! A History of the AIDS Action Council of the ACT*, AIDS Action Council of the ACT, Canberra.

---

47 Woolcock, 1999; Goddard, Martyn 1993, 'Across the Great Divide', *National AIDS Bulletin*, December 1992 – January 1993, pp. 15–17; Ariss, 1997.

I've never known an issue to scare health ministers as much as AIDS. I remember working with Labor Ministers, down in Victoria and nationally, good lefties (Brian Howe and Caroline Hogg and her successor, Maureen Lyster) and being in meetings and they were quite scared because there was an ACT UP demo outside. Not only because of the power of performance over media—the media was all over this disease, it was part of this disease—but the counter media was also, the theatre and the nature of ACT UP and its wit and sharpness was something that was very post-modern. That dynamic was really fascinating to watch. They really had political power, even though they were a very small group. They were visible and they were intelligent...I think the politicians were very much intimidated by ACT UP. (We never told them, we didn't want them to get swelled heads!) Besides [ACT UP's] fundamental role in the epidemic was different. ACT UP in America was necessary, it was actually vital. If ACT UP hadn't been in America it would have been crazy. ACT UP in Australia, half of them were public servants, half of them were employed by the health department. Our relationship was different. It wasn't 'you murderers'. They knew that we weren't bad people. They were making points to the media and the general community more than to us as the enemy. So that was really interesting.

— Phil Carswell (2005a)

Treating the System: The Baume Review

In November 1987, two days after ACON had held its demonstration to demand greater funding for AZT trials, more money was provided by the NSW Government to allow an extra 20 participants into the AZT trial. This of course did not solve the problem of an exceedingly slow drug-approval process in Australia—an issue that was escalated in the minds of activists in March 1990 when the American FDA approved AZT for general prescription in that country.[48]

Endorsement by the FDA or other overseas authorities does not ensure a drug will be made available in Australia. Rather, all new medications must undergo an Australian-specific trial process and gain TGA approval. The TGA, with its stringent testing regimes, was set up in response to the infamous 'thalidomide scandal' of the early 1960s in which an approved drug turned out to have devastating side effects on children whose mothers had taken it while pregnant (as thalidomide was prescribed for morning sickness, there were many such cases). While TGA regulations were put in place for obviously sound reasons, it did mean that in the 1980s the process for approving new drugs took two to

---

48 Sendziuk, 2003.

three years and required significant financial investment from pharmaceutical manufacturers. Given the relatively small Australian market for pharmaceuticals, many companies were not willing to make that investment.[49]

Communication between AIDS activists in Australia and those in the United States meant people in Australia were well aware of the availability and efficacy of AZT. For Australian activists, there did not seem to be any convincing reason why it should not be similarly available in Australia when it was clear many hundreds of people would die (and were already dying) from AIDS while waiting for TGA approval. Australian activists were also inspired by the US treatment-action campaign when activists had been successful in speeding up the FDA approval process for HIV drugs.[50]

Towards the end of 1990, in response to activist demands, Health Minister Brian Howe directed the Australian National Council on AIDS (ANCA) to facilitate an inquiry into how best to hasten the process of drug approval in Australia. The ANCA report was completed in December 1990. It made 37 recommendations that focused on fast-tracking experimental drugs. It also highlighted impediments to the approval of new drugs including limited resources and the strict formatting requirements for ADEC submissions. The report concluded that the process that manufacturers had to follow in order for new pharmaceutical products to be approved was overly slow and cumbersome.[51] But also—perhaps more significantly—ANCA recommended that pharmaceuticals approved by British or American authorities should be accepted by Australia without local trials. While activists generally supported ANCA's findings, it was on this point that the report was widely criticised by medical researchers and health department officials. The proposal was seen as a breach of Australia's sovereignty in this area, a threat to the nation's capacity to govern its health system in the context of an international pharmaceutical market. Many also felt that it was a potentially high-risk venture, as Australia had no control over the regulations applied by other countries.[52] Largely on this basis, Minister Howe did not accept ANCA's findings.

Frustrated by Howe's lack of action on the report, ACT UP announced what they called their 'D-Day' Campaign. D-Day centred on an ultimatum delivered to Howe to increase funding for drug trials and ease restrictions on pharmaceutical

---

49   Carr, Adam 1992, 'What is AIDS?', in Eric Timewell, Victor Minichiello and David Plummer (eds), *AIDS in Australia*, Prentice Hall, Sydney; Sendziuk, 2003.
50   In the United States, before HIV/AIDS campaigns were successful in changing regulations, it took on average 12 years to gain FDA approval for new drugs and cost the sponsor about US$231 million. Young, James Harvey 1995, 'AIDS and the FDA', in Caroline Hannaway, Victoria Harden and John Parascandola (eds), *AIDS and the Public Debate*, ISO Press, Amsterdam.
51   Carr, 1992.
52   Prue Power, Interview with the author, 25 May 2004.

approvals before a set date—the allotted D-Day: 6 June 1991.[53] There was a long lead-up to D-Day in which ACT UP built its campaign. But when the day arrived, the Federal Government had not responded to the demands. The threatened series of D-Day actions took place, including paint-bombing the offices of Brian Howe and uprooting a prominent floral clock in Melbourne, replacing it with a miniature graveyard of wooden crosses.[54] Also—in perhaps the most dramatic and well-remembered ACT UP protest—activists in Canberra abseiled from the public gallery into the main House of Representatives in Federal Parliament House while Brian Howe was speaking during Question Time. They threw red streamers (to symbolise red tape) and blew whistles. As activists were thrown out of Parliament House by security guards, they lit orange flares and staged a 'die-in' on the front concourse. On the same day, the Sydney chapter of ACT UP mailed a letter to every Member of Parliament containing a single obituary of a person who had died from AIDS in 1991, together with a note stating, 'This name is for you'.[55] A statement from ACT UP prepared for the media on D-Day read:

> The most important way for people with HIV/AIDS to get access to new treatments is through drug trials. There are not enough trials of new drugs occurring in Australia. This has been acknowledged everywhere, including [by] Minister Howe. Yet his only response to this situation, which has been glaringly obvious for over three years, is to appoint yet another committee…The medical profession chooses to see drug trials as pure medical research to evaluate the efficacy of new pharmaceuticals. However, when there are no other pharmaceuticals available, and when the pharmaceuticals being trialed have already proven to be of benefit, this view is immoral. The drug trialing system must be viewed as a means of giving access to treatments and as such it must ensure that is [sic] accessible and equitable to all people with HIV/AIDS.[56]

ACT UP's D-Day media briefing also made the point that the beginning of trials for another new drug, DDI, had been delayed by seven months and that the DDI trial protocols meant it was not as widely available as activists believed was ethically warranted. The media kit argued that the Government needed to account for the fact that a small population made Australia a relatively

53   Carr, Adam 1991, 'Once More Unto the Breach', *Outrage*, June, pp. 42–4.
54   Woolcock, 1999.
55   Brown, 1991; Anonymous 1991, 'Diary of a D-Day Full of Daredevil Drama', *Melbourne Star Observer*, 14 June, p. 3; McDougall, Michael 1991, 'D-Day Attack Sydney', *Sydney Star Observer*, 14 June, pp. 1 and 9.
56   AIDS Coalition to Unleash Power (ACT UP) 1991, Cut the Red Tape, Media briefing, ACT UP Demonstration, Sydney.

insignificant market for large pharmaceutical companies, and, as such, there needed to be incentives for companies to submit their products to the Australian approval process.

> [One] of the strong points about ACT UP is the amount of research which goes into each issue before there is any action taken. So there's a real responsible approach taken in terms of gaining all of the information first. And I think that's been ACT UP's strength everywhere in the world; in that it's easy to dismiss someone who is out there waving a placard as a ratbag, however, when they can sit around a table with a pharmaceutical company executive and argue trials, it becomes much more difficult to dismiss them as a lunatic or a fanatic. And that's been our top strength, that we can come right in off the street and meet with the Deputy Prime Minister or the Therapeutic Goods Administration and they know that they are dealing with some very substantial activists there who are just as capable of negotiation and argument around the meeting table as they are at doing staged public protests for the media and the general populace.
>
> — Bruce Brown (1991)

Although their response was less radical than ACT UP's, other AIDS activists were also frustrated by the outcome of the ANCA report and continued to lobby on the issue. When Howe announced the formation of a new committee to begin another review, activists were cynical but also pleased to accept invitations to participate. The second review was headed by Peter Baume, a professor of community medicine at the University of New South Wales and former (Liberal) Federal Health Minister. Its findings were released in July 1991.[57]

Baume's review rejected ANCA's proposal to endorse drugs on the basis of overseas approvals, but recommended significant expansion of clinical trials to facilitate much greater access to experimental drugs. Baume also proposed setting in place a strict, and limited, time frame for approvals to which the TGA would be compelled to adhere. Shortly after the report was released, Minister Howe announced that he would implement all of Baume's recommendations. Both activists and many members of the medical profession welcomed Baume's approach to the problem.[58]

---

57   Altman, Dennis 1992, 'The Most Political of Diseases', in Eric Timewell, Victor Minichiello and David Plummer (eds), *AIDS in Australia*, Prentice Hall, Sydney.
58   Goddard, Martyn 1991, 'Howe Moves on Drugs', *Melbourne Star Observer*, 12 July, p. 1.

> Mainly what [the Baume Review] helped with was the reform of the clinical trials system in Australia. Prior to that you had to submit this enormous amount of ridiculous documentation to the TGA which held up the start of the trial for many, many months. What Baume suggested was a new system where if an ethics committee approves the trial, the TGA allows it to go ahead as a notification. And this really speeded up the process. Australia at the time in the late '80s really wasn't on the map in terms of participation in clinical trials in any therapeutic area because, you know, Australia is only 1 per cent of the world pharmaceutical market and companies didn't see it as cost effective— it took a lot of money. That speeding up of the process and a good medical system and committed doctors and patients to do studies in a cost effective way meant that industry became a lot more interested and to this day they remain so. Trials are done in Australia even though we are still only 1 per cent of the pharmaceutical market. That system is still in place and that was brought about because of HIV/AIDS and I think it has worked through, to a certain extent, to other therapeutic areas into cancer and rheumatoid arthritis and Crohn's disease, where the issue is really [about] expensive drugs and how do you get access to them. I don't think those patient groups are as well organised as gay men but they certainly have taken lessons.
>
> — Anonymous (2005)*
>
> ─────────
>
> * This quotation is an extract from an interview conducted by the author in 2005 with a medical practitioner who worked in the AIDS sector during the 1980s and 1990s.

The fact that the Baume Review happened at all—together with the changes that it led to—is regularly cited (by activists as well as by many people working in government and medicine at the time) as one of the greatest achievements of the AIDS movement. Without agitation by AIDS activists, there would have been no reason for the Government to initiate any changes to the TGA system. Indeed, the issues that Baume considered were certainly not ones that medical professionals or bureaucrats were campaigning on. In many cases, people in these groups actively opposed change.

> [Activists] influenced the report and the implementation of it…[There] were issues about Australia still having sovereign rights to test and approve its own medications rather than taking it straight from America. It was obvious that it would have been too controversial to change that. But the way around it was to allow trials, many trials, so that the drugs can come in anyway. It was really quite an interesting way through. So that all the groups, those that wanted to maintain sovereign right, those that wanted access…there were some issues around access still, it didn't please everybody. But on the whole, it was [a] good way around.
>
> — Prue Power (2004)

Activists felt that their concerns had been taken into consideration within the Baume Review and cautiously welcomed its findings. In a public address, the President of AFAO at the time, Bill Whittaker, stated:

> It's a major restructure of the drug regulatory system. It's major surgery if you like, on a system that is long overdue for such action. I'm very proud that almost all of the points brought forward to Professor Baume by AFAO on behalf of our constituents were taken up and I think the reasons for this is [sic] two fold—firstly they were very sound and sensible and secondly we had enormous support right around the country from AIDS councils, the PLWA groups, from ACT UP and from doctors and from nurses and many other concerned people in keeping this issue on treatments before the public over the past 18 months. So I think Baume's report is a culmination of the delivery of a very good result. As a result of a lot of hard work that we put into it.[59]

Similarly, Tony Kennan, the then President of the VAC, reported:

> The release of the Baume report on the future of drug evaluation in Australia saw the efforts of a long and hard campaign come to fruition. Whilst there are still some concerns about the implementation of the recommendations, the report signals a significant victory for people living with AIDS/HIV.[60]

The Baume Review reflected the success of the AIDS movement in influencing government regulation of pharmaceuticals. This was significant because it was the first time lay-people had held such influence over a major institution within the medical system. AIDS activists also, however, gained authority within the health system at lower levels. The organised dissemination of information about HIV treatments by AIDS activists meant that people with HIV/AIDS were a highly informed patient population, who were able to challenge the advice of their doctors on the basis of their own medical knowledge. Activists had also begun to challenge the authority of doctors and medical researchers who were running clinical trials. This was a powerful position for health consumers to be in, which was carried on in future years as people living with HIV/AIDS established their presence within the HIV sector.

---

59   Whittaker, Bill 1991, Transcript of a Public Meeting, 16 August, Victorian AIDS Council, Melbourne.
60   Keenan, Tony 1992, 'President's Report', *Annual Report*, Victorian AIDS Council, Melbourne.

[There] had been 11 reviews of the TGA and ADEC processes of varying degrees and none of them had produced anything useful in the way of reforming the drug approval and clinical trial processes. And what generated this was the fact that new treatments were coming along and Australia wasn't going to get to trial them or it would be years until they were put on the PBS and people would die. So you can understand it was pretty easy to ferment a lot of heat in the media and everywhere else around that issue...I think we created the heat, but we had a very sophisticated and well-developed set of arguments to put to the bureaucrats and to the ministers. And we were able to propose a way forward, which led to the Baume report and we were part of that review.

— Bill Whittaker (2004)

There were many sections of the department that were absolutely with us but...[not] the TGA and those old medical bureaucrats who'd been there for decades and who had created all this mythology about how unique and wonderful the Australian system is. And the Australian public I think were led to believe that every time there was an application for a new drug in the Health Department there would be lab tests and Bunsen burners and rats would be tested and of course it was all nonsense, all they really did was review data from well conducted clinical trials. All that sort of mythology, it was immense opposition and the lines were coming from people in the department: 'Oh we will release all these unsafe drugs too early and people will die', and all this sort of stuff. So that's where the opposition was coming from. I think there was tremendous support from politicians of all persuasions, backbenchers... 'cause we lobbied them all. To overcome 12 years, 12 reviews and 20 years of attempts required a sophisticated effort, but it was the emotion, the passion, the concern and the hype—if you want—you could generate around an epidemic where people were dying that cracked the nut. Then it was getting the right people to work around it, and some of those people were community people, [who took] it forward and having a minister who was committed to it, a very brave minister. I think Brian Howe is one of the unsung heroes; we always talk about Blewett, who needs great credit, and his advisors. But Howe delivered a whole set of other stuff, which was continuing a strong strategy and reforming clinical trials and drug approval processes and that flowed on to things...like consumer reps on ADEC.

— Bill Whittaker (2004)

The Expertise of Experience: People living with AIDS

In the late 1980s people living with HIV began to organise separately from the broader AIDS movement, and a national organisation, the National People Living With AIDS Coalition (commonly referred to by its catchy acronym, NPLWAC, pronounced 'nipple-wack'), was formed in 1988, later to be renamed the National Association of People With AIDS (NAPWA). The first meeting of NPLWAC was held in November 1988 and many State-based coalitions emerged from this. The aim of People Living With AIDS (PLWA) organisations was to construct a visible presence for people with HIV both within the HIV sector and among the broader public.[61] PLWA activists became central to 'treatment action' because, apart from the fact that they clearly had the greatest personal stake in the outcomes of any clinical research, they were able to claim 'expertise' about HIV/AIDS on the basis of their personal experience of living with the virus.

Coming out

A visit by American activist Michael Callen was one of the inspirations for NPLWAC and other PLWA organisations. Callen had been instrumental in the formation of a movement of 'self-empowerment' among people living with HIV in the United States and advocated, as a political strategy, HIV-positive people 'coming out' and publicly declaring their HIV status.[62] At the end of the Third National Conference on AIDS, held in Hobart during August 1988, where Michael Callen had been speaking, people with AIDS were asked to take the stage.[63] As PLWA activist Ross Duffin recalls:

> It is interesting to look at the positioning of people with HIV and AIDS [at the National AIDS conferences]. At the first two national conferences there were very few, if any, visible people with HIV and AIDS. At Hobart people with AIDS were visible by badges which said, 'Talk with us—not about us'. Four years ago being that visible was a very brave

---

61 Menadue, David 2003a, Opening Plenary Session Address, The Art of Living: Ninth Biennial Conference of the National Association of People Living With AIDS, 27–28 October, Cairns, Qld; Woolcock, 1999; McQuarrie, Vanessa 1993, '"Keep on Acting" Says Richardson', *Sydney Star Observer*, 12 November, p. 7.
62 Ariss, 1997.
63 Duffin, Ross 1993, 'People with HIV and the National Conference', *The National AIDS Bulletin*, December–January, pp. 20–3; McCallum, Lou 2003, *Review of Paper by Neal Blewett*, Australian Health Policy Institute Commissioned Paper Series 7, University of Sydney, NSW, viewed 5 May 2006, <http://www.ahpi.health.usyd.edu.au/pdfs/colloquia2003/AIDSpaper.pdf>

act. People with HIV and AIDS were asked to take the stage and I think this was a real watershed in terms of visibility of people with HIV and AIDS in the AIDS movement.[64]

In the United States, the 'empowerment movement' for people with AIDS established a set of principles to guide their activism: the 'Denver Principles'. The Denver Principles were founded around the goal of increasing the public visibility of people with AIDS. They also sought to challenge the portrayal of people with AIDS as 'victims' or 'sufferers' of AIDS—terms commonly used in media discourse at the time. It was felt that these terms positioned people with AIDS as subservient and passive in their relationship with the medical profession, the Government and people who cared for them.[65]

Australian PWA organisations followed similar principles and part of their early work involved efforts to reconstruct public perceptions of people with AIDS—recasting negative stereotypes and also encouraging the media to use the term 'people *living* with AIDS' rather than 'victims', 'sufferers' or 'people *dying* from AIDS'. During the late 1980s, State-based PWA groups and NPLWAC obtained many media opportunities through which they could pursue their objectives. One example of this included a spread in the *Sydney Morning Herald*'s weekend magazine, *Good Weekend*, on 26 November 1988. The article told the stories of several people with AIDS who were trying alternatives to 'synthetic drugs'. The author emphasised the way in which these men had adopted an inquiring approach to their health care, experimenting with alternative therapies and questioning conventional medical advice. The article managed to present an image of people with AIDS as empowered, and capable of making informed, intelligent decisions about their health.[66]

NPLWAC/NAPWA also sought to influence the nature of medical and social research being conducted around HIV/AIDS. For example, in the mid-1990s they began to agitate for more research that looked at the everyday experiences of people living with HIV/AIDS, resulting in an innovative idea for a study that came to be known as the 'HIV Futures' study. Beginning in 1997, the Futures study looked at the health, lifestyle, safe-sex practices, utilisation of services and treatment uptake of people living with HIV/AIDS. The survey has been repeated at regular intervals since this time and has come to be an important source of information about people living with HIV/AIDS that is used regularly by HIV-advocacy organisations and policy makers as well as within government.[67]

---

64   Ibid.
65   Ariss, 1997.
66   Ibid.
67   HIV Futures is run by the Australian Research Centre in Sex, Health and Society at La Trobe University. Hurley, Michael 2003, Boundaries and Borders: Researchers and Researched in NAPWA, Presentation to The Art of Living: Ninth Biennial Conference of the National Association of People Living With AIDS, 27–28 October, Cairns, Qld.

In terms of clinical studies of new HIV treatments, people living with AIDS clearly had a very personal stake (indeed a 'life or death' stake) in the development of effective antiviral medications.[68] For this reason, many people with HIV/AIDS were willing to participate as research subjects in the clinical trials of any new therapies. The fact that there were a large number of people involved in HIV clinical trials who were also part of an organised social movement meant, however, that the way in which those trials were conducted became a subject of movement attention. PLWA organisations became organised advocacy bodies for people involved in HIV trials. These organisations lobbied for increased involvement of people with HIV/AIDS in the design and implementation of clinical research. The position of NPLWAC/NAPWA on this is articulated well in the following quotation taken from a presentation by the former convener (health and treatments portfolio) of NAPWA, Peter Canavan:

> Sometimes, just being present as a positive person can in itself function as a reminder that research deals with flesh-and-blood people, who live daily with the reality that is HIV. We know about lipodystrophy not necessarily because we understand how or why it develops—but because we are the ones who have stood in front of the mirror, and observed the changes over time to the bodies in which we live. When a piece of research involves a high number of hospital visits, or that we are hooked up to an intravenous drug delivery machine, we are the ones who know what that means and what that will feel like, or how various treatments might affect your capacity to work or play or have sex or generally get on with the business of life. It's not that doctors and clinicians aren't aware of it or haven't thought of it: mostly, they are really sensitive towards this stuff, especially in HIV—which in itself is a testament to the power of a partnership between community and researchers for which we have fought and struggled. But the research process involves people whose perspectives and priorities are not always coincidental with our own, at least in the practical sense. I am not suggesting here that anyone wants to do bad or harmful research. But all research disciplines—whether social or clinical science—require people to conform to certain principles about research design, or 'how things get done', or indeed, to answer to particular political, academic or cultural agendas, and these may not always sit comfortably with how HIV positive people see their lives.[69]

---

68   In 1996, Highly Active Anti-Retroviral Therapy (HAART) was introduced. HAART involves the use of several antiviral medications in combination. The rate of mortality and morbidity associated with AIDS dropped dramatically with the introduction of HAART. Stewart, Graeme 1998, 'You've Gotta Have HAART', *Medical Journal of Australia*, 169, pp. 456–7.

69   Canavan, Peter 2003, Reflecting on 'Our' Involvement in NAPWA, Presentation to The Art of Living: Ninth Biennial Conference of the National Association of People Living With AIDS, 27–28 October, Cairns, Qld.

The relatively small number of HIV-positive people in Australia meant that there was only a small pool of possible research participants for any HIV drug trial. If patients were unhappy with trial protocols, they could elect not to participate or withdraw from the study, and there were not necessarily other people to replace them. Hence, negotiating with activists meant medical researchers had continued access to HIV-positive people who were willing to participate in research. This placed activists in a strong position to negotiate with medical researchers and doctors.

One major issue that brought activists into contest with the medical profession was the use of placebo pills in randomised control trials (RCTs). There were concerns that the use of placebos in RCTs meant some people enrolled in the trial missed out on potentially life-saving medication.[70] Many activists insisted that placebos were unjustified in the case of a drug such as AZT, which overseas trials had already demonstrated to be effective.[71] There were several occasions where activists threatened to undermine the validity of some placebo-based trials by having their pills tested to see if they were active or not. Those with active doses would halve theirs in order to share it with people on the placebo pill.[72] Through actions such as this, or the refusal of large numbers of people with AIDS to participate in a trial, community support became virtually a basic requirement if a trial was to go ahead. Hence, the medical community in Australia was pushed into a position where they had to accept greater community involvement in HIV clinical research. As a result, by the end of the 1990s, both NAPWA and AFAO had representatives on the National Centre in HIV Epidemiology and Clinical Research (NCHECR) Protocol Working Group. They also participated regularly in various NCHECR working groups and advisory committees.[73]

---

70 Randomised control trials (RCT) were initially developed in the 1940s to test the effects of various drugs on tuberculosis. In RCTs, patients are randomly assigned either to the trial group, where they receive the medication being tested, or to the control group, where they receive a placebo pill. To control for any possible 'placebo effect', patients do not know to which group they have been assigned (in a double-blind trial, the clinician does not know this either). The idea of clinical trials is to remove uncertainty—including that which might come from human emotion or subjectivity—from the process of testing therapies. RCTs are claimed to remove any 'guesswork' from scientific assessment. They are still considered the 'gold standard' in biomedical research—the most effective method of accurately and objectively assessing the efficacy of a treatment regime. Epstein 1996; Willis, Evan 1989, *Medical Dominance: The Division of Labour in Australian Health Care*, Allen & Unwin, Sydney.

71 ACT UP, 1990b.

72 Professor Peter Baume, Interview with Dr John Ballard, Oral History Project: The Australian Response to AIDS, TRC 2815/1, NLA.

73 Canavan, 2003.

> The issue of the ethics of [RCTs] using placebos still pops up occasionally. There is still the basic belief in the science community that RCT is the only standard—gold standard. However, the fact that Australia has such a small community weighs in against this for the medical profession. If a trial is perceived to be unethical by the community they will be unlikely to get enough research participants.
>
> — Ian Rankin (2004)

The position of NAPWA was that the personal experiences and opinions of HIV-positive people were just as relevant to clinical trials involving human subjects as medical or scientific knowledge. 'Medical dominance' is sustained by the medical profession's claim to a greater level of expertise over health issues than other groups or individuals. The fact that there was now a patient population which was organised and articulate about their own basis of knowledge, and which had already achieved a legitimate role in the AIDS sector through their earlier campaigns and their role on NACAIDS, represented a significant challenge to medical autonomy. AIDS activists forced medical authorities to take them seriously by continually presenting their position on the ethics and processes of clinical trials. They also threatened to take organised action to undermine the trials.

Contest and Collaboration: Boundaries between medicine and activism

At the 2003 NAPWA Conference, reflecting on relations between the community and medical researchers, Professor John Kaldor stated:

> Back in the late 1980s when it was clear AZT was not going to work on its own, there was a sense of urgency. Research had to deliver in a way that I think is hard to comprehend in today's environment…It was also, as some will remember, a very confrontational environment in many respects…there were hurried and agitated meetings with ACT UP representatives, and there was always someone getting up at every meeting asking: 'Why not now?'…So it is a sign of incredible progress to be in this situation in Australia. The relationship between researchers and community in Australia is I think, amazingly healthy.[74]

---

74 Kaldor, John 2003, Personal Reflections, Presentation to The Art of Living: Ninth Biennial Conference of the National Association of People Living With AIDS, 27–28 October, Cairns, Qld. Professor John Kaldor, PhD, is Deputy Director and Professor of Epidemiology of the National Centre in HIV Epidemiology and Clinical

The 'treatment action' campaigning of the AIDS movement pushed activists and the medical profession towards working more closely together in an increasing number of forums. AIDS activists, particularly representatives from PLWHA organisations, established a regular presence in all aspects of HIV health delivery including prevention and health promotion through to working with pharmaceutical companies.[75] It is now common practice for community representatives (lay-people) to be consulted about the ethics and processes of clinical trials, and community-based AIDS organisations are routinely represented on the working committees of research organisations such as the NCHECR. The TGA's ADEC also now has a community representative and community consultation has also been extended to other disease groups—a shift in medical practice that is often attributed to the work of the AIDS movement.[76]

Although this style of community participation in health has become increasingly commonplace and easy to negotiate, when they were first being established in relation to HIV/AIDS there was a significant amount of tension coming from both activists and doctors. As Peter Canavan recalls: 'At first these [partnerships] were tentative and nervous. There was some mutual suspicion, and a sense of being off "familiar" turf.'[77] An alliance of this type between doctors and activists had no historical precedent and although their relationship was ostensibly 'professional', trust still needed to be established. A number of doctors in the field had to confront their own personal prejudices. The medical profession is historically quite conservative, and, in the early 1980s, many medical doctors had never known any gay men and had only ever formed opinions about them within the context of negative stereotypes and assumptions about homosexuality.

According to one medical practitioner working in the AIDS sector at the time:

> I think more of the tension was within the health system itself where the sort of reaction against HIV/AIDS was well: 'Infectious disease, gay men, don't like gay men'—particularly among conservative surgeons, it was: 'Why should we be treating them, we might be getting this infection by treating them, so why should we treat them?'[78]

Research. He has been responsible for coordinating national surveillance for HIV/AIDS since 1989. He has also worked on a range of epidemiological research programs in blood-borne viruses and sexually transmissible diseases.

75 Canavan, Peter 2004, 'Because It's Personal: What Good Advocacy Can Achieve, and How', *The Australian Health Consumer*, (1) (2003–04), pp. 17–20.

76 Bill Whittaker, Interview with the author, 5 November 2004.

77 Canavan, 2004.

78 This quotation is an extract from an interview conducted by the author in 2005 with a medical practitioner who worked in the AIDS sector during the 1980s and 1990s.

When AIDS emerged, these doctors were suddenly expected to not only acknowledge and accept gay men as patients, but to form professional alliances with openly gay activists. One medical doctor described the tensions, stating:

> In the medical system we've never had [the orthodox medical system has never had] contact with gay men in the way that the AIDS epidemic brought out because most gay men at the time were cared for, for their STDs, by either the public STD clinics or the private general clinics that specialised in STDs. They were generally run by gay men and obviously gay men felt comfortable going there because they were non-judgmental, because homosexuality wasn't really out of the closet in the late '70s, early '80s. So I think the medical system never really experienced gay men and it was pretty confronting—confronting for all of us. I think for someone like Penington, or Gordon Archer, it was particularly confronting for them, being older straight men, probably grew up in an era when homosexuality was not a good thing in terms of their societal norms...But having said that I think they respected the dialogue because it was obviously coming from men who were well educated and knew the issues. But it was certainly tense for a while.[79]

As the above quotation suggests, one of the means by which the social divide was bridged between activists and doctors was the capacity of activists to engage in medical discussion. Activists had worked hard to become literate in medical jargon and could comprehend the biological processes related to HIV/AIDS and HIV treatments. To some extent this undermined the power of the medical profession to control debates about HIV/AIDS. The 'mystical' and elite status of medical knowledge was destabilised. But perhaps more importantly, activists' self-education won them much respect among medical professionals, loosening some of the boundaries between 'doctors' and 'lay-people'.

> The combination of media portrayals of 'AIDS victims' together with a paternalistic and highly technological medical system were powerful forces against seeing people with AIDS as active agents in control of their lives. The battle fought by people living with AIDS has revolutionised the relationship between the medical system and a group of erstwhile 'patients'.
>
> — Victorian AIDS Council (1993)*
>
> ---
>
> * Victorian AIDS Council 1993, *A Dangerous Decade: Ten Years of AIDS*, Victorian AIDS Council, Melbourne.

---

79 Ibid.

On this basis, the AIDS movement ushered into the Australian health system a new set of expectations about the role of non-medical people, and patients, in health issues. The medical profession was forced to confront their reluctance to engage professionally with lay-people. As one medical doctor stated:

> It would have been fair to say that we were a little bit imperious about the whole thing, you know, patients shouldn't be interfering in what doctors do. I think that was a fairly common attitude at the time because we had never confronted that. We felt that we were delivering effective health care in the medical system and patients didn't generally query too much our recommendations. And when patient advocacy groups start to do that, it is a bit threatening to a lot of doctors. But we got over it and now they're engaged and extremely helpful in many of the things we do—particularly about whether trials will be acceptable to certain patient populations.[80]

[Community activists and the medical community] worked hugely closely together—often behind the scenes. Often one telling the other what was going on so that, say, ACT UP could be at the right place at the right time to interfere with discussions with a drug company who was saying, you know: 'We'll do this but…we won't make it available to the people who are really sick.' And so their talks would get interfered with because the people…the medical fraternity would make sure the community sector knew what was going on so they could be there. Other examples [were] making sure the community sector were involved in things like drug trial planning, importation of drugs, lobbying for expanded access, increased number of people being able to prescribe [more GPs] and working together to get that information out.

— Levinia Crooks (2005)

Boundary Crossers

Conversely, while the medical profession was forced to accept the involvement of activists in their work, activists had to learn to work productively within the medical system and institutions to which they had demanded entry. This was facilitated by mutual goals between some sections of the medical profession and activists. For instance, general practitioners supported AIDS activists to lobby for faster approval of AZT. As long as AZT prescriptions were available only within a clinical trial, GPs were limited in the treatment options they could offer

---

80   Ibid.

and locked out of the loop in terms of HIV treatment. So, in part for their own interests, GPs often lobbied in support of activists.[81] Also, doctors and activists came to rely on support from each other to attract funding into the HIV sector.

Health social movements have been referred to as 'boundary crossers'.[82] While health activists generally engage in protest activities such as street demonstrations and lobbying, they also often partake in formal collaboration with scientific and research institutions. This blurs the traditional boundaries between 'medicine' and 'lay-people'. But by working with medical institutions, health social movements also move beyond commonly agreed definitions of social-movement activity, collaborating with the 'opposition' and adopting an 'expert' identity of their own. This distinctive characteristic of health social movements occurs in part because activists are dependent on science. There are few, if any, other social-movement 'issues' where individual movement actors are dependent on the 'targets' of their political action (their political opponents) for treatment or even survival. For this reason, health social movements generate a culture of action that is not simply focused on sparring with opposing forces. Building collaborative relationships is part of their political strategy. Collaboration between activists and doctors is, in this sense, a radical manoeuvre.[83]

The increasing alliance between AIDS activists and the medical profession that developed through the 1980s and 1990s is testament to the way in which AIDS activists challenged the dominance of the medical profession, not only through political contest, but through finding ways for lay-people to participate in the health system. The professional boundaries of the medical establishment were impinged upon by activists not only through overt political contest, but through their cooperative participation in the health system.

Boundaries were also crossed, however, by the number of gay doctors who became involved in the HIV/AIDS sector. Not surprisingly, the massive impact HIV/AIDS had on the Australian gay community was of personal interest to gay men with medical training. These doctors became active participants in both HIV/AIDS medical treatment and community activism.[84]

---

81   Ariss, 1997.
82   Brown, Phil, Zavaestoski, Stephen, McCormick, Sabrina, Mayer, Brian, Morello-Frosch, Rachel and Gasior, Rebecca 2004, 'Embodied Health Movements: New Approaches to Social Movements in Health', *Sociology of Health and Illness*, 26(1), pp. 50–80.
83   Ibid.
84   David Lowe, Interview with the author, 12 July 2005.

> To capture an accurate picture of it you have to capture the complexity of it and the fact that there were people on both sides of the fence who wore two hats...There was a tension between powerful medical academics and grassroots medical people who [had] greater insights into the grassroots practicality... [There] was greater interest in the power and politics from the others. That was the sort of tension. So you'd often see this dichotomy referred to between people like David Penington, representing medical academics with no real reason to be involved apart from the fact that they considered themselves to be important, [and] the more grassroots medical people, many of whom were gay, who had lots of good reasons to be involved and were much closer to what was going on in a practical sense. To me, that was a big tension.
>
> — David Plummer (2004)

The boundaries of any profession are determined by who is allowed 'in' and who is not. Once people are 'in'—a legitimate member of the profession— they are expected to adhere to a particular set of cultural and moral norms. Steven Shapin discusses this point with reference to what he terms the 'thought collective' of medicine.[85] The thought collective is a 'fund of knowledge' from which individuals draw and to which they contribute. Ideas and information are shared and new knowledge is formed as part of a group process of dialogue and discussion. To remain part of the thought collective, members must adhere to its conventions.[86]

The culture of the medical 'thought collective' is to a large extent sustained by the standardised training process through which all doctors must pass. Doctors are, in a sense, trained in the cultural norms of the medical profession. But beyond this, there are bonds of trust within the group. Doctors trust that other members of the collective operate within a similar framework of knowledge and cultural norms to their own, and that the knowledge contributed to the thought collective is legitimate in terms of the expectations of the medical profession. As Shapin describes, 'in order for that knowledge to be effectively accessible to an individual—for an individual to have it—there needs to be some kind of moral bond between the individual and other members of the community'.[87]

Gay doctors sat within two groups: the medical profession and the gay community. In effect, they had access to the *moral bonds* of both collectives, thus providing a bridge between the AIDS movement and the medical world. Gay doctors effectively gave the AIDS movement a cultural 'in' to the medical establishment and provided a more legitimate basis from which activists could contribute to

---

85   Shapin, Steven 1994, *A Social History of Truth*, University of Chicago Press, London.
86   Ibid.
87   Ibid.

medical knowledge. As well as being a source of medical information for the gay community, 'gay doctors' contributed to the capacity of the AIDS movement to speak 'credibly' on AIDS in medical circles. For this reason, 'gay doctors' played an immensely important role in establishing relations of trust between the medical profession and AIDS activists.

> [Amongst] heterosexual scientists and doctors who then needed to become involved there was of course understandably a little uncertainty dealing with this new group. It's not a paradigm that they had worked with either dealing with the community, not to mention gay men. In any case the 'doctor knows best' mentality is very, very strong. And a lot of them were fairly shocked by having a verdict challenged or being forced to work with activists. So...there were tensions at times. But again trust was built up fairly quickly...because [of] money, community activism was delivering money for doctors, community services and hospitals...they are not good at that sort of lobbying, we did that sort of lobbying, we did that for them. We were lobbying government with them but generally more effectively to enable research and services to happen. So I think that partnership is really one of the strongest aspects of the Australian response and that continues.
>
> — Bill Whittaker (2004)

Mistrust and Medical Activism

The development of trust between AIDS activists and the medical profession marked an interesting progression in the social history of gay men in Australia. The history of homosexuality meant that gay men were less likely to trust medical science than many other social groups might have been. Gay men were reluctant to leave decisions about treatment of a disease that affected them so intimately in the hands of scientists, even when potential 'miracle drugs' were on the scientific horizon. Mistrust of scientific interests also rested on a legitimate fear of discrimination. As has been described in previous chapters, the medical establishment had historically been involved in attempts to 'cure' homosexuality through barbaric practices such as electroshock therapy. Whether or not this history came directly to the minds of AIDS activists, it certainly meant that there was no prior relationship of trust between the gay community and (heterosexual) doctors. When AIDS hit, gay men doubted the confidentiality of medical practices and were therefore wary of clinical interventions such as HIV testing. There was also a general concern that the objectives of scientific research often overrode the personal interests and needs of gay men.[88]

---

88 Misztal, Barbara 1996, *Trust in Modern Societies*, Polity Press, Cambridge; Kimsma, Gerrit 1990, 'Frames of Reference and the Growth of Medical Knowledge: L. Fleck and M. Foucault', in Henk Ten Have, Gerrit

AIDS activists' mistrust of doctors and of science was highly important in determining the course of the AIDS movement.[89] Two key strategies adopted by the AIDS movement throughout its treatment-action campaigns were: 1) to assert an alternative basis of expertise, grounded in personal experience and community need, which challenged the autonomy of medical intervention: and 2) to ensure activists gained enough technical knowledge about the physiology of AIDS and the processes of clinical trials to engage effectively in medical dialogue. AIDS activists ensured that they fully comprehended the scientific aspects of HIV/AIDS and the processes of the medical system because they did not trust it to act in their interests otherwise.

What is interesting about the AIDS movement, however, is that over time relations of trust—or at least working relations that involved some level of trust—were established between the AIDS activists in the gay community and medical doctors and researchers working in the area of AIDS. This was not uncontested trust, or what could be termed 'blind faith' in medical institutions on behalf of activists. Rather trust was built on the basis of a negotiated relationship. What the AIDS movement achieved was a renegotiation of the trust relationship between lay-people and the medical profession.

Kimsma and Stuart Spicker (eds), *The Growth of Medical Knowledge*, Kluwer Academic Publishers, Dordrecht.
89   It is also worth noting that gay men and lesbians often have the experience of feeling 'outside' mainstream culture. Whether or not this is based on mistrust of the mainstream, it has meant that the gay community has developed its own facilities. In the 1980s, this included a network of gay-friendly GPs. Phil Carswell, Personal communication, 25 October 2006, Melbourne.

Part Three: Grief and Activism

5. Rites of Belonging: The AIDS Memorial Quilt[1]

Each year in Australia, and throughout the Western world, candlelight memorials are held in remembrance of people who have died from AIDS. These memorials and solemn and silent processions followed by a vigil are often accompanied by a public reading of names of people who have died from AIDS.

Inaugurated in this country by AIDS activist Phil Carswell and a nurse at the Melbourne Communicable Diseases Centre, Tom Carter, the first Australian candlelight memorial was held in 1985 when these two men stood silently with lit candles in a Melbourne city square. From this, the event grew in magnitude and scope to the point where, 10 years later, the estimated attendance at candlelight memorials across the country had grown into the tens of thousands.

Memorials have been an important part of AIDS activism. Indeed, candlelight memorials and the AIDS Memorial Quilt today form part of the most iconic imagery of the AIDS era.

The AIDS Memorial Quilt is a series of cloth panels—each produced in memory of a person or persons who has died from AIDS—stitched together in the format of a traditional 'comfort quilt'. When laid side-by-side, the panels of the quilt can carpet literally hundreds of square metres. Each panel is 1.8 x 0.9 m (6 x 3 ft) in size—deliberately the average dimensions of a grave plot and the size of a human body.[2] The panels are sewn together in groups of eight.

The first Australian AIDS Quilt was launched in Sydney on World AIDS Day in December 1988 in a ceremony hosted by well-known media personality, and former NACAIDS Chairwoman, Ita Buttrose. When the Australian quilt was first launched, it had 35 panels. Today there are well more than 700, each of which has been produced by the family, partners, friends or carers of people who have died from AIDS.[3] Personal items are often stitched into the panels: old theatre tickets, favourite T-shirts, soft toys, photographs, jewellery. The 'Quilt Project' holds regular workshops at which volunteers assist people with the technicalities of producing their panel. Many panels include personal statements about, and dedications to, those who have died:

---

1   A version of this chapter has been published previously as: Power, Jennifer 2009, 'Rites of Belonging: Grief, Memorial and Social Action', *Health Sociology Review*, 18(3), pp. 260–72.
2   Fuchs, E. 1996, 'On the AIDS Quilt: The Performance of Mourning', in E. Fuchs (ed.), *The Death of Character, Perspectives in Theatre After Modernism*, Indiana University Press, Bloomington.
3   Australian AIDS Memorial Quilt Project 2004, *History of the Australian AIDS Memorial Quilt Project*, Australian AIDS Memorial Quilt web site, viewed 2 December 2005, <http://www.AIDSquilt.org.au>

I could read it quite clearly in his palm. There would be a terrible tragedy. My love could not protect him, DM.

[He] loved the Australian lifesavers, the Iron Man competitions and the world's most beautiful, yet dangerous, beaches.

Mr Cha Cha Heels. Teardrops on the dance floor.

The Quilt invites its viewers to wonder about those to whom each panel is dedicated. The details of the textiles, the images, words and personal objects provide enough of a glimpse into the life of an individual to lead one to reflect further about who they were and how they lived their lives. In this way, the Quilt is both memorial and storyteller. As former coordinator of the Quilt Project Terry Thorley describes: the panels 'just say, "That's him" or her, and it just becomes like a portrait really. It just becomes a little time capsule of those people and who they were, what they were, what their character was like.'[4]

The Quilt was originally an American project that drew on the long tradition of quilting as a folk art: quilts are traditionally passed through generations, symbolising heritage, family loyalty and connection to place. The American AIDS Quilt deliberately sought to tap into (and perhaps subvert) a sentiment of nostalgia, reminiscent of nineteenth-century sewing bees, community and rural tradition.[5] While textile work finds its way into some Australian traditions—most notably, the rich history of painted trade union banners—a quilt does not hold the same symbolic position in Australian culture as it did in the United States.[6] Despite some initial criticism of the Quilt being an American import, however, both the Quilt and candlelight memorials became rallying points for people who had been directly affected by HIV/AIDS.[7]

> When new panels are revealed, this is the most moving thing. One time there were 15 people walking out with their panel all crying, sometimes it is the mums and dads, sometimes lovers handing over the panel. It is the most emotional, moving event. It is the epidemic happening (growing) in front of our eyes. Apart from someone dying, which most people outside the gay community don't see, all the news stories and articles are lifeless. The Quilt makes it real. It has a heartbeat.
>
> — Phil Carswell (2005b)

---

4   Terry Thorley, Interview with Diana Ritch, 25 August 1993, Oral History Project: The Australian Response to AIDS, TRC 2815/54, National Library of Australia, Canberra [hereinafter NLA].

5   Hawkins, Peter 1993, 'Naming Names: The Art of Memory and the Names Project', *Critical Inquiry*, 19(4), pp. 752–79.

6   Hawkes, Ponch, Yardley, Ainslie and Langley, Kim 1994, *Unfolding: The Story of the Australian and New Zealand AIDS Quilt Project*, McPhee Gribble, Melbourne.

7   Phil Carswell, Interview with the author, 17 December 2005.

Memorial as Political Strategy

In his book on the bubonic plague, Johannes Nohl writes that one of the major contributory factors to the evolution of social institutions and burial rites during this period was the community's 'loss of confidence in the establishments' (medical, church and state) powers to control or cure these deadly diseases'.[8] A loss of faith in formal traditions and institutions led to new practices for both commemorating death and protecting the living. The establishment of AIDS memorials invites a similar analysis of history. The stigma surrounding HIV/AIDS meant there was no formal recognition of HIV/AIDS as a 'national tragedy', nor would there be moves to commemorate formally those who had died from the virus in a manner that often occurs following events such as natural disasters or wars. The Quilt and candlelight vigils gave people an opportunity to grieve collectively and publicly.

AIDS memorials also functioned as a ritual of remembrance, akin in many ways to collective funeral rites. Throughout the 1980s, the gay community was enduring the illness and loss of large numbers of its members, yet there was a void of institutional recognition of this. While the individual funerals of many who died from AIDS were undoubtedly held in churches, collectively, the gay community was ostracised from the central institutions through which funerals are performed. Certainly, the mainstream churches would have been unlikely to play a leadership role in any formal memorialising of people killed by AIDS. AIDS memorials played a role in filling this voice, as Gerard Lawrence, organiser of the 1993 Sydney Candlelight Memorial, explains:

> We have to find ways of dealing with our losses...Many find funerals are too religious and do not work for them. With the AIDS Memorial Quilt, wakes, and with Candlelight, people have found new ways of arranging the needed ceremony, a framework for the process of death that is appropriate for us.[9]

Public memorials and monuments influence both the collective memory of a society and public attitudes towards the present. War memorials, for instance, generate an image of soldiers as brave heroes or martyrs. Acts of memorial, such as the Gallipoli dawn service, serve not only to define Australian history but to influence attitudes towards war in the present day. Modern soldiers are 'remembered' alongside those from World War I as heroes deserving of respect

---

8   Quoted in Lewis, Lynette and Ross, Michael 1995, *A Select Body: The Gay Dance Party Subculture and the HIV/AIDS Pandemic*, Cassell, London, p. 124.
9   Lawrence cited in Editorial, '5000 March in Sydney Candlelight AIDS Rally', *The Canberra Times*, 24 May 1993, p. 3.

and recognition. Gallipoli is signified as a defining moment in Australia's history.[10] Memorials, in this sense, are highly political in that they directly contribute to the shaping of history and identity.

The term 'counter-memorial' is sometimes used to describe memorials that attempt to challenge mainstream attitudes or draw attention to an alternative conception of reality.[11] The Quilt Project and candlelight memorials can be seen as counter-memorials in that they form part of a political protest—a reaction to mainstream institutions. Yet their intention is not dissimilar to that of state memorials. In the same way that the Gallipoli ceremonies construct a particular image and collective memory of that battle and the soldiers who fought it, AIDS memorials seek to influence public perceptions of people who have died from AIDS. What makes a project such as the AIDS Quilt a 'counter-memorial' is that fact that it challenges much of the public imagery around HIV/AIDS and the stigma cast upon people with AIDS. The very act of memorialising an individual, or group of individuals, is in itself a declaration that they deserve to be remembered in a way that is dignified and celebrated. It asserts that people who die from AIDS are morally worthy of a public memorial.[12]

According to Phil Carswell: 'The Quilt could make a profoundly political statement just by the positioning of panels. Having gay men next to children who had died of AIDS made a statement (about AIDS affecting everyone, the egalitarian nature of the Quilt, everyone deserving equal respect).'[13]

The AIDS Quilt also worked to confront negative stereotypes associated with gay men and people with AIDS through its design, which emphasises the lives and deaths of individuals, as well as the group. The intention of the Quilt project—originally called 'The Names Project'—from its inception in the United States was for the names of individuals who had died from AIDS to be memorialised as a way of reducing the anonymity and secrecy surrounding AIDS.[14] In part, this was because the creators of the Quilt wanted public acknowledgment of

10   Capozzolo, Christopher 2002, 'A Very American Epidemic: Memory Politics and Identity Politics in the AIDS Memorial Quilt, 1985–1993', *Radical History Review*, 82 (Winter), pp. 91–109; Hawkins, 1993.

11   Bold, Christine, Knowles, Ric and Leach, Belinda 2002, 'Feminist Memorialising and Cultural Countermemory: The Case of Marianne's Park', *Signs*, 28(1), pp. 125–48.

12   Olick, Jeffrey and Robbins, Joyce 1998, 'Social Memory Studies: From "Collective Memory" to the Historical Sociology of Mnemonic Practices', *Annual Review of Sociology*, 24, pp. 105–40.

13   Phil Carswell, Interview with the author, 17 December 2005.

14   Rand, E. 2007, 'Repeated Remembrance: Commemorating the AIDS Quilt and Resuscitating the Mourned Subject', *Rhetoric and Public Affairs*, 10(4), pp. 655–80; Names Project Foundation 2008, '*History of the Quilt': The AIDS Memorial Quilt*, Names Project Foundation, Atlanta, Ga, viewed 15 October 2008, <http://www.aidsquilt.org/history.htm>; Melbourne Candlelight Vigil Committee 1992, *Remember Their Names*, Melbourne Candlelight Vigil Committee, Melbourne.

the deaths of their own friends and partners. But also, the Quilt as a whole is designed to visually represent the total number of AIDS-related deaths. It is a monument to large-scale loss.[15]

In this context, viewings of the Quilt and candlelight memorials were often politically charged events. They became a chance to connect the grief and loss being experienced by individuals with demands for tangible political change. This was articulated well by Justice Michael Kirby, who presented a formal address at the unfolding of the Quilt in the Sydney Convention and Exhibition Centre at Darling Harbour in 1999. Kirby said:

> I think of the friends that I have lost. I go through their names like a Rosary (and this despite a stern Protestant upbringing). A Rosary of much loved human spirits. Of Peter, a school friend. Of Daniel, the artist in Paris. Of another Peter from England…But remembering and thinking is not enough. Celebrating their lives and recalling their strengths and joys and little foibles, recorded in these cloths, is not enough. These quilts, and the people they remember, propel us to action…On this last note we should dedicate ourselves here and now. We should do so in the presence of these quilts and the spirits that they memorialise. We should demand an end to the last vestiges of prejudice and discrimination that still lurk in the hidden, and not so hidden, corners of Australian society…Remembrance is not enough. Sorrow, is not enough…These are days for action, lest receding memories and apathy and political time-serving take over.[16]

Internationally, AIDS quilts reached almost iconic status for their striking representation of the mortal impact of HIV/AIDS. The American Quilt found its way into popular culture as a feature on the television talk show *Nightline* in 1988. It also appeared in an episode of daytime soap opera *All My Children*. A documentary film, *Common Thread: Stories from the Quilt*, made in 1989, received an Academy Award. The same year, the Quilt was nominated for a Nobel Peace Prize.[17]

---

15   Brown, M. 1997, 'The Cultural Saliency of Radical Democracy: Moments from the AIDS Quilt', *Cultural Geographies*, 4(1), pp. 27–45.

16   Kirby, Michael 1999, Once Again, The Australian AIDS Memorial Quilt, Opening address to The Quilt Project Sydney Australian AIDS Memorial Quilt Display, 10 April, Sydney Convention and Exhibition Centre, Darling Harbour, NSW.

17   Stull, Gregg 2001, 'The AIDS Memorial Quilt: Performing Memory, Piecing Action', *American Art*, 15(2), pp. 84–9.

> First and foremost [the purpose of the Quilt is] to be there for those people to create the Quilt. But if we just created a Quilt that was static, that would defeat the purpose of being…we'd just have a room full of quilts and what's the point of that? It's the ability then to take the Quilt back into the community, to give it back to the community and to utilise it for really positive reasons…To make people aware. To use it to support safe sex education. That's very important.
>
> — Terry Thorley (1993)

In Australia, AIDS memorials—particularly the Quilt—received wide-scale public attention, becoming part of HIV/AIDS prevention education as well as being integrated into political protest strategies. Opportunities were created for broad sectors of the community to view the Quilt—in public libraries, schools, museums and galleries. Candlelight memorials have attracted up to 8000 people in any one city, and up to 60 000 across the country. Arguably, these two initiatives have reached the broader public to a greater extent than any other actions of the AIDS movement.

The Quilt has been the subject of numerous news and feature articles. In 1989, *ITA Magazine* featured a five-page spread including interviews with mothers and children of people who had died of AIDS, as well as with the lovers of gay men.[18] The Quilt also tended to attract interest from the mainstream media, which generally produced articles that were supportive of the Quilt Project. These usually featured anecdotes about the families who produced panels for their children, running headlines such as, 'Honour the Courage of Those Living with AIDS'[19] and 'AIDS Quilt Brings Comfort to Community'.[20] The Quilt has been displayed in numerous public locations, including Sydney's Darling Harbour and the National Gallery of Victoria. Several panels were also displayed at the National Gallery of Australia in 1994 as part of an exhibition, *Don't Leave Me This Way: Art in the Age of AIDS*. The Quilt has regularly been taken into schools and in some cases school students have made panels, either dedicated to a person they knew or a general panel acknowledging their support for people with AIDS.[21]

Alongside this, by involving the extended families of people who have died from AIDS, the Quilt has been an important outreach tool—a link between the gay community and the broader public. This link is evident in the Quilt panels themselves, many of which have been made by community groups, hospices and jails. Quilt panels read: 'Mount Alvernia (hospital). Keeping the flame of

---

18   Woodhouse, Ursula 1989, 'The Quilt Project', *ITA*, 1(4), pp. 106–10.
19   Frith, Marion 1993, 'Honour the Courage of Those Living with AIDS', *The Canberra Times*, 23 May, p. 2.
20   Dennis, Jenny 2001, 'AIDS Quilt Brings Comfort to Community', *Illawarra Mercury*, 26 November, p. 7.
21   Woodhouse, 1989.

compassion alive...Maitland Gaol. In memory of all those Inmates who have passed on: Family Planning NSW—Health Promise Promotion Unity Unit: The Continuing Care Unit. Alfred Hospital, Melbourne. 1997: Royal Melbourne Nurses, Care and Remember...'

AIDS memorials also encouraged people within the gay community to become involved. Candlelight memorials/vigils became the largest public rallies seen in Australia around HIV/AIDS. As activist Phil Carswell describes:

> People came to Candlelight Vigils who never came to other AIDS events. The bars in Melbourne would advertise them, put together clips to play on their video screens. It was a community event, one of those things everyone assumed you would go to—like a dance party. People would go to [the Sydney Gay and Lesbian] Mardi Gras and they'd go to the Vigil.[22]

The Politics of Empathy

The Quilt illustrates the human side of HIV/AIDS. The inclusion of individual memorials on the Quilt allows its viewers to find personal connections between their own lives and the lives of people who have died from AIDS. Rather than didactically informing people about the number of AIDS deaths or the nature of HIV transmission, it is a device for storytelling, introducing viewers of the Quilt to some intimate details of the lives of people with AIDS. Someone who previously had no association with HIV/AIDS can suddenly find a connection between themselves and someone on the Quilt—the same birthdate, similar interests, the same name.[23]

Terry Thorley says:

> [One of the Quilt volunteers/presenters] used to tell the story that there was this little boy, and [the volunteer had] taken down one of the panels with a pair of jeans on it. And this little boy became fascinated with them and, you know, kept coming back: 'Were they his favourite pair of jeans?' 'Yes'. And a little bit later came back: 'He must've loved those jeans.' And just this little cycle of this boy connecting with the jeans...I mean, if his knowledge of AIDS comes through connecting with that pair of jeans then, you know, it's a learning thing.[24]

---

22   Phil Carswell, Interview with the author, 17 December 2005.
23   Melbourne Candlelight Vigil Committee, 1992; Hawkes et al., 1994; Capozzolo, 2002.
24   Terry Thorley, TRC 2815/54, NLA.

Phil Carswell explains:

> You could take a Quilt panel to a public event and immediately have people on side. I've done dozens of school talks, and as soon as you tell a story behind a Quilt panel the kids start to make a connection—a connection that all the leaflets and badges can't make. One student saw a panel of a person who had the same birthdate as her and I bet she still thinks about that person on World AIDS Day. We would take videos of the Quilt to public talks—we made up a 10-minute video. The visual nature of these made it very easy to start a talk with. You saw images of these beautiful young people who just shouldn't have died as early as they did.[25]

By encouraging viewers to make an empathetic connection to people who have died from AIDS through the details depicted on its panels, the Quilt plays a role in extending the emotional impact of the AIDS epidemic beyond the borders of the gay community. People might react to viewing the Quilt with feelings of sadness or loss, or even happiness or interest, for those whom they might previously have understood only as part of a stigmatised minority: gay men, drug users, people with AIDS. Empathy and emotion have political impact in this context because they humanise AIDS, which in turn implies that AIDS affects ordinary people and is therefore a problem for the whole community. By encouraging an emotional reaction from its viewers, the Quilt has the potential to recast prejudice towards both gay men and people with HIV/AIDS.

In her analysis of public memorials, Marita Sturken describes the Quilt as 'bright, colourful, easy to understand, and moving, a perfect human interest story on the evening news or in the local paper'.[26] She goes on to discuss how this has created some cynicism among US activists for sanitising the experience of AIDS. The mainstream public accepts the Quilt because it does not make many references to the sexuality or sex lives of gay men. Nor does it carry imagery associated with sickness and death. In this sense, the Quilt does not challenge deep-seated homophobia and AIDS-related stigma. Even critics of the Quilt, however, acknowledge its capacity to personalise and humanise the plight of people with AIDS.[27] AIDS memorials might not directly tackle homophobia and prejudice, but they do introduce an alternative moral framework. It is this that makes memorials a profound form of cultural activism. They are concerned not with formal political engagement, but with the production of social and moral

---

25   Phil Carswell, Interview with the author, 17 December 2005.
26   Sturken, Marita 1997, *Tangled Memories: The Vietnam War, the AIDS Epidemic and the Politics of Remembering*, University of California Press, Berkeley, p. 213.
27   Ibid.

codes. They also tap directly into emotional sentiment as a means of challenging the social reality of people outside the movement (or the community most directly affected).

The Right to Grieve

Challenging 'emotional codes' has been part of the explicit agenda of many social movements. The Gay Pride Movement, for instance, and the Civil Rights Movement both sought to make visible 'bad' feelings associated with stigmatised identities—such as shame and guilt—and replace them with a sense of pride in one's identity. The Gay Pride Movement asserted that feelings of self-esteem and happiness should be the acceptable and 'rational' way to feel towards gay identity, rather than the sense of shame, distress or sadness that had become the 'normalised' reaction to being gay (certainly, people had not always been encouraged to feel proud about discovering they had homosexual desires). Both these movements sought to rewrite the 'feeling rules'—or the cultural norms that guide individuals in the expression and sensation of emotion—associated with particular identities.[28] The aim of a social movement in this context is not just to change the way in which a social group is perceived by society, but also to change the experience of belonging to that group—to assert that the experience of being gay is positive and worthy of pride. In this sense, the targets of the movement are its own constituents as much as it is the mainstream public. Indeed, the very act of developing a sense of solidarity with others might in itself become a positive emotional experience, more conducive to feelings of pleasure and confidence than shame or ambivalence.[29]

The social stigma of AIDS complicated the process of grief for many people, especially the families of gay men who lived in mainstream, heterosexual society without connection to others affected by HIV/AIDS. The usual sources of support that might be present following the death of a child, sibling, friend

---

28 Hochschild, Arlie Russell 1998, 'The Sociology of Emotion as a Way of Seeing', in Gillian Bendelow and Simon Williams (eds), *Emotions in Social Life: Critical Themes and Contemporary Issues*, Routledge, London; Jasper, James 1998, 'The Emotions of Protest: Affective and Reactive Emotions in and Around Social Movements', *Sociological Forum*, 13(3), pp. 397–424; Flam, Helena 2005, 'Emotions Map: A Research Agenda', in Helena Flam and Debra King (eds), *Emotions and Social Movements*, Routledge, Abingdon, UK; Taylor, Verta and Rupp, Leila 2002, 'Living Internationalism: The Emotion Culture of Transnational Women's Organisations 1888–1945', *Mobilization*, 7(2), pp. 141–58.
29 Taylor, Verta 2000, 'Emotions and Identity in Women's Self Help Movements', in Sheldon Stryker, Timothy Owens and Robert White (eds), *Self, Identity, and Social Movements*, University of Minnesota Press, Minneapolis; Caron, Bruce 2003, 'Festivals and Social Movements—Event Centred Solidarity', *Community, Democracy and Performance, The Urban Practice of Kyoto's Higashi-Kujo Madang*, viewed 2 December 2005, <http://junana.com/CDP/corpus/D511.html>; Nugteren, Albertina 2001, Collective/Public Ritual Behaviour After Disasters: An Emerging Manifestation of Civil Religion?, Presentation to Spiritual Supermarket Conference, April, London School of Economics, viewed 2 December 2005, <http://www.cesnur.org/2001/london2001/nugteren.htm>

or parent were not necessarily available in the case of AIDS, where community attitudes were often hostile. Even where support was present, the experience of grief could be overshadowed by a sense of indignity or dishonour that came with a family member's death from AIDS. In some instances, families would deny publicly that HIV had been the cause of death, blaming another illness such as cancer. For the lovers of gay men, their grief was often not acknowledged by the biological families of those who had died. In many cases, gay men were excluded from their partner's funeral or other family-controlled burial rites.[30]

There is a strong moral code that guides grieving in societies—a 'morality of loss'.[31] The social value placed on an individual's relationship with a person whom they have lost (through death or separation) tends to influence the respect paid to, and concessions made for, an individual's grief. For example, the loss of a marriage through death is generally greatly respected by the community. Widows and widowers are presumed to be—indeed are expected to be—suffering great sadness, while funeral rituals include paying homage to their bereavement. When a relationship does not fit into accepted moral codes, however, such as with an adulterous affair or in many cases with homosexual relationships, the community generally does not recognise or acknowledge the grief of a partner following loss. Also, where the individual who has died has breached certain social or moral expectations—as would have been the case with many gay men who died from AIDS—there are generally fewer accommodations made for grieving loved ones. Indeed, the sense of loss an individual experiences in these cases might be recorded as illegitimate. Martha Fowlkes describes this process, writing: 'The "spoiled identity" of which stigma is constructed has the power to contravene or cancel out the meaning of loss *even* where kinship is concerned. The mourner encounters hostility and disregard, and these add to and underscore the pain of the loss itself' (emphasis in original).[32]

AIDS memorials were created to provide support to people who had lost loved ones to AIDS. But also, through creating a forum where grief for people with AIDS was legitimised, AIDS memorials sought to change an experience that was, for many people, filled with feelings of shame. Moreover, they created space for those whose sense of loss might not have been recognised in other forums—namely, the friends and lovers of gay men—to grieve.

The nature of AIDS means, however, that these memorials were highly politicised acts. Experienced individually, grief is a personal process, but the collective

---

30 Holst-Warhaft, Gail 2005, *The Cue for Passion: Grief and Its Political Uses*, Harvard University Press, Cambridge, Mass.; Wettergren, Asa 2005, 'Mobilization and the Moral Shock', in Helena Flam and Debra King (eds), *Emotions and Social Movements*, Routledge, Abingdon, UK; Fowlkes, Martha R. 1990, 'The Social Regulation of Grief', *Sociological Forum*, 5(4), pp. 635–52.

31 Fowlkes, 1990, p. 648.

32 Ibid., p. 648.

expression of grief and mourning facilitated by AIDS memorials demonstrated a refusal by large numbers of people to yield to the stigma around AIDS. The political power of collective action in this instance is asserted through the creation of space within which the expression of a particular emotional state is legitimised and respected—a space that did not previously exist within the stigma of AIDS. By asserting the right to grieve and acknowledging that grief, AIDS activists challenged the negative cultural and moral status of HIV/AIDS and the people most affected by it.

Breaching the Moral Code

In her analysis of the 'Women in Black' vigils, Tova Benski is interested in the possibility for social-movement performances to become 'breaching events'.[33] By this she means that movement action can present a moral or ethical stance that contradicts common assumptions or social norms. Social movements pose symbolic resistance to the social order when they expose the social and moral codes that are ingrained in cultural processes by presenting a different reading of reality. The Women in Black vigils were a series of peace protests held by a group of women in Israel calling for Israeli/Palestinian reconciliation. Benski suggests that the significance of a 'breaching event' can be witnessed in the emotional reaction of spectators. Negative reactions from observers tend to follow a significant violation of moral codes. In her study of viewers of the Women in Black vigils, Benski found that the majority of people who witnessed the vigils expressed anger or contempt towards protestors, shouting at them or making angry gestures. Benski argues that the protestors incited anger amongst spectators because their actions breached dominant and deeply ingrained attitudes towards both Israeli/Palestinian politics and the role of women in politics. Women publicly expressing a political position in this context confronted the moral sensibilities of spectators.[34]

AIDS activists were well aware that AIDS memorials challenged mainstream moral attitudes towards both gay men and HIV/AIDS. The very act of commemorating people who had died from AIDS was confronting in terms of the stigma surrounding HIV/AIDS. But Quilt Project organisers sought to control as much as possible the reaction of outsiders and spectators by creating a particular 'mood' at Quilt events. A series of rituals was[35] performed at Quilt

---

33 Benski, Tova 2005, 'Breaching Events and the Emotional Reactions of the Public: Women in Black in Israel', in Helena Flam and Debra King (eds), *Emotions and Social Movements*, Routledge, Abingdon, UK.
34 Ibid.
35 I use the past tense in this chapter because I am referring specifically to events that took place in the 1980s and 1990s. To my knowledge, however, these rituals are still practised when new Quilt panels are unveiled.

unfoldings to solemnise the process of handing over new quilt panels from those who made them to the 'public project'. Trained volunteers encircled each Quilt panel and unfolded it in choreographed unison. People wore simple, white outfits to ensure their dress did not detract from the detail of panels. The unfolding was accompanied by a public recitation of names from the Quilt, often read by prominent community figures.[36] The rituals around Quilt unfoldings and viewings, along with the visual impact of a candlelight procession, were designed to be deliberately quiet and calming—setting up a particular emotional experience for both participants and spectators. The rituals were similar to those that govern action in a church or sacred site, and the mood evoked was similar. By creating such an atmosphere, the emotional reaction of participants and spectators tends towards sadness or quiet reflection, leaving limited room for public heckling or derision. As Quilt organiser Phil Carswell describes: 'There is something approaching reverence for the Quilt. People are always extremely respectful. Even children always behave at the Quilt, they pick up on the atmosphere.'[37] Activists worked to counter the possibility of antagonistic reactions to the 'breaching event' by controlling the environment—using visual and emotional codes to illicit a particular response. As Carswell says: 'People participated in the Quilt because the "aura" of the Quilt overtook the fear of vilification or other stigma. When all the panels were displayed together it was amazing. Like an oasis of amazing tranquility.'[38]

The emotional dynamics of grief and loss are personally and culturally familiar to most people. One does not have to be gay or affected by HIV/AIDS to understand sadness and loss. AIDS memorials tapped into a common moral framework of 'respect for the dead' and utilised the familiar cultural cues that have developed around rituals such as funerals and religious services.[39] In other words, outsiders respected the Quilt and the candlelight memorial because they used common cultural codes to invoke respect and solemnity.

AIDS memorials were not a confrontational form of political activism. But this does not mean they were apolitical. Since their inception, AIDS memorials have involved literally thousands of people—many from outside the gay community—in a form of community protest against stigma and discrimination. These memorials have captured the attention of political leaders and the broader community and have become a focal point of both the politics of HIV/AIDS and HIV-prevention education.

---

36   Australian AIDS Memorial Quilt Project, 2004.
37   Phil Carswell, Interview with the author, 17 December 2005.
38   Ibid.
39   Collins, Randall 2001, 'Social Movements and the Focus of Emotional Attention', in Jeff Goodwin, James Jasper and Francesca Polletta (eds), *Passionate Politics: Emotions and Social Movements*, University of Chicago Press, Ill.

According to Phil Carswell:

> What we were fighting [against] for so long was invisibility. We had sensationalist stories in the media and images of skeletal people dying of AIDS. But most people never knew anyone dying from AIDS. The Quilt gave visibility to the real lives of people. It made that gut-level, primal connection that people in the gay community had from knowing people who had died from AIDS. But those in the broader community hadn't been up close and personal. The Quilt was as up close and personal as you can get without holding them in your arms.[40]

Through paying tribute to people who had died from AIDS, and respectfully acknowledging those grieving for them, the Quilt Project and candlelight memorials recast the moral context of HIV/AIDS. They insisted that people who had died from AIDS deserved public memorial even in cases where the virus had been acquired through perceived 'immoral' means. As well as supporting individuals in their grief, the public display of respect for both those who had died and those who were grieving challenged the stigma surrounding both HIV/AIDS and homosexuality.

AIDS memorials were successful in drawing people into the AIDS movement and engaging observers and people outside the movement through their drama and art. But more importantly, the ritual of the memorials, which drew on familiar cultural imagery of funerals and commemorations, evoked a particular emotional reaction for both outsiders and participants that encouraged respect for people who had died from AIDS. In this way, they challenged the stigma surrounding HIV/AIDS, particularly in the late 1980s and early 1990s.

The success of the Quilt itself might indeed be evidence of the fact that public attitudes towards gay men have been changed over the course of the AIDS epidemic. The public was willing to accept and be involved with the Quilt and with gay men in a way they might not have been early in the 1980s when fear and uncertainly about HIV/AIDS were at their height. Over time, the fear of being publicly outed as a person with AIDS was also mitigated—indicated through the greater willingness of people to be identified on Quilt panels over time.

Terry Thorley recalls:

> Back in the '80s when the project…was first started there was still a lot of fear and secrecy and discrimination surrounding AIDS. So a lot of the panels weren't clearly personally identifying, in that they would come in with initials or just Christian names. Now I think there has been a

---

40   Phil Carswell, Interview with the author, 17 December 2005.

change in that circumstance. I mean, it's still not ideal but there has been a change. But the panels are becoming more elaborate, more openly expressive of personality and character.[41]

Social movements are a part of history and are engaged in a social process of 'knowledge making'. They seek to influence the cultural and moral scripts that frame everyday life. AIDS memorialising—as a social-movement strategy—became a means through which the AIDS-movement 'frame' was expressed. That is, AIDS memorials both reflected and reinforced the ideological stance of the AIDS movement using imagery and emotion rather than an articulated ideological argument. In this context, social movements can be seen as concurrently intellectually and emotionally driven.

---

41   Terry Thorley, TRC 2815/54, NLA.

Epilogue: Bug Chasers and Criminals

Events disrupt the operative systems of ideas, beliefs, values, roles, and institutional practices of a given society. In so doing, events change the way in which social actors think about the meaning and importance they assign to modes of action and the rules that govern interaction, groups and their discourses, symbols, and rituals. In the event, the meanings carried by cultural objects are embodied in historic consequences (real or perceived) the event has for particular actors.

— Stephen Ellingson[1]

Large-scale or unpredictable events can rupture social convention and change people's attitudes towards the world. Everyday modes of being—the habits, customs and patterns of thought that frame our everyday existence—are rarely questioned unless something happens to disrupt them or expose their arbitrariness. Pierre Bourdieu described as 'doxa' the framework of knowledge through which we think. Doxa is not a reference to the conscious ideas that we have or the particular arguments and thoughts that fill our conversation, but the underlying assumptions that inform and structure our ways of thinking. That which is in the realm of doxa is knowledge so taken for granted and ubiquitous that it is virtually invisible.[2] Public debate usually sits within the framework of 'what is known' about the way the world is, even when there is argument or dissent within that framework. According to Bourdieu,[3] social knowledge does not move from the realm of doxa into conscious awareness and discussion as a consequence of the thoughts or ideas of individuals. Rather, the potential for new or previously unspoken knowledge to enter 'discursive consciousness' is created through a change in social conditions. Bourdieu sees a materially based dialectic between social conditions and knowledge. The assumptions that underlie the way we think are questioned only when something forces those assumptions to be made visible.

In this text, I have explored the impact of HIV/AIDS on various aspects of Australian society. While for most Australians HIV/AIDS probably sat only on the periphery of their everyday world, for those close to it the virus produced massive social and emotional upheaval. It was perhaps the most significant event ever to affect communities of gay men, not only because it threatened lives but

---

1   Ellingson, Stephen 1995, 'Understanding the Dialectic of Discourse and Collective Action: Public Debate and Rioting in Antebellum Cincinnati', *The American Journal of Sociology*, 101(1), pp. 100–44, at p. 103.
2   Bourdieu, Pierre 1977, *Outline of a Theory of Practice*, Cambridge Studies in Social Anthropology, Cambridge; Charlesworth, Simon 2000, *A Phenomenology of Working Class Experience*, Cambridge University Press, Cambridge.
3   Bourdieu, 1977.

also because ideas about the nature and morality of homosexuality were pushed so starkly into the public spotlight. While this might not have exposed on any grand scale the 'doxic framework' into which knowledge about homosexuality is formed, HIV interrupted 'everyday' social patterns long enough to create opportunities for gay men to influence public knowledge of, and attitudes towards, homosexuality in a way that they had never previously been able.

By the 1990s, those in the AIDS movement had developed confidence in their own capacity as 'AIDS experts'. They had also achieved a certain level of credibility and legitimacy within the AIDS sector of the medical fraternity. Activists were formally recognised and funded by the Federal and State governments and had an established media presence on HIV/AIDS matters. Their alternative, community-based model of disease prevention had also gained recognition and acceptance by public health and medical officials as well as government. As such, the AIDS movement was in a position to challenge the notion that medical knowledge was the only form of legitimate knowledge about HIV/AIDS and, indeed, about the way in which clinical trials are conducted.[4]

Author and activist Robert Ariss argues that the development of working relationships between doctors and activists was not necessarily an example of 'relationship building' between these two groups. Rather, he sees the development of doctor–activist partnerships as simply serving the function of rescuing 'science from the threat of non-compliance'.[5] The threat of non-compliance was, however, an important challenge to medical dominance. Even if the ultimate priority of doctors and scientists was to maintain the scientific integrity of their research, the AIDS movement did force the medical system as a whole to change its processes. Indeed, Ariss concedes that 'AIDS activism has transformed the practices of clinical science from one that prioritises the demands of science itself, to one that is more responsive to the needs of human beings'.[6]

This was a significant achievement for the AIDS movement. Medical knowledge has a cultural authority rarely challenged. The autonomy and status of the medical profession are ingrained in the modern social order, and the capacity or credibility of doctors is rarely questioned. The process by which the AIDS movement successfully challenged this authority and shifted many of the long-established boundaries separating lay-people from the medical profession represents an important story in the history of the Australian medical system. It

---

4 Treichler, Paula 1988, 'AIDS, Homophobia and Biomedical Discourse', in Douglas Crimp (ed.), *AIDS Cultural Analysis, Cultural Activism*, The MIT Press, Cambridge, Mass.

5 Ariss, Robert 1997, *Against Death: The Practice of Living with AIDS*, Gordon and Breach, Amsterdam, p. 199.

6 Ibid., p. 200.

also demonstrates that the development of alternative forms of expertise (in this case, a form of expertise based on personal experience and 'felt knowledge') has radical potential for social movements.

The power to determine the way in which the social world is perceived—to make one's 'truth' accepted as universal and natural—is to a large extent what is at stake in political struggle.[7] At issue for all social movements is how to achieve wide-scale acceptance for their political position and for their social and cultural values and ideas. To this end, all social movements engage in 'identity politics' of a sort. A high-profile scientist, for instance, is often more likely to gain media airplay for an argument about the dangers of global warming than an environmental activist. Social-movement actors will use their 'expert' supporters and public intellectuals strategically. But for the AIDS movement, the public presence of gay men themselves, rather than 'experts' representing them, was central to achieving the shift in public attitudes towards gay men and lesbians that it did—even if many of these gay men and lesbians were also doctors or medical experts in their own right. What had been absent from previous public discussion about homosexuality was any sort of high-profile, regular presence of gay people talking about homosexuality. Through AIDS activism, 'gay identity' achieved greater legitimacy and visibility in the public realm. In this sense, as well as influencing the direction of HIV/AIDS policy, a large part of the impact of the AIDS movement could be described as cultural—an influence directed more towards civil society than the state, one that challenged cultural codes and conventions.[8] The cultural impact of the AIDS movement was witnessed in such things as the increasing acknowledgment of gay youth in mainstream health and welfare services and education as well as in the increasing acceptance of 'lay-people' within the medical establishment. The paradox of HIV/AIDS for gay men was that such a terrible tragedy contributed to significant social and political gains for the gay community.

In making this point, in no way do I wish to suggest that the AIDS movement was miraculously able to eradicate homophobia or inequality based on sexuality from Australian culture. Violence is a lingering threat in the background, and unfortunately occasionally the foreground, of the lives of all gay men and women. Homophobic attitudes underlie much of Australian culture, with 'poofter jokes' and derogatory references to gay men a commonplace part of the Australian vernacular. That being said, the situation for gay men and lesbians in Australia today has changed dramatically from the time when any public

---

7   Lovell, Terry 2004, 'Bourdieu, Class and Gender: "The Return of the Living Dead"?', *The Sociological Review*, 52(s2), pp. 35–56; Bourdieu, Pierre 1985, 'The Social Space and the Genesis of Groups', *Theory and Society*, 14(6), pp. 723–44; Melucci, Alberto and Avritzer, Leonardo 2000, 'Complexity, Cultural Pluralism and Democracy: Collective Action in the Public Space', *Social Science Information*, 39(4), pp. 507–27.
8   Melucci and Avritzer, 2000, p. 509.

discussion about gay people occurred in the context of how to punish or cure the 'affliction' of misdirected sexuality. But the story of the Australian AIDS movement and homosexual liberation is not one that, as yet, has an end.

Bug Chasers and Criminals

Every so often, the relationship between gay men and HIV/AIDS finds its way back into the media. While media hysteria in Australia around these issues has never again reached the fever pitch of the 1980s, there still tends to be an undercurrent of blame and mistrust of gay men.

In 2007, the Australian media picked up on the idea of 'gift giving' and 'bug chasing'—terms used to refer to HIV-positive men who deliberately seek to give others HIV through unprotected sex and HIV-negative men who have sex with positive men in the hope of catching HIV. The extent to which either gift giving or bug chasing are common enough to be credited as a 'phenomenon' is a subject of debate among HIV organisations, health educators and academics, with most concluding that if this does occur it involves only a minority of individuals.[9] The idea of a subculture of HIV 'conversion' parties, however, translated well into sensationalist media articles that implied some sort of sordid undercurrent had recently been uncovered among the Australian gay community.[10]

The Herald Sun's Brendan Roberts, for example, reported:

> What appeared to be a run-of-the-mill investigation turned out to be a much wider probe that took police on an eye opening journey through the seedy underbelly of Melbourne's gay community. It opened up a perverse world of high-risk sex where [the] human immunodeficiency virus, HIV, was often an accepted risk, sometimes worn by carriers... as a badge of honour. Exposed was a bizarre culture inhabited by 'bug chasers'—healthy men actively seeking to be infected with HIV—and 'breeders' who infected them at depraved 'conversion parties'. One veteran detective said he had no idea of the bounds the investigation would reach...'I'd describe it as surprisingly shocking'.[11]

9   Hurley, Michael and Croy, Samantha 2009, 'The Neal Case: HIV Infection, Gay Men, the Media and the Law', in Sally Cameron and John Rule (eds), *The Criminalisation of HIV Transmission in Australia; Legality, Morality and Reality*, NAPWA Monograph, National Association of People Living With HIV/AIDS, Sydney.
10   Medew, Julia and Kissane, Karen 2007, 'Gays in HIV "Bug Chase"', *The Age*, 21 April, p. 1; Roberts, Brendan 2007, 'Seedy World Unravels', *The Herald Sun*, 31 March, p. 1; Medew, Julia and Stark, Jill 2007, 'In Pursuit of HIV: Real or Just Fantasy?', *The Age*, 31 March, p. 2.
11   Roberts, 2007, p. 1.

In *The Age*, Julia Medew and Karen Kissane reported that:

> A Melbourne man who fantasised about catching HIV before he contracted the virus has spoken out about a gay subculture in which infection is seen as desirable. The young professional, who does not want to be named, told *The Age* a combination of complacency about the virus and the wish to have unprotected sex with an HIV-positive man he loved led him to become infected...He is the first to speak publicly about taking part in a behaviour known in the gay community as 'bug chasing'.[12]

A lot of the media attention on 'bug chasing' was linked with the high-profile Victorian trial of a man alleged to have deliberately infected others with HIV. The Michael Neal case went before the courts over a two-month period in 2008, following a committal hearing in April 2007. Neal faced 106 criminal charges including intentionally spreading a deadly disease, attempting to intentionally spread a deadly disease, rape and possession of child pornography.[13] In their opening address to the jury, the prosecution spoke of how Neal used the promise of drugs to lure men to 'conversion parties'.[14] Throughout the trial, witnesses were called to describe their involvement in these parties. Media reporting of the trial focused heavily on these witness statements, presenting the experiences of this handful of men as evidence of this supposed new gay subculture in Australia:[15]

> A witness told the court Mr Neal hosted a 'conversion' party at which a 15 year old boy was injected with crystal methamphetamine and then 'bred' (infected with HIV) by about 15 HIV-positive men who had sex with him.[16]

> The court also heard there was a 'bug chaser' movement in Melbourne's gay community who wanted to contract the disease and 'breed' it.[17]

> Though gay community advocates weren't aware that the subculture had arrived here [in Australia], a steady stream of witnesses in the Neal case told the court they were familiar with terms such as 'gift giving' and 'breeding' (passing on HIV).[18]

---

12   Medew and Kissane, 2007, p. 1.

13   Robinson, Natasha 2007c, 'HIV Policies Flawed as Officials Miss a Bare Reality', *The Australian*, 21 April, p. 2.

14   Rout, Melinda 2007 'Piercing Used "to Help Spread HIV"', *The Australian*, 20 June, p. 7.

15   D, Tim 2007, 'Chasing Bugs in the News', *SameSame*, 21 April, <http://www.samesame.com.au/news/local/650/Chasing_Bugs_In_The_News>; Hurley and Croy, 2009.

16   Robinson, Natasha 2007a, 'Five Years to Tell Police of HIV Case', *The Australian*, 23 March, p. 5.

17   Medew, Julia 2007, 'Court Hears of Psychiatrist's Plea', *The Age*, 23 March, p. 3.

18   Robinson, 2007c, p. 2.

Irrespective of whether Neal was guilty or innocent of the charges against him,[19] the case became an occasion for a resurgence of media headlines depicting gay men and people with HIV/AIDS as untrustworthy and dangerous.[20] Through the construct of a courtroom trial, with its requisite victims and perpetrator, the once-familiar discourse of 'innocents' versus 'blameworthy' deviants was shown to be lurking not too far beneath the surface of contemporary media attitudes toward HIV/AIDS.[21]

That being said, the issue of bug chasing came and went from the media quite quickly[22] and was in fact diverted by a political scandal linked to the Neal case that resulted in the Chief Health Officer at the time being sacked.[23] The Victorian Department of Human Services allegedly mishandled several confidential files relating to HIV-positive individuals, allowing them to be handed to police investigating the Neal case.[24] Further, there were allegations that the Chief Health Officer had not responded to advice from the Victorian HIV Case Advisory Panel to detain Neal several months before his arrest. As a result, some of Neal's alleged 'victims' were threatening to file a law suit against the Health Department.[25] This all occurred in the context of the first reported increases in new cases of HIV in Australia in more than a decade. Victoria, where Neal was a resident, had experienced greater increases than other States and Territories.[26] In fact, in March 2006, two months before Neal was arrested, the Victorian Health Minister, Bronwyn Pike, had announced that Victoria was to host a summit of health officials to discuss the issue of rising HIV notifications in the eastern states of Australia.[27]

The focus on the departmental handling of the Neal case and HIV in general had a tinge of the punitive, legalistic approach to HIV prevention seen in the 1980s. Conservative commentators ran with the idea that civil libertarianism was clearly a threat to public health,[28] arguing the Government needed to do more to contain 'HIV Spreaders'.[29]

---

19   Neal was sentenced to 18 years' imprisonment in January 2009.

20   Menadue, David 2007, 'Under Attack', *Poslink*, 34, pp. 4 and 27.

21   Persson, Asha and Newman, Christy 2008, 'Making Monsters: Heterosexuality, Crime and Race in Recent Western Media Coverage of HIV/AIDS', *Sociology of Health and Illness*, 30(4), pp. 632–46.

22   Hurley and Croy (2009) identified 118 articles relating to the Neal case between May 2006 and January 2009. Just more than half of these were about the Neal story and the court case, about 40 per cent were about the political fallout from the case and seven articles were on the national HIV response and gay sex cultures.

23   Medew, Julia 2007b, 'Health Chief Apologised Over Failure to Act on HIV Advice', *The Age*, 19 April, p. 2.

24   Hurley and Croy, 2009.

25   Medew, 2007b.

26   Pike, Bronwyn 2006b, Victorian Strategy Tackles Rising HIV Rates, Media release, Government of Victoria, Melbourne.

27   Pike, Bronwyn 2006a, National Summit to Discuss Increase in HIV Notifications, Media release, Government of Victoria, Melbourne.

28   Ackerman, Piers 2007, 'Deadly Game of Privacy Protection', *The Age*, 12 April, p. 21.

29   Robinson, Natasha 2007b, 'Officials Told: Dob in HIV Spreaders', *The Australian*, 2 April, p. 5.

The reporting did not, however, have the same 'bite' that it would have had in the 1980s. While the salacious details of the Neal case were clearly irresistible fodder for journalists, there were few suggestions that the Neal case represented a threat to the community at large. This is perhaps reflective of the changing public perception of HIV in Australia—from a disease affecting 'us' to a disease affecting the developing world; from an unknown, deadly disease to a manageable chronic condition.[30]

It is most likely also indicative of the ongoing work of HIV-prevention agencies that governments and journalists take a measured and largely sensible approach to HIV/AIDS in Australia. Although the media did not seem particularly interested in the question of whether there was any actual evidence, or lack thereof, of practices such as bug chasing in Australia or the extent to which safer sex is practised by most HIV-positive individuals, gay and lesbian community advocates and HIV organisations did have a presence in media reporting on the Neal case. There was an effort made by some journalists to link the story to broader discussion about the adequacy of current funding for HIV prevention in Victoria. This had successful outcomes.[31] National public health governance systems are being reviewed with respect to the best way to manage individuals known to be intentionally risking the health of others with regards to infectious diseases. More money has also been allocated to HIV prevention in Victoria.

Conclusion

There is a large and varied collection of publications on the topic of Australia's response to HIV/AIDS, much of it written by researchers and activists who began their analysis *in situ* in the 1980s. Australia's response to HIV/AIDS was so unique and successful that there will always be more that can be learned from this particular part of Australia's history. This history can teach policy makers a lot about the importance of collaboration with communities; it can teach sociologists about the way in which communities exert power; it can teach historians of the present why the rate of HIV in Australia has not exploded the way it has in some other countries. For the lesbian and gay community in Australia (as with many other Western countries), the emergence of HIV/AIDS marked a political, social and legal turning point. The tragedy and threat of HIV/AIDS galvanised communities like nothing had previously. The ramifications of this are still evident in the way in which HIV is managed today—with the continued involvement of affected communities, albeit with more professionalised

---

30   This is not to suggest that HIV should be considered a manageable chronic condition or that it is a disease affecting only developing countries. Rather, I am referring to anecdotal evidence that HIV is often seen in this context by many members of the Australian public.

31   Hurley and Croy, 2009.

community organisations at the helm. The impact of a galvanised community is also evident in the increasing cultural visibility and acceptance of gay men and lesbians in Australia. It might be that this would have occurred regardless of HIV/AIDS. But that will never be known. Either way, the fight against HIV/AIDS clearly brought resources and attention to the Australian lesbian and gay community—not really a 'silver lining' to the devastation of HIV/AIDS, but certainly an unparalleled achievement for community action.

Bibliography

Interviews

Altman, Dennis 1993, Dennis Altman Interviewed by Heather Rusden on 7 July, Oral History Project: The Australian Response to AIDS, TRC 2815/37, Oral History Section, National Library of Australia, Canberra.

Anonymous 2005, Medical practitioner interviewed by Jennifer Power, 27 May, Unpublished transcript.

Baume, Peter 1992, Professor Peter Baume, Head of the School of Public Health, University of New South Wales and former Liberal Senator for New South Wales, Interviewed by Dr John Ballard, 18 March, Oral History Project: The Australian Response to AIDS, TRC 2815/1, Oral History Section, National Library of Australia, Canberra.

Baxter, Don 1993, Don Baxter, former President of the AIDS Council of NSW, Interviewed by James Waites, 26 November, Oral History Project: The Australian Response to AIDS, TRC 2815/75, Oral History Section, National Library of Australia, Canberra.

Bowtell, Bill 2005a, Bill Bowtell interviewed by Jennifer Power, 28 May, Unpublished transcript.

Brown, Bruce 1992, Bruce Brown, Interviewed by Martyn Goddard, 7 June, Oral History Project: The Australian Response to AIDS, TRC 2815/6, Oral History Section, National Library of Australia, Canberra.

Carswell, Phil 2005a, Phil Carswell interviewed by Jennifer Power, 23 July, Unpublished transcript.

Carswell, Phil 2005b, Phil Carswell interviewed by Jennifer Power, 17 December, Unpublished transcript.

Carswell, Phil 2005c, Unpublished speaking notes for presentation at conference Retrospectives: HIV/AIDS in Australia, Historical Perspectives on an Epidemic, 27 May 2002, University of New South Wales, Unpublished notes and personal communication with Jennifer Power, 23 July 2005.

Carswell, Phil 2006, Personal communication with Jennifer Power, 25 October, Melbourne.

Crooks, Levinia 2005, Levinia Crooks interviewed by Jennifer Power, 28 January, Unpublished transcript.

Davis, Ken 2004, Ken Davis interviewed by Jennifer Power, 4 November, Unpublished transcript.

Dwyer, John 1993, Interview with Professor John Dwyer, Clinical Director, Prince of Wales Hospital and member of NACAIDS, Interviewed by Stewart Harris, Oral History Project: The Australian Response to AIDS, TRC 2815/51, Oral History Section, National Library of Australia, Canberra.

Lowe, David 2005, David Lowe interviewed by Jennifer Power, 12 July, Unpublished transcript.

Mark, Steve 1993, Interview with Steven Mark, lawyer and President, NSW Anti-Discrimination Board, Interviewed by Diana Ritch, 12 August, Oral History Project: The Australian Response to AIDS, TRC 2815/52, Oral History Section, National Library of Australia, Canberra.

Plummer, David 2004, David Plummer interviewed by Jennifer Power, 30 August, Unpublished transcript.

Power, Prue 2004, Prue Power interviewed by Jennifer Power, 25 May, Unpublished transcript.

Power, Prue 2006, Personal communication with Jennifer Power, 26 May, Unpublished transcript.

Rankin, Ian 2004, Ian Rankin interviewed by Jennifer Power, 26 July, Unpublished transcript.

Ross, Jennifer 1993, Jennifer Ross, Executive Director, Haemophilia Foundation of Australia, Interviewed by Heather Rusden, 11 February, Oral History Project: The Australian Response to AIDS, TRC 2815/18, Oral History Section, National Library of Australia, Canberra.

Thorley, Terry 1993, Terry Thorley, Interviewed by Diana Ritch, 25 August, Oral History Project: The Australian Response to AIDS, TRC 2815/54, Oral History Section, National Library of Australia, Canberra.

Whittaker, Bill 2004, Bill Whittaker interviewed by Jennifer Power, 6 November, Unpublished transcript.

AIDS Movement Campaign Materials and Community-Generated Information

AIDS Coalition to Unleash Power (ACT UP) 1990a, Campaign Poster for 'Kiss In', AIDS Coalition to Unleash Power, Victorian Chapter, Melbourne.

AIDS Coalition to Unleash Power (ACT UP) 1990b, Cut the Red Tape, Media briefing, AIDS Coalition to Unleash Power, Sydney.

AIDS Coalition to Unleash Power (ACT UP) 1991, Cut the Red Tape, Media briefing, ACT UP Demonstration, Sydney.

AIDS Council of NSW (ACON) 1989, *Future Directions for the AIDS Council of NSW: A Strategic Planning Document*, AIDS Council of NSW, Sydney.

AIDS Council of NSW (ACON) 2006, *Community Support Network*, AIDS Council of NSW web site, viewed 20 May 2006, <http://www.acon.org.au>

AIDS Treatment Action Committee (ATAC) 1991a, National Media Kit, July, AIDS Treatment Action Committee, Sydney.

AIDS Treatment Action Committee (ATAC) 1991b, *The Economic, Social and Ethical Costs of HIV/AIDS, Adapted from AIDS Council of NSW 1990 'The Trialing, approval and marketing of treatments and therapies for HIV/AIDS and related diseases: a policy document' ACON, Sydney*, AIDS Treatment Action Committee, Sydney.

Andrews, Dean 1991, 'HIV and AIDS Treatments: Action Campaign Gears Up', *Sydney Star Observer*, 28 June, p. 1.

Anonymous 1991, 'Diary of a D-Day Full of Daredevil Drama', *Melbourne Star Observer*, 14 June, p. 3.

Ariss, Robert 1989, 'Convener's Report, PLWHA NSW', *Annual Report*, People Living With HIV/AIDS NSW, Sydney.

Australian AIDS Memorial Quilt Project 2004, *History of the Australian AIDS Memorial Quilt Project*, Australian AIDS Memorial Quilt web site, viewed 2 December 2005, <http://www.AIDSquilt.org.au>

Australian Federation of AIDS Organisations (AFAO) 1992, *HIV/AIDS and Australia's Community-Based Sector: A Success Story in Prevention*, Paper commissioned by the Commonwealth Department of Health, Housing and Community Services for the National HIV/AIDS Strategy Evaluation, Australian Federation of AIDS Organisations, Canberra.

Australian Federation of AIDS Organisations (AFAO) 2003, HIV on the Rise in Three States: Australia's National AIDS Strategy Must Be Revitalised, Press release, 29 May, Australian Federation of AIDS Organisations, Newtown, NSW, viewed 2 June 2003, <http://www.afao.org.au>

Bobby Goldsmith Foundation (BGF) 1999, Who Was Bobby Goldsmith?, Bobby Goldsmith Foundation web site, viewed 24 April 2004, <http://www.bgf. org>

Brown, Bruce 1991, Acting Up Down Under (ACT UP Campaign Sheet), AIDS Coalition to Unleash Power, Sydney [paper held at the Noel Butlin Archives, Ref. H3N/12, No. 174/8].

Carr, Adam 1987, 'President's Report', Annual Report, Victorian AIDS Council, Melbourne.

Carr, Adam 1991, 'Once More Unto the Breach', Outrage, June, pp. 42–4.

Carr, Adam 1998, 'Outrage at 15 or the Rise and Fall of Practically Everyone', Outrage, April [republished by the author on his personal web site: <http:// www.adam-carr.net>].

Carswell, Phil 1985a, 'Gay Men Should Ignore This Test', Outrage, February, pp. 5–7.

Carswell, Phil 1986, 'President's Report: Where We've Been, Where We're Going', Annual Report, Victorian AIDS Council, Melbourne.

Croome, Rodney 1992, 'AIDS as a Euphemism for Homosexuality', Sydney Star Observer, 1 May, p. 15.

D, Tim 2007, 'Chasing Bugs in the News', SameSame, 21 April, <http://www. samesame.com.au/news/local/650/Chasing_Bugs_In_The_News>

Gamma Project Victoria (GAMMA) n.d., GAMMA Project: AIDS Bisexual Men and Their Female Partners, Publicity flyer, Gamma Project Victoria.

Gamma Project Victoria (GAMMA) 1986, GAMMA Melbourne AIDS Public Education and Awareness Project, Media release, Gamma Project Victoria.

Goddard, Martyn 1991, 'Howe Moves on Drugs', Melbourne Star Observer, 12 July, p. 1.

Grant, Peter 1987, 'The Education Working Group', Annual Report, Victorian AIDS Council, Melbourne.

Keenan, Tony 1992, 'President's Report', Annual Report, Victorian AIDS Council, Melbourne.

McDougall, Michael 1991, 'D-Day Attack Sydney', *Sydney Star Observer*, 14 June, pp. 1 and 9.

McQuarrie, Vanessa 1993, '"Keep on Acting" Says Richardson', *Sydney Star Observer*, 12 November, p. 7.

Malcom, Anne 1991, 'Community Services Report', *Annual Report*, AIDS Council of NSW, Sydney.

Menadue, David 2007, 'Under Attack', *poslink*, (34), pp. 4 and 27.

Michael, Dean 1987, 'The Political Action Working Group', *Annual Report*, Victorian AIDS Council, Melbourne.

Morcos, Monica 1986, 'Money Matters', *Annual Report*, Victorian AIDS Council, Melbourne.

Positive Living 2002, 'Twenty Years', Editorial, *Positive Living*, November–December, viewed 21 March 2011, <http://www.afao.com.au>

Tabone, Joey 2004, Australia's Response to HIV/AIDS at Risk Through Lack of Leadership from the Commonwealth Government, Media release, 18 May, AIDS Action Council of the ACT, Canberra, viewed 20 November 2005, <http://www.AIDSaction.org.au/content/media/2004/responsetohivAIDS.php>

Tasmania Gay and Lesbian Rights Group (TGLRG) 1997, It's Over: Nine Year Gay Law Reform Campaign Ends in Victory, Press release, Tasmania Gay and Lesbian Rights Group, viewed 24 June 2005, <http://www.tased.edu.au/tasonline/tasqueer/flash.html>

Tobias, Sandy 1988, AIDSLINE—A Profile, Unpublished paper, Victorian AIDS Council, Melbourne.

Victorian AIDS Council (VAC) 1986, 'President's Report: Where We've Been, Where We're Going: An Interview with Phil Carswell, VAC President', *Annual Report*, Victorian AIDS Council, Melbourne.

Victorian AIDS Council (VAC) 1993, *A Dangerous Decade: Ten Years of AIDS*, Victorian AIDS Council, Melbourne.

Watson, Lex 1985, 'Antibody Testing Unquestionably Has Some Value', *Outrage*, 21 (February), pp. 5 and 7.

Whittaker, Bill 1990, Treatment Issues—Updates on AZT and DDI, Letter to members of the Australian Federation of AIDS Organisations from the National President, 25 June.

Whittaker, Bill 1991, Transcript of a public meeting, 16 August, Victorian AIDS Council, Melbourne.

Newspaper Articles and Other Popular Media

Ackerman, Piers 2007, 'Deadly Game of Privacy Protection', *The Age*, 12 April, p. 21.

Bagwell, Sheryle 1985, 'The Van Grafhosts Learn How to Cope', *The Australian*, 18 November, p. 8.

Bagwell, Sheryle and Leser, David 1985, 'Crisis Point in Gay, Doctor Relationship', *The Weekend Australian*, 2 March, p. 3.

Barnard, Michael 1985, 'AIDS: A Time to Get Tough?', *The Age*, 19 March, p. 19.

Barnett, David 1989, 'Surgeons Alarmed at AIDS Risk', *The Bulletin*, 25 April, pp. 38–41.

Border Morning Mail 1983, 'Gay March on Police Station After Raids', *Border Morning Mail*, 28 February, p. 8.

Brown, Malcolm 1985, 'Homosexuals' Angry Ad: AIDS Chief Speaks Out', *Sydney Morning Herald*, 7 August, p. 13.

Carney, Sean 1988a, 'AIDS: Most Support Marriage and Hospital Tests', *The Age*, 3 December, p. 1.

Carney, Sean 1988b, 'Support for Wider Use of AIDS Tests', *The Age*, 5 December, p. 1.

Carswell, Phil 1985b, 'Homosexuals Active Against AIDS', *The Age*, 26 March, p. 13.

Chadwick, Paul 1982, 'States Warned of Mystery Killer Disease', *The Age*, 20 July, p. 16.

Cook, Sue 1983, 'Disease Fear Leads Red Cross to Ban Gays as Donors', *The Australian*, 10 May, pp. 1–2.

Coultan, Mark 1983, 'Police Raid on Club Angers Homosexual Community', *Sydney MorningHerald*, 31 January, p. 3.

Croft, David 1997, 'Homosexuals in Schools', Letter to the Editor, *West Australian*, 6 August, p. 14.

Cumming, Fia 1982, 'Homosexual Study Urged Law Reform', *The Australian*, 6 July, p. 3.

Daily Telegraph 1989, 'Tough Action the Only Way to Fight AIDS', Editorial, *Daily Telegraph*, 2 August, p. 10.

Darby, Andrew 1990, 'Tas to Look at AIDS Laws', *Sydney Morning Herald*, 28 June, p. 6.

Date, Margot 1992, 'Storm Continues Over Hollows AIDS Speech', *Sydney Morning Herald*, 4 March, p. 2.

Date, Margot 1993, 'Patient With HIV Denied Surgery', *Sydney Morning Herald*, 18 January, p. 5.

Davis, Ian and Birnbauer, Bill 1984, 'Sinclair Links Labor With Deaths of Three Babies', *The Age*, 17 November, p. 1.

Davis, Ken 1992, 'AIDS: The Right Unveils its Agenda', *Green Left Weekly*, (59), 17 June, p. 10.

Dawson, Jim and Dawson, Lyn 1997, 'Dangers of Indifference', Letter to the Editor, *West Australian*, p. 14.

Dennis, Jenny 2001, 'AIDS Quilt Brings Comfort to Community', *Illawarra Mercury*, 26 November, p. 7.

Dewsbury, Ruth 1989a, 'AIDS Test Urged for Health Workers', *Sydney Morning Herald*, 9 March, p. 10.

Dewsbury, Ruth 1989b, 'Doctors Accused of Silence Over AIDS', *Sydney Morning Herald*, 29 April, p. 7.

Dewsbury, Ruth 1989c, 'Blewett Launches Defamation Actions', *Sydney Morning Herald*, 22 July, p. 11.

Dickie, Phil 2004, 'Probing Shady Places', *The Age*, 6 June, p. 13.

Frail, Rod 1985, '50,000 Sydney Men Now Carry AIDS', *Sydney Morning Herald*, 31 January, p. 1.

Frith, Marion 1993, 'Honour the Courage of Those Living with AIDS', *The Canberra Times*, 23 May, p. 2.

Green, Roger 1985, 'With Compulsion, Victims Go Underground', *The Canberra Times*, 6 September, p. 10.

Heary, Monica 1989, 'Gay Man Fights AIDS Test Demand', *The Australian*, 16 May, p. 7.

Heath, Sally 1990, 'AIDS Poster Starts a Row Over Safe-Sex Campaign', *The Age*, 26 July, p. 6.

Hole, Jacquelyn 1991, 'HIV Sufferers United in Condemning Report', *Sydney Morning Herald*, 5 October, p. 2.

Kent, Simon 1992, 'Fred Wants to Tell AIDS Story Like It Is', *The Sun-Herald*, 22 March, p. 15.

Kraft, Scott 1982, 'New Illness Strikes Gays', *Launceston Examiner*, 13 July, p. 6.

Langley, George and Rice, Margaret 1984, 'Three Babies Die of Suspected AIDS: QLD Acts Against Donors', *The Australian*, 16 November, p. 1.

Lawrence, Tess 1989, 'AIDS: MPs Soft on the Fight', *Sunday Press*, 25 June, p. 9.

McCauley, Carmel 1988, 'Opposition Looks at Mandatory AIDS Test', *The Age*, 1 September, p. 4.

McClelland, Jim 1991, 'Both Sides Wrong in Outing Case', *Sydney Morning Herald*, 14 August, p. 12.

Macdonald, Janine 1997, 'Anti-Suicide Program "Had Gay Message"', *West Australian*, 15 August, p. 11.

McDonnell, Dan 1985, 'Patient Panic on AIDS Law', *The Sun*, 28 September, p. 13.

Mandle, Bill 1993, 'AIDS Gets Too Much Unjustified Attention', *The Canberra Times*, 17 January, p. 26.

Margo, Jill 1989, 'Safe Sex Hailed as AIDS Cases Drop', *Sydney Morning Herald*, 5 June, p. 8.

Medew, Julia 2007a, 'Court Hears of Psychiatrist's Plea', *The Age*, 23 March, p. 3.

Medew, Julia 2007b, 'Health Chief Apologised Over Failure to Act on HIV Advice', *The Age*, 19 April, p. 2.

Medew, Julia and Kissane, Karen 2007, 'Gays in HIV "Bug Chase"', *The Age*, 21 April, p. 1.

Medew, Julia and Stark, Jill 2007, 'In Pursuit of HIV: Real or Just Fantasy?', *The Age*, 31 March, p. 2.

Mercer, Neil 1982, 'Board Reports on Homosexuality', *Sydney Morning Herald*, 6 July, p. 2.

Mercer, Neil 1983, 'Anti-Labor Threat After Homosexual Club Raid', *Sydney Morning Herald*, 28 February, p. 3.

Midweek Truth 1985, 'Die, You Deviate', *Midweek Truth*, 8 December, p. 1.

Needham, Paul 1983, 'Homosexuals to Fight Lethal AIDS', *Launceston Examiner*, 31 May, p. 6.

Newcastle Herald 1985a, '7 Children Lend Their Support', Editorial, *NewcastleHerald*, 1 October, p. 1.

Newcastle Herald 1985b, 'AIDS Girl Banned on Biting Count', Editorial, *Newcastle Herald*, 14 October, p. 6.

Northern Territory Times 1984, 'Now Labor Party Blamed for AIDS', *Northern Territory Times*, 4 December, p. 1.

Olszewski, Peter 1985, 'X-Rated Posters Mark Gay AIDS War', *Melbourne Truth*, 26 January, p. 13.

Pirrie, Michael 1988, 'AIDS Experts Reject Compulsory Tests', *The Age*, 2 September, p. 10.

Pratt, L. 1997, 'They Deserve A Future', Letter to the Editor, *West Australian*, 7 August, p. 13.

Riley, Mark 1990, 'Holly is Farewelled, But the Grief Stays', *Sydney Morning Herald*, 6 September, p. 9.

Roberts, Brendan 2007, 'Seedy World Unravels', *The Herald Sun*, 31 March, p. 1.

Robinson, Natasha 2007a, 'Five Years to Tell Police of HIV Case', *The Australian*, 23 March, p. 5.

Robinson, Natasha 2007b, 'Officials Told: Dob in HIV Spreaders', *The Australian*, 2 April, p. 5.

Robinson, Natasha 2007c, 'HIV Policies Flawed as Officials Miss a Bare Reality', *The Australian*, 21 April, p. 2.

Rout, Melinda 2008, 'Piercing Used "To Help Spread HIV"', *The Australian*, 20 June, p. 7.

Sampson, John 1989, 'Date Set for AIDS Summit', *Sydney Morning Herald*, 10 April, p. 9.

Sanderson, Wayne 1985, 'Gays May Refuse AIDS Test', *Daily Telegraph*, 14 January, p. 5.

Santamaria, B. A. 1984, 'AIDS: Public Reaction and the Gay Community', *The Australian*, 27 November, p. 11.

Sattler, Howard 1991, 'Silence Is Not So Golden', *Sunday Times*, 24 March, p. 39.

Stannard, Bruce and Murphy, Kevin 1989, 'More Than a Million Australians? Still Glad to be Gay?', *The Bulletin*, 10 October, pp. 50–7.

Stapleton, John and McCarthy, Phillip 1991, 'Gay Guerillas Come Out to Prey', *Sydney Morning Herald*, 10 August, p. 36.

Sydney Morning Herald 1983, 'Homosexuals March', *Sydney Morning Herald*, 1 February, p. 10.

Sydney Morning Herald 1987, 'Managing the Truth on AIDS', Editorial, *Sydney Morning Herald*, 8 June, p. 6.

Sydney Morning Herald 1991, 'AIDS Victims Receive Little Sympathy, Survey Shows', Editorial, *Sydney Morning Herald*, 30 September, p. 5.

Sydney Morning Herald 1993, 'Shame and Grief Mark the Death of a Small Teacher', *Sydney Morning Herald*, 22 November, p. 3.

Synnott, John 1985, 'Board Blames Hysteria for Gay Sackings', *Illawarra Mercury*, 1 August, p. 5.

The Age 1982, 'Homosexuals Should Get Rights, Says NSW Board', *The Age*, 6 July, p. 5.

The Age 1983, 'Gays Form AIDS Group', *The Age*, 8 August, p. 5.

The Age 1989, 'A Tougher Approach to AIDS Prevention', Editorial, *The Age*, 10 June, p. 11.

The Australian 1984, 'The New Plague', Editorial, *The Australian*, 17 November, p. 24.

The Canberra Times 1982, 'Law Change on Homosexuality Recommended', *The Canberra Times*, 6 July, p. 6.

The Canberra Times 1983, 'Gay Protest', *The Canberra Times*, 6 February, p. 3.

The Canberra Times 1984, 'QLD Considers Manslaughter Charges: Sir Joh Cites ALP on AIDS', *The Canberra Times*, 4 December, p. 1.

The Canberra Times 1993, '5000 March in Sydney Candlelight AIDS Rally', Editorial, *The Canberra Times*, 24 May, p. 3.

The Courier-Mail 1984, 'AIDS and Responsibilities', Editorial, *The Courier-Mail*, 17 November, p. 4.

The Courier-Mail 1989, 'AIDS Isolation Might Be Necessary: Church', *The Courier-Mail*, 15 February, p. 16.

The Mercury 1989, 'Making it Tougher in War on AIDS', Editorial, *The Mercury* [Hobart], 23 November, p. 8.

Tsitas, Evelyn 1988, 'Married and Having a Gay Old Time', *Australasian Post*, 2 July.

Warren, Matthew 1988, 'Gay Men Embrace "Safe Sex" Practices', *The Australian*, 26 December, p. 3.

Watson, Lex 1983, 'Facts on AIDS', Letter to the Editor, *Sydney Morning Herald*, 30 June, p. 8.

West Australian 1983, 'WA's Homosexuals Warned on AIDS', *West Australian*, 21 May, p. 23.

Whelan, Judith 1990, 'The AIDS Baby Who Made It', [Agenda Section], *The Sunday Age*, 15 July, p. 2.

Wilmoth, Peter 1990, 'Keeping AIDS in the News', *The Age*, 13 October, pp. 8–9.

Woodhouse, Ursula 1989, 'The Quilt Project', *ITA*, 1(4), pp. 106–10.

General Reference List

Abercrombie, Nicholas 1980, *Class, Structure and Knowledge: Problems with the Sociology of Knowledge*, Basil Blackwell, Oxford.

Alford, Robert 1975, *Health Care Politics: Ideological and Interest Group Barriers to Reform*, University of Chicago Press, Ill.

Altman, Dennis 1988, 'Legitimation Through Disaster: AIDS and the Gay Movement', in Elizabeth Fee and Daniel Fox (eds), *AIDS: The Burdens of History*, University of California Press, Berkeley.

Altman, Dennis 1989, 'The Emergence of Gay Identity in the USA and Australia', in Christine Jennet and Stewart Randal (eds), *Politics of the Future: The Role of Social Movements*, Macmillan, Melbourne.

Altman, Dennis 1990, 'Introduction', in Richard Clayton (ed.), *Gay Now, Play Safe*, Victorian AIDS Council/Gay Men's Community Health Centre, Melbourne.

Altman, Dennis 1992, 'The Most Political of Diseases', in Eric Timewell, Victor Minichiello and David Plummer (eds), *AIDS in Australia*, Prentice Hall, Sydney.

Altman, Dennis 1994, *Power and Community: Organizational and Cultural Responses to AIDS*, Taylor & Francis, London.

Antonian, L., Shinitzky, M., Samuel, D. and Lippa, A. 1987, 'AL721, A Novel Membrane Fluidizer', *Neuroscience and Biobehavioral Reviews*, 11(4), pp. 399–413.

Ariss, Robert 1993, 'Performing Anger: Emotion in Strategic Responses to AIDS', *Australian Journal of Anthropology*, 4(1), pp. 18–30.

Ariss, Robert 1997, *Against Death: The Practice of Living with AIDS*, Gordon and Breach, Amsterdam.

Australian National Council on AIDS, Hepatitis C and Related Diseases (ANCAHRD) 1998, *1997 Report to the Minister for Health and Family Services*, Australian National Council on AIDS, Hepatitis C and Related Diseases, Canberra.

AVERT 2005, *The Different Stages of HIV Infection*, AVERT web site, viewed 20 March 2006, <http://www.avert.org/hivstages.htm>

AVERT 2006, *The History of AIDS 1987–1992*, AVERT web site, viewed 18 April 2006, <http://www.avert.org/his87_92.htm>

Ballard, John 1989, 'The Politics of AIDS', in Heather Gardner (ed.), *The Politics of Health: The Australian Experience*, Churchill Livingstone, Melbourne.

Ballard, John 1992, 'Australia: Participation and Innovation in a Federal System', in David Kirp and Ronald Bayer (eds), *AIDS in the Industrialised Democracies: Passions, Politics and Policies*, Rutgers University Press, New Brunswick, NJ.

Ballard, John 1998, 'The Constitution of AIDS in Australia: Taking Government at a Distance Seriously', in Mitchell Dean and Barry Hindess (eds), *Governing Australia: Studies in Contemporary Rationalities of Government*, Cambridge University Press, Melbourne.

Ballard, John 1999, 'HIV Contaminated Blood and Australian Policy', in Eric Feldman and Ronald Bayer (eds), *AIDS, Blood and the Politics of Medical Disaster*, Oxford University Press, New York.

Barbalet, Jack 2001, Emotion in Social Life and Social Theory: Recovering the Leicester Tradition, Inaugural lecture, 20 November, University of Leicester, UK.

Basham, Kenn 2006, 'Speech Given at the "Reflections" Exhibition at the Canberra Museum and Gallery 8 December 2004', in Ian Rankin (ed.), *AIDS Action! A History of the AIDS Action Council of the ACT*, AIDS Action Council of the ACT, Canberra.

Bates, Benjamin and Harris, Tina 2004, 'The Tuskegee Study of Untreated Syphilis and Public Perceptions of Biomedical Research: A Focus Group Study', *Journal of the National Medical Association*, 96(8), pp. 1051–64.

Bates, Erica and Linder-Pelz, Susie 1990, *Health Care Issues*, (Second edition), Allen & Unwin, Sydney.

Benford, Robert and Snow, David 2000, 'Framing Processes and Social Movements: An Overview and Assessment', *Annual Review of Sociology*, 26, pp. 611–39.

Benski, Tova 2005, 'Breaching Events and the Emotional Reactions of the Public: Women in Black in Israel', in Helena Flam and Debra King (eds), *Emotions and Social Movements*, Routledge, Abingdon, UK.

Blain, Michael 1994, 'Power, War and Melodrama in the Discourses of Political Movements', *Theory and Society*, 23(6), pp. 805–37.

Blewett, Neal 2003, *AIDS in Australia: The Primitive Years, Reflections on Australia's Policy Response to the AIDS Epidemic*, Australian Health Policy

Institute Commissioned Paper Series 7, University of Sydney, NSW, viewed 5 May 2006, <http://www.ahpi.health.usyd.edu.au/pdfs/colloquia2003/AIDSpaper.pdf>

Bold, Christine, Knowles, Ric and Leach, Belinda 2002, 'Feminist Memorialising and Cultural Countermemory: The Case of Marianne's Park', *Signs*, 28(1), pp. 125–48.

Bourdieu, Pierre 1977, *Outline of A Theory of Practice*, Cambridge Studies in Social Anthropology, Cambridge.

Bourdieu, Pierre 1985, 'The Social Space and the Genesis of Groups', *Theory and Society*, 14(6), pp. 723–44.

Bowtell, Bill 2005, Marshalling Political Will and Effective Policy Responses to the HIV/AIDS Epidemic: Making it Better, Presentation to the Effective Public Health Advocacy Conference, Cancer Council of New South Wales, 29 August, Northcott Centre, Parramatta, NSW.

Brandt, Allan 1997, 'Behaviour, Disease, and Health in the Twentieth Century United States', in Allan Brandt and Paul Rozin (eds), *Morality and Health*, Routledge, New York.

Bray, Fiona and Chapman, Simon 1991, 'Community Knowledge, Attitudes and Media Recall About AIDS, Sydney 1988 and 1989', *Australian Journal of Public Health*, 15(2), pp. 107–13.

Brier, Jennifer 2002, Infectious Ideas: AIDS and Conservatism in America 1980–1992, Unpublished PhD Thesis, Rutgers University, New Brunswick, NJ.

Briscoe, Gordon 1996, Disease, Health and Healing: Aspects of Indigenous Health in Western Australia and Queensland, 1900–1940, PhD Thesis, The Australian National University, Canberra, viewed 22 May 2006, <http://histrsss.anu.edu.au/briscoe/intro.html>

Britt, Lory and Heise, David 2000, 'From Shame to Pride in Identity Politics', in Sheldon Stryker, Timothy Owens and Robert White (eds), *Self, Identity, and Social Movements*, University of Minnesota Press, Minneapolis.

Brown, M. 1997, 'The Cultural Saliency of Radical Democracy: Moments From the AIDS Quilt', *Cultural Geographies*, 4(1), pp. 27–45.

Brown, Phil, Zavaestoski, Stephen, McCormick, Sabrina, Mayer, Brian, Morello-Frosch, Rachel and Gasior, Rebecca 2004, 'Embodied Health Movements: New Approaches to Social Movements', *Health in Sociology of Health and Illness*, 26(1), pp. 50–80.

Browning, Bob 1992, *Exploiting Health: Activists and Government Versus the People*, Canobury Press, Melbourne.

Bull, Melissa, Pinto, Susan and Wilson, Paul 1991, 'Homosexual Law Reform in Australia', *Australian Institute of Criminology Trends and Issues in Crime and Criminal Justice*, 29, <http://aic.gov.au>

Burstein, Paul, Einwohner, Rachel and Hollander, Jocelyn 1995, 'The Success of Political Movements: A Bargaining Perspective', in Craig Jenkins and Bert Klandermans (eds), *The Politics of Social Protest*, University of Minnesota Press, Minneapolis.

Cabassi, Julia 2001, *Barriers to Access and Effective Use of Anti-Discrimination Remedies for People Living with HIV and HCV*, Occasional Paper No. 1, Australian National Council on Hepatitis C, AIDS and Related Diseases, Canberra.

Canavan, Peter 2003, Reflecting on 'Our' Involvement in NAPWA, Presentation to The Art of Living: Ninth Biennial Conference of the National Association of People Living With AIDS, 27–28 October, Cairns, Qld.

Canavan, Peter 2004, 'Because It's Personal: What Good Advocacy Can Achieve, and How', *The Australian Health Consumer*, (1) (2003–04), pp. 17–20.

Canel, Eduardo 1997, 'New Social Movement Theory and Resource Mobilization Theory: The Need for Integration', in M. Kaufman and H. Dilla Alfonso (eds), *Community Power and Grassroots Democracy: The Transformation of Social Life*, International Development Research Centre, Ottawa, <http://www.idrc.ca>

Capozzolo, Christopher 2002, 'A Very American Epidemic: Memory Politics and Identity Politics in the AIDS Memorial Quilt, 1985–1993', *Radical History Review*, 82 (Winter), pp. 91–109.

Caron, Bruce 2003, 'Festivals and Social Movements—Event Centred Solidarity', *Community, Democracy and Performance, The Urban Practice of Kyoto's Higashi-Kujo Madang*, viewed 2 December 2005, <http://junana.com/CDP/corpus/D511.html>

Carr, Adam 1992, 'What is AIDS?', in Eric Timewell, Victor Minichiello and David Plummer (eds), *AIDS in Australia*, Prentice Hall, Sydney.

Carter, Meredith and O'Connor, Debra 2003, 'Consumers and Health Policy Reform', in P. Liamputtong and H. Gardner (eds), *Health, Social Change and Communities*, Oxford University Press, Melbourne.

Centers for Disease Control (CDC) 1985, *Acquired Immunodeficiency Syndrome (AIDS) Weekly Surveillance Report—December 30*, United States AIDS Activity Center for Infectious Diseases, Centers for Disease Control, Atlanta, Ga.

Centers for Disease Control (CDC) 2005, *HIV/AIDS Surveillance Report 2004*, United States Department of Health and Human Services, Centers for Disease Control and Prevention, Atlanta, Ga, viewed 21 November 2005, <http://www.cdc.gov/hiv/topics/surveillance/resources/reports/2004report/>

Charlesworth, Simon 2000, *A Phenomenology of Working Class Experience*, Cambridge University Press, Cambridge.

Cohen, Peter 1988, *Love and Anger: Essays on AIDS, Activism and Politics*, Harrington Park Press, New York.

Collins, Randall 2001, 'Social Movements and the Focus of Emotional Attention', in Jeff Goodwin, James Jasper and Francesca Polletta (eds), *Passionate Politics: Emotions and Social Movements*, University of Chicago Press, Ill.

Commonwealth of Australia 1988, *AIDS: A Time to Care, A Time to Act: Towards a Strategy for Australians*, Policy Discussion Paper, Department of Community Services and Health, Canberra.

Commonwealth of Australia 1989, *Report of the Working Panel on Discrimination and Other Legal Issues—HIV/AIDS*, Consultation Paper No. 2, Department of Community Services and Health, Canberra.

Conrad, Peter 1992, 'Medicalization and Social Control', *Annual Review of Sociology*, 18, pp. 209–32.

Crichton, Anne 1990, *Slowly Taking Control? Australian Governments and Health Care Provision, 1788–1988*, Allen & Unwin, Sydney.

Croome, Rodney 2003, 'Relationship Law Reform in Tasmania', *Word is Out*, June, <http://www.wordisout.info>, pp. 1–7.

Crossley, Michelle 1998, '"Sick Role" or "Empowerment"? The Ambiguities of Life with an HIV Positive Diagnosis', *Sociology of Health and Illness*, 20(4), pp. 507–31.

Crossley, Nick 2003, 'From Reproduction to Transformation: Social Movement Fields and the Radical Habitus', *Theory, Culture and Society*, 20(6), pp. 43–68.

Daniel, Ann 1998, 'Trust in Medical Authority', in Alan Petersen and Charles Waddell (eds), *Health Matters: A Sociology of Illness, Prevention and Care*, Allen & Unwin, Sydney.

Dant, Tim 1991, *Knowledge, Ideology and Discourse: A Sociological Perspective*, Routledge, London.

Davenport-Hines, Richard 1990, *Sex, Death and Punishment*, Collins, London.

Della Porta, Donatella and Diani, Mario 1999, *Social Movements: An Introduction*, Blackwell, Oxford.

De Waal, Peter, Black, Ian, Trebilco, Peter and Wills, Sue 1994, *A Review of the 1976 Tribunal on Homosexuals and Discrimination*, The Tribunal Working Group, Sydney.

Dowsett, Gary 1998, 'Pink Conspiracies: Australia's Gay Communities and National HIV/AIDS Policies, 1983–1996', in Anna Yeatman (ed.), *Activism and the Policy Process*, Allen & Unwin, Sydney.

Drummond, Michael, Health Outcomes International and National Centre for HIV Epidemiology and Clinical Research 2002, *Return on Investment in Needle and Syringe Programs in Australia*, Department of Health and Ageing, Canberra.

Duffin, Ross 1993, 'People with HIV and the National Conference', *The National AIDS Bulletin*, December–January, pp. 20–3.

Edwards, Mark 1997, 'AIDS Policy Communities in Australia', in Peter Aggleton, Peter Davies and Graham Hart (eds), *AIDS Activism and Alliances*, Taylor & Francis, London.

Ellingson, Stephen 1995, 'Understanding the Dialectic of Discourse and Collective Action: Public Debate and Rioting in Antebellum Cincinnati', *The American Journal of Sociology*, 101(1), pp. 100–44.

Emke, Ivan 1992, 'Medical Authority and its Discontents: A Case of Organised Non-Compliance', *Critical Sociology*, 19(3), pp. 57–80.

Epstein, Steven 1995, 'The Construction of Lay Expertise: AIDS Activism and the Forging of Credibility in the Reform of Clinical Trials', *Science, Technology and Human Values*, 20(4), pp. 408–37.

Epstein, Steven 1996, *Impure Science: AIDS, Activism and the Politics of Knowledge*, University of California Press, London.

Eyerman, Ron 2005, 'How Social Movements Move: Emotions and Social Movements', in Helena Flam and Debra King (eds), *Emotions and Social Movements*, Routledge, Abingdon, UK.

Eyerman, Ron and Jamison, Andrew 1991, *Social Movements: A Cognitive Approach*, Polity Press, Cambridge.

Feachem, Richard 1995, *Valuing the Past—Investing in the Future: Evaluation of the National HIV/AIDS Strategy 1993–94 to 1995–96*, Department of Human Services and Health, Canberra.

Flam, Helena 2005, 'Emotions Map: A Research Agenda', in Helena Flam and Debra King (eds), *Emotions and Social Movements*, Routledge, Abingdon, UK.

Fogarty, Walter 1992, '"Certain Habits": The Development of a Concept of the Male Homosexual in New South Wales Law, 1788–1900', in Robert Aldrich and Gary Wotherspoon (eds), *Gay Perspectives: Essays in Australian Gay Culture*, Department of Economic History, University of Sydney, NSW.

Foster, John 1993, *Take Me to Paris, Johnny*, Black Inc., Melbourne.

Foucault, Michel 1976, *The History of Sexuality. Volume 1: An Introduction*, Penguin Books, London.

Foucault, Michel 1980, *Power/Knowledge: Selected Interviews and Other Writings 1972–1977*, Pantheon Books, New York.

Foucault, Michel 1994 [1963], *The Birth of the Clinic*, Vintage Books, New York.

Fowlkes, Martha R. 1990, 'The Social Regulation of Grief', *Sociological Forum*, 5(4), pp. 635–52.

Fraser, Nancy 1998, 'Heterosexism, Misrecognition and Capitalism', *New Left Review*, 228, pp. 140–50.

Freidson, Eliot 1988, *Profession of Medicine: A Study of the Sociology of Applied Knowledge*, University of Chicago Press, Ill.

French, Robert 1993, *Camping by a Billabong*, Blackwattle Press, Sydney.

Frohlich, Katherine, Corin, Ellen and Potvin, Louise 2001, 'A Theoretical Proposal for the Relationship Between Context and Disease', *Sociology of Health and Illness*, 23(6), pp. 776–97.

Fuchs, E. 1996, 'On the AIDS Quilt: The Performance of Mourning', in E. Fuchs (ed.), *The Death of Character, Perspectives in Theatre After Modernism*, Indiana University Press, Bloomington.

Gamson, Josh 1989, 'Silence, Death, and the Invisible Enemy: AIDS Activism and Social Movement "Newness"', *Social Problems*, 36(4), pp. 351–67.

Gamson, William and Modigliani, Andre 1989, 'Media Discourse and Public Opinion on Nuclear Power: A Constructionist Approach', *American Journal of Sociology*, 95(1), pp. 1–37.

Germov, John 2002, 'Challenges to Medical Dominance', in John Germov (ed.), *Second Opinion: An Introduction to Health Sociology*, Oxford University Press, Melbourne.

Giugni, Marco 1998, 'Was it Worth the Effort? The Outcomes and Consequences of Social Movements', *Annual Review of Sociology*, 24, pp. 371–93.

Goddard, Martyn 1993, 'Across the Great Divide', *National AIDS Bulletin*, December 1992 – January 1993, pp. 15–17.

Goodwin, Jeff, Jasper, James and Polletta, Francesca 2001, 'Why Emotions Matter', in Jeff Goodwin, James Jasper and Francesca Polletta (eds), *Passionate Politics: Emotions and Social Movements*, University of Chicago Press, Ill.

Gould, Deborah 2000, Sex, Death and the Politics of Anger, Unpublished PhD Thesis, University of Chicago, Ill.

Gould, Deborah 2002, 'Life During Wartime: Emotions and the Development of ACT UP', *Mobilization*, 7(2), pp. 177–200.

Gray, Gwendolyn 1991, *Federalism and Health Policy*, University of Toronto Press, Ont.

Grey, Sandra 2002, Can We Measure the Influence of Social Movements?, Political Science Program Seminar, 18 September, The Australian National University, Canberra.

Griffin, Christine 1993, *Representations of Youth: The Study of Youth and Adolescence in Britain and America*, Polity Press, Cambridge.

Hall, Ananda 1998, *A Risky Business: Criminalising the Transmission of HIV*, Faculty of Law, The Australian National University, Canberra, <http://law.anu.edu/criminet/ananda's_thesis.html>

Hansen, Helena 2003, 'Human Immunodeficiency Virus and Quarantine in Cuba', *JAMA*, 290, p. 2875.

Harris, Fredrick 2006, 'It Takes Tragedy to Arouse Them: Collective Memory and Collective Action During the Civil Rights Movement', *Social Movement Studies*, 5(1), pp. 19–43.

Hawkes, Ponch, Yardley, Ainslie and Langley, Kim 1994, *Unfolding: The Story of the Australian and New Zealand AIDS Quilt Project*, McPhee Gribble, Melbourne.

Hawkins, Peter 1993, 'Naming Names: The Art of Memory and the Names Project', *Critical Inquiry*, 19(4), pp. 752–79.

Hilliard, David 1997, 'Church, Family and Sexuality in Australia in the 1950s', *Australian Historical Studies*, 28(109), pp. 133–46.

Hochschild, Arlie Russell 1998, 'The Sociology of Emotion as a Way of Seeing', in Gillian Bendelow and Simon Williams (eds), *Emotions in Social Life: Critical Themes and Contemporary Issues*, Routledge, London.

Hollibaugh, Amber, Karp, Mitchell, Taylor, Katy and Crimp, Douglas 1988, 'The Second Epidemic', in Douglas Crimp (ed.), *AIDS Cultural Analysis, Cultural Activism*, The MIT Press, Cambridge, Mass.

Holst-Warhaft, Gail 2000, *The Cue for Passion: Grief and Its Political Uses*, Harvard University Press, Cambridge, Mass.

Hurley, Michael 1992, 'AIDS Narratives, Gay Sex and the Hygenics of Innocence', *Southern Review*, 25(2), pp. 141–59.

Hurley, Michael 2001, *Strategic and Conceptual Issues for Community Based, HIV/AIDS Treatments Media*, Researchers in Residence Program, Working Paper 3, Australian Federation of AIDS Organisations, Newtown, NSW, and Australian Research Centre in Sex, Health and Society, La Trobe University, Melbourne.

Hurley, Michael 2003, Boundaries and Borders: Researchers and Researched in NAPWA, Presentation to The Art of Living: Ninth Biennial Conference of the National Association of People Living With AIDS, 27–28 October, Cairns, Qld.

Hurley, Michael and Croy, Samantha 2009, 'The Neal Case: HIV Infection, Gay Men, the Media and the Law', in Sally Cameron and John Rule (eds), *The Criminalisation of HIV Transmission in Australia; Legality, Morality and Reality*, NAPWA Monograph, National Association of People Living With HIV/AIDS, Sydney.

Irvine, Janice 1994, 'Sexual Cultures and the Construction of Adolescent Identities', in Janice Irvine (ed.), *Sexual Cultures and the Construction of Adolescent Identities*, Temple University Press, Philadelphia.

Jasper, James 1998, 'The Emotions of Protest: Affective and Reactive Emotions In and Around Social Movements', *Sociological Forum*, 13(3), pp. 397–424.

Jones, James 1992, 'The Tuskagee Legacy: AIDS and the Black Community', *Hastings Centre Report*, November–December, pp. 38–40.

Kaldor, John 2003, Personal Reflections, Presentation to The Art of Living: Ninth Biennial Conference of the National Association of People Living With HIV/AIDS, 27–28 October, Cairns, Qld.

Kayal, Philip 1993, *Bearing Witness: Gay Men's Health Crisis and the Politics of AIDS*, Westview Press, Boulder, Colo.

Kehoe, Jean 1992, Medicine, Sexuality and Imperialism: British Medical Discourses Surrounding Venereal Disease in New Zealand and Japan: A Socio-Historical and Comparative Study, Unpublished PhD Thesis, Victoria University of Wellington, New Zealand.

Kelleher, David, Gabe, Jonathan and Williams, Gareth 1994, 'Understanding Medical Dominance in the Modern World', in Jonathan Gabe, David Kelleher and Gareth Williams (eds), *Challenging Medicine*, Routledge, London.

Kelley, Jonothan 2001, 'Attitudes Towards Homosexuality in 29 Nations', *Australian Social Monitor Online Journal*, <http://www.international-survey.org/A_Soc_M/>, pp. 15–22.

Kendell, Christopher and Walker, Sonia 1998, 'Teen Suicide, Sexuality and Silence', *Alternative Law Journal*, 23(5), pp. 216–21.

Kimsma, Gerrit 1990, 'Frames of Reference and the Growth of Medical Knowledge: L. Fleck and M. Foucault', in Henk Ten Have, Gerrit Kimsma and Stuart Spicker (eds), *The Growth of Medical Knowledge*, Kluwer Academic Publishers, Dordrecht.

Kippax, S., Connell, R. W., Dowsett, G. W. and Crawford, J. 1993, *Sustaining Safe Sex: Gay Communities Respond to AIDS*, Falmer Press, London.

Kippax, S., Tillet, G., Crawford, J. and Cregan, J. 1991, *Discrimination in the Context of AIDS*, Macquarie University Research Unit, National Centre for HIV Social Research, Sydney.

Kirby, Michael 1999, Once Again, The Australian AIDS Memorial Quilt, Opening address to The Quilt Project Sydney Australian AIDS Memorial Quilt Display, 10 April, Sydney Convention and Exhibition Centre, Darling Harbour, NSW.

Kitschelt, Herbert 1986, 'Political Opportunity Structures and Political Protest: Anti-Nuclear Movements in Four Democracies', *British Journal of Political Science*, 16(1), pp. 57–85.

Klandermans, Bert 1992, 'The Social Construction of Protest and Multiorganizational Fields', in Aldon Morris and Carol Mueller (eds), *Frontiers in Social Movement Theory*, Yale University Press, New Haven, Conn.

Kolker, Emily 2004, 'Framing as a Cultural Resource in the Health Social Movements: Funding Activism and the Breast Cancer Movement in the US 1990–1993', *Sociology of Health and Illness*, 26(6), pp. 820–44.

Lawler, Steph 2004, 'Rules of Engagement: Habitus, Power and Resistance', *The Sociological Review*, 52(s2), pp. 110–18.

Leech, Tim 2005, 'Gay Men and the Response: Political, Legal and Health Promotion Perspectives', in J. Godwin, D. Puls, J. Cabassi, L. Crooks and M. Carman (eds), *HIV and Hepatitis C: Policy, Discrimination, Legal and Ethical Issues*, Australian Society for HIV Medicine, Sydney.

Lewis, Lynette and Ross, Michael 1995, *A Select Body: The Gay Dance Party Subculture and the HIV/AIDS Pandemic*, Cassell, London.

Lewis, Milton 1998, *Thorns on the Rose: The History of Sexually Transmitted Disease in Australia in International Perspective*, Australian Government Publishing Service, Canberra.

Lovell, Terry 2004, 'Bourdieu, Class and Gender: "The Return of the Living Dead"?', *The Sociological Review*, 52(s2), pp. 35–56.

Lupton, Deborah 1993, Moral Threats, Sexual Punishment: Discourses on AIDS in the Australian Press, Unpublished PhD Thesis, University of Sydney, NSW.

Lupton, Deborah 1995, *The Imperative of Health*, Sage Publications, London.

McCallum, Lou 2003, *Review of Paper by Neal Blewett*, Australian Health Policy Institute Commissioned Paper Series 7, University of Sydney, NSW, viewed 5 May 2006, <http://www.ahpi.health.usyd.edu.au/pdfs/colloquia2003/AIDSpaper.pdf>

McCarthy, E. Doyle 1996, *Knowledge as Culture: The New Sociology of Knowledge*, Routledge, London.

McCarthy, John and Zald, Mayer 1977, 'Resource Mobilization and Social Movements: A Partial Theory', *The American Journal of Sociology*, 82(6), pp. 1212–41.

McKenzie, James 1992, *When You Say Yes*, Young People From the Victorian AIDS Council and the Gay Men's Community Health Centre, Melbourne.

McVeigh, Rory, Myers, Daniel and Sikkink, David 2004, 'Corn, Klansmen, and Coolidge: Structures and Framing in Social Movements', *Social Forces*, 83(2), pp. 653–90.

Marsh, I. and Galbraith, L. 1995, 'The Political Impact of the Sydney Gay and Lesbian Mardi Gras', *Australian Journal of Political Science*, 30(2), pp. 300–20.

Marx, Jean L. 1982, 'New Disease Baffles Medical Community', *Science, Technology and Human Values*, 217 (13 August), pp. 618–22.

Melbourne Candlelight Vigil Committee 1992, *Remember Their Names*, Melbourne Candlelight Vigil Committee, Melbourne.

Melucci, Alberto 1989, *Nomads of the Present: Social Movements and Individual Needs in Contemporary Society*, Edited by John Keane and Paul Mier, Hutchinson Radius, London.

Melucci, Alberto and Avritzer, Leonardo 2000, 'Complexity, Cultural Pluralism and Democracy: Collective Action in the Public Space', *Social Science Information*, 39(4), pp. 507–27.

Menadue, David 2003a, Opening Plenary Session Address, The Art of Living: Ninth Biennial Conference of the National Association of People Living With AIDS, 27–28 October, Cairns, Qld.

Menadue, David 2003b, *Positive*, Allen & Unwin, Sydney.

Miller, Timothy 1991, *The Hippies and American Values*, University of Tennessee Press, Memphis.

Misztal, Barbara 1990, 'AIDS in Australia: Diffusion of Power and Making of Policy', in Barbara Misztal and David Moss (eds), *Action on AIDS: National Policies in Comparative Perspective*, Greenwood Press, New York.

Misztal, Barbara 1991, 'HIV/AIDS Policies in Australia: Bureaucracy and Collective Action', *International Journal of Sociology and Social Policy*, 11(4), pp. 62–82.

Misztal, Barbara 1996, *Trust in Modern Societies*, Polity Press, Cambridge.

Moore, Kate 2006, 'Consumer Participation: A Personal Reflection', *Health Issues*, (89), pp. 14–17.

Names Project Foundation 2008, 'History of the Quilt', *The AIDS Memorial Quilt*, Names Project Foundation, Atlanta, Ga, viewed 15 October 2008, <http://www.aidsquilt.org/history.htm>

National Centre in HIV Epidemiology and Clinical Research (NCHECR) 2006, *Australian HIV Surveillance Report*, 22(2), National Centre in HIV Epidemiology and Clinical Research, University of New South Wales, Sydney, pp. 1–16.

National Centre in HIV Epidemiology and Clinical Research (NCHECR) 2010, *HIV Viral Hepatitis and Sexually Transmissible Infections in Australia Annual Surveillance Report 2010*, National Centre in HIV Epidemiology and Clinical Research, University of New South Wales, Sydney.

Nettleton, Sarah 1995, *The Sociology of Health and Illness*, Polity Press, Cambridge.

New South Wales Anti-Discrimination Board 1992, *Discrimination—The Other Epidemic*, NSW Anti-Discrimination Board, Sydney.

Nile, Fred 1983, *The Facts on AIDS—'The Gay Plague'*, Australian Christian Solidarity, Sydney [held in Noel Butlin Archives, H3N No. 181, Box 13].

Nugteren, Albertina 2001, Collective/Public Ritual Behaviour After Disasters: An Emerging Manifestation of Civil Religion?, Presented at the Spiritual Supermarket Conference, April, London School of Economics, viewed 2 December 2005, <http://www.cesnur.org/2001/london2001/nugteren.htm>

Olick, Jeffrey and Robbins, Joyce 1998, 'Social Memory Studies: From "Collective Memory" to the Historical Sociology of Mnemonic Practices', *Annual Review of Sociology*, 24, pp. 105–40.

Parliament of New South Wales 1991, *Legislative Council Notices of Motions and Orders of The Day First Session of The Fiftieth Parliament Wednesday 3 July*, Parliament of New South Wales, Sydney.

Patton, Cindy 1990, *Inventing AIDS*, Routledge, New York.

Pereira, Darryl 1999, 'HIV/AIDS and its "Willing Executioners": The Impact of Discrimination', *Murdoch University Electronic Journal of Law*, 6(4), viewed 24 June 2004, <http://www.murdoch.edu.au/elaw/issues/v6n4/pereira64nf.html>

Perkins, Roberta 1991, 'Working Girls: Prostitutes, Their Life and Social Control', *Australian Studies in Law, Crime and Justice Series*, Australian Institute of Criminology, Canberra, viewed 12 November 2006, <http://www.aic.gov.au/publications/lcj/working/ch2-5.html>

Persson, Asha and Newman, Christy 2008, 'Making Monsters: Heterosexuality, Crime and Race in Recent Western Media Coverage of HIV/AIDS', *Sociology of Health and Illness*, 30(4), pp. 632–46.

Phillips, Dr Bryce 1988, The Role of the Australian Medical Association, Presented to Living With AIDS Toward the Year 2000: Third National Conference on AIDS, Department of Community Services and Health, 4–6 August, Hobart.

Pichardo, Nelson 1997, 'New Social Movements: A Critical Review', *Annual Review of Sociology*, 23, pp. 411–30.

Pike, Bronwyn 2006a, National Summit to Discuss Increase in HIV Notifications, Media release, Government of Victoria, Melbourne.

Pike, Bronwyn 2006b, Victorian Strategy Tackles Rising HIV Rates, Media release, Government of Victoria, Melbourne.

Plummer, David and Irwin, Lyn 2004, Grassroots Activities, National Initiatives and HIV Prevention: Clues to Explain Australia's Dramatic Early Success in Controlling HIV, Paper presented at TASA Conference, 8–11 December, La Trobe University, Beechworth, Vic.

Prestage, Garrett 2002, Investigating Sexuality: A Personal View of Homosexual Behaviour, Identities and Subcultures in Social Research, Unpublished PhD Thesis, University of New South Wales, Sydney.

Quibell, Ruth 2004, Unmasking the Other: Discourses on Intellectual Disability in Contemporary Society, Unpublished PhD Thesis, Swinburne University of Technology, Melbourne.

Rand, E. 2007, 'Repeated Remembrance: Commemorating the AIDS Quilt and Resuscitating the Mourned Subject', *Rhetoric and Public Affairs*, 10(4), pp. 655–80.

Rawling, Alison 1998, Corporatism, Risk and the Construction of Australian HIV/AIDS Policy, Unpublished PhD Thesis, University of Sydney, NSW.

Rose, Nikolas 1994, 'Medicine, History and the Present', in Colin Jones and Roy Porter (eds), *Reassessing Foucault: Power, Medicine and the Body*, Routledge, London.

Rosenberg, Charles 1988, 'Disease and Social Order in America: Perceptions and Expectations', in Elizabeth Fee and Daniel Fox (eds), *AIDS: The Burdens of History*, University of California Press, Berkeley.

Rumesberg, Don 2002, 'The Early Years of Gay Youth', *The Advocate* [Los Angeles], 25 June, p. 26.

Seidman, Steven 2002, 'AIDS and the Discursive Construction of Homosexuality', in Kim Phillips and Barry Reay (eds), *Sexualities in History: A Reader*, Routledge, New York.

Sendziuk, Paul 2001, 'Bad Blood: The Contamination of Australia's Blood Supply and the Emergence of Gay Activism in the Age of AIDS', in Elizabeth Ruinard and Elspeth Tilley (eds), *Fresh Cuts: New Talents 2001*, API Network and University of Queensland Press, Sydney, viewed 24 June 2005, <http://www.api-network.com/articles/index.php?jas67_sendziuk>

Sendziuk, Paul 2003, *Learning to Trust: Australian Responses to AIDS*, UNSW Press, Sydney.

Shapin, Steven 1994, *A Social History of Truth*, University of Chicago Press, London.

Simes, Gary 1992, 'The Language of Homosexuality in Australia', in Robert Aldrich and Gary Wotherspoon (eds), *Gay Perspectives: Essays in Australian Gay Culture*, Department of Economic History, University of Sydney, NSW.

Smith, F. B. 1996, 'Beating Mortality: Health Transition in Australia', *Eureka Street*, 6(9), pp. 54–6.

Snow, David and Robert Benford 1992, 'Master Frames and Cycles of Protest', in Aldon Morris and Carol McClung (eds), *Frontiers in Social Movement Theory*, Yale University Press, New Haven, Conn.

South-East Sydney Area Health Service (SESAHS) 2006, *Ankali*, South-East Sydney Area Health Service web site, viewed 21 November 2005, <http://www.sesahs.nsw.gov.au/albionstcentre/Ankali/index.asp>

Staples, Joan 2006, *NGOs Out in the Cold: The Howard Government Policy Toward NGOs in Democratic Audit of Australia*, Discussion Paper 19/06, Faculty of Law, University of New South Wales, Sydney, viewed 3 June 2006, <http://democratic.audit.anu.edu.au/papers/20060615_staples_ngos.pdf>

Stewart, Graeme 1998, 'You've Gotta Have HAART', *Medical Journal of Australia*, 169, pp. 456–7.

Stockdill, Brett 2001, 'Forging a Multidimensional Oppositional Consciousness: Lessons from Community-based AIDS Activism', in Jane Mansbridge and Aldon Morris (eds), *Oppositional Consciousness: The Subjective Roots of Social Protest*, University of Chicago Press, Ill.

Stryker, Sheldon 2000, 'Identity Competition: Key to Differential Social Movement Participation', in Sheldon Stryker, Timothy Owens and Robert White (eds), *Self, Identity, and Social Movements*, University of Minnesota Press, Minneapolis.

Stull, Gregg 2001, 'The AIDS Memorial Quilt: Performing Memory, Piecing Action', *American Art*, 15(2), pp. 84–9.

Sturken, Marita 1997, *Tangled Memories: The Vietnam War, the AIDS Epidemic and the Politics of Remembering*, University of California Press, Berkeley.

Swain, Ashok 2002, *Social Networks and Social Movements*, Uppsala Peace Research Paper No. 4, Department of Peace and Conflict Research, Uppsala University, Sweden.

Swidler, Ann and Arditi, Jorge 1994, 'The New Sociology of Knowledge', *Annual Review of Sociology*, 20, pp. 305–29.

Tarrow, Sidney 1992, 'Mentalities, Political Cultures, and Collective Action Frames: Constructing Meaning Through Action', in Aldon Morris and Carol Mueller (eds), *Frontiers in Social Movement Theory*, Yale University Press, New Haven, Conn.

Tarrow, Sidney 1998, *Power in Movement: Social Movement and Contentious Politics*, Cambridge University Press, Cambridge.

Taylor, Verta 2000, 'Emotions and Identity in Women's Self Help Movements', in Sheldon Stryker, Timothy Owens and Robert White (eds), *Self, Identity, and Social Movements*, University of Minnesota Press, Minneapolis.

Taylor, Verta and Rupp, Leila 2002, 'Living Internationalism: The Emotion Culture of Transnational Women's Organisations 1888–1945', *Mobilization*, 7(2), pp. 141–58.

Tesh, Sylvia 2000, *Uncertain Hazards: Environmental Activists and Scientific Proof*, Cornell University Press, Ithaca, NY.

Thompson, Denise 1985, *Flaws in the Social Fabric: Homosexuals and Society in Sydney*, George Allen & Unwin, Sydney.

Touraine, Alain 2002, 'The Importance of Social Movements', *Social Movement Studies*, 1(1), pp. 89–95.

Treichler, Paula 1988, 'AIDS, Homophobia and Biomedical Discourse', in Douglas Crimp (ed.), *AIDS Cultural Analysis, Cultural Activism*, The MIT Press, Cambridge, Mass.

Tuckey, Wilson 1988, Address to Living With AIDS Toward the Year 2000: Third National Conference on AIDS, Department of Community Services and Health, 4-6 August, Hobart.

Vittelone, Nicole 2001, 'Watching AIDS, Condoms and Serial Killers in the Australian "Grim Reaper" TV Campaign', *Continuum: Journal of Media and Cultural Studies*, 15(1), pp. 33–48.

Wachter, R. 1996, 'AIDS, Activism, and the Politics of Health', in Stella Theodoulou (ed.), *AIDS: The Politics and Policy of Disease*, Prentice Hall, Upper Saddle River, NJ.

Waldby, Cathy, Kippax, Susan and Crawford, June 1990, 'Theory in the Bedroom: A Report from the Macquarie University AIDS and Heterosexuality Project', *Journal of Social Issues*, 25(3), pp. 177–85.

Watchirs, Helen 2002, *Reforming the Law to Ensure Appropriate Responses to the Risk of Disease Transmission*, Occasional Papers No. 2, ANCAHRD Position Paper, Australian National Council on AIDS, Hepatitis C and Related Diseases, Canberra, viewed 15 April 2006, <http://www.ancahrd.org/pubs/pdfs/op_2_may02.pdf>

Watney, Simon 1994, *Practices of Freedom*, Rivers Oram Press, London.

Watson, Lex 1988, 'Life After AIDS', *Australian Left Review*, October–November, pp. 12–15.

Wearing, Michael 2004, 'Medical Dominance and the Division of Labour in the Health Professions', in Carol Grbich (ed.), *Health in Australia: Sociological Concepts and Issues*, Pearson, Sydney.

Weeks, Jeffrey 1981, *Sex, Politics and Society: The Regulation of Sexuality Since 1800*, Longman, London.

Wellings, Kaye 1988, 'Perceptions of Risk—Media Treatment of AIDS', in Peter Aggleton and Hilary Homans (eds), *Social Aspects of AIDS*, The Falmer Press, London.

Westlund, John 2006, 'Address to Public Meeting by Co-Ordinator of the AIDS Action Council of the ACT, 23 June 1987, Canberra', in Ian Rankin (ed.), *AIDS Action: A History of the AIDS Action Council of the ACT*, AIDS Action Council of the ACT, Canberra.

Wettergren, Asa 2005, 'Mobilization and the Moral Shock', in Helena Flam and Debra King (eds), *Emotions and Social Movements*, Routledge, Abingdon, UK.

White, Kevin 1996, 'The Social Origins of Illness and the Development of the Sociology of Health', in Carol Grbich (ed.), *Health in Australia: Sociological Concepts and Issues*, Prentice Hall, Sydney.

White, Kevin and Willis, Evan 1992, 'The Languages of AIDS', *New Zealand Sociology*, 7(2), pp. 127–49.

World Health Organisation (WHO) 2002, *Australia 2002 Update*, Epidemiological Fact Sheets on HIV/AIDS and Sexually Transmitted Infections, World Health Organisation, Geneva, viewed 2 June 2003, <http://www.unAIDS.org>

Willett, Graham 1997, 'The Darkest Decade: Homophobia in 1950s Australia', *Australian Historical Studies*, 28(109), pp. 120–32.

Willett, Graham 2000, *Living Out Loud: A History of Gay and Lesbian Activism in Australia*, Allen & Unwin, Sydney.

Willet, Graham 2005, 'Psyched In: Psychology, Psychiatry and Homosexuality in Australia', *Gay and Lesbian Issues and Psychology Review*, 1(2), pp. 53–7.

Wilkinson, David and Dore, Greg 2000, 'An Unbridgeable Gap? Comparing the HIV/AIDS Epidemics in Australia and Sub Saharan Africa', *Australian and New Zealand Journal of Public Health*, 24(3), pp. 276–80.

Williams, Melissa 1998, *Voice, Trust and Memory*, Princeton University Press, Princeton, NJ.

Willis, Evan 1989, *Medical Dominance: The Division of Labour in Australian Health Care*, Allen & Unwin, Sydney.

Wilson, Paul, Walker, John and Mukherjee, Satyanshu 1986, 'How the Public Sees Crime: An Australian Survey', *Trends and Issues in Australian Crime and Criminal Reporting Series No. 2*, Australian Institute of Criminology, Canberra.

Woolcock, Geoffrey 1999, A Vector of Identity Transmission: AIDS Activism and Social Movement Theory, Unpublished PhD Thesis, La Trobe University, Melbourne.

Wotherspoon, Garry 1991, 'From Sub-Culture to Mainstream Culture: Some Impacts of Homosexual and Gay Sub-Cultures in Australia', *Journal of Australian Studies*, 15(28), pp. 56–62.

Young, James Harvey 1995, 'AIDS and the FDA', in Caroline Hannaway, Victoria Harden and John Parascandola (eds), *AIDS and the Public Debate*, ISO Press, Amsterdam.

Index